AUTHORING

AUTHORING

An Essay for the English Profession on Potentiality and Singularity

JANIS HASWELL
RICHARD HASWELL

UTAH STATE UNIVERSITY PRESS
Logan, Utah
2010

Utah State University Press
Logan, Utah 84322-7800

Manufactured in the United States of America
Cover design by Barbara Yale-Read

Library of Congress Cataloging-in-Publication Data

Haswell, Janis Tedesco.
  Authoring : an essay for the English profession on potentiality and singularity / Janis Haswell,
Richard Haswell.
     p. cm.
  Includes bibliographical references and index.
  ISBN 978-0-87421-771-1 (pbk. : alk. paper) -- ISBN 978-0-87421-772-8 (e-book)
  1. English language--Rhetoric--Study and teaching (Higher) 2. Report writing--Study and teach-
ing (Higher) 3. English language--Study and teaching (Higher) 4. College prose--Evaluation. I.
Haswell, Richard H. II. Title.
  PE1404.H37 2010
  808'.0420711--dc22
                              2010000770

This book is dedicated to
VICTORIA, KEVIN, NORA, AND BOB
authors all.

CONTENTS

ACKNOWLEDGMENTS

A special few out of the deserving many: Glenn Blalock, Tiane Donahue, Carol Scott, Sally Scott. "Knotty timber needs sharp wedges."

And for financial support and permissions: the College of Liberal Arts, Texas A&M University, Corpus Christi; the Harry Ransom Research Center, University of Texas at Austin; the Department of Special Collections & University Archives, McFarlin Library, University of Tulsa.

INTRODUCTION
English Studies and Black Boxes

"What a box I'm in," he would cry, looking up from the gutter the next morning.

John Gardner, *Vlemk the Box-Painter*

In information science, when input is known and output is known but the process that connects the two remains unknown, the situation is called a black box. This essay opens some black boxes safeguarded by the higher-education project called "English."

Education and black boxes, of course, are joined by symbiosis in every department and discipline. This is because it takes black boxes to learn about black boxes. Fixers routinely use computerized tools about which they care to know little in order to diagnose problems—is there radon in the basement?—about which they hope to learn more. Bruno Latour (1987) shows that even in the enlightened field of the hard sciences, questioning of unquestioned procedures always uncovers more unquestioned procedures, like a Russian doll with no end to the parade of inner dolls. Yet as fixers and working scientists will respond, black boxes have to be taken for granted to get on with the investigation. That is why black boxes abound and abide. They are ideational as well as material, and they come in all shapes and sizes, as atomic as intuitions, as nebulous as presuppositions. Some of the most encompassing are the stuff our Enlightenment-Romantic-Modern-Postmodern dreams have been made on: Faraday's ether, Kant's categories, Hegel's Geist, Hopkins' inscape, Freud's libido, Bergson's life force, Skinner's mentalism, Derrida's presence. Every discipline has its black boxes it doesn't want to plumb because the work has to get done, and work would have to wait while the basement is being tested.

Every discipline including English.

Authoring, the human inner act of making texts, is the one term that most unites the four divisions of English studies—composition, literature, linguistics, and creative writing. Yet in English departments authoring is currently a remarkably black box. Akin to the behaviorist concept of mentalism, which can only be inferred through measurable stimulus and measurable response, authoring—the inward act that triggers the outward act of writing—may be the one concept in the toolkit of the English trade that teachers of writing and written discourse least question. Those of us in literature and composition have often scoffed at stimulus-response methodology. Yet we think continually of input in terms of cultural environment, ethnic given, academic site, and instructional activity, and we think continually of output in the form of text, learning, grades, and test results. What lies in between we bracket as authoring: the internal human process of turning background, experience, and imagination into something written. It is not so much the author who is dead as the act of authoring.

It is not a death, of course, but a truism (the logical equivalent of a black box) or—the same thing—a suspending of attention. No doubt the suspension has aided four decades of our field's profitable investigation into society and culture on the one end, and text and response on the other end. Authoring is the dark synapse that lies between. This essay hopes to throw a little light into it.

We investigate authoring from two different angles. One angle, philosophical in nature, is the idea of potentiality. Famously, potentiality is another black box. It does not stand as a fact since the concrete evidence for it, its actualization, alters it, sometimes destroys it. Like the black boxes of presence in literary deconstruction or intention in literary criticism, potentiality is irremediably altered by its expression. Nonetheless, that expression allows ready inference of potentiality as a human element of authoring. Whoever scribed a word without first, the inkling that it was scribable, and second, without imagining the potential of its imprint on readers?

Our second angle, factual in nature, is the verifiable human condition of singularity. A writer is unlike any other writer and a reader unlike any other reader, because only one person fits inside her or his skin. Especially writers know this, and, as we will soon show, that knowledge of individual uniqueness moves them to write. As they touch felt tip to paper or finger tip to keyboard, they intuit that no one at this particular moment is in their particular spot, and that therefore no one has ever written what they are about to write, and they are correct.

Potentiality and *singularity*—two black boxes inside the black box of *authoring*.[1] Familiar as home, our three companion terms feel estranged from English departments. Yet instruction and scholarship that avoid these three human realities—this is our contention—make an English studies that will tend to be unmotivated, jejune, and aloof. Since we will also contend that in the last couple of decades the profession has indeed avoided the concepts, perforce much of our critique will run countercurrent. But if there is a little bloodletting in these pages, we feel it is for the good of the patient. This book is an essay for the discipline of English, not against it—a discipline to which the two of us have devoted almost seventy years of our collective lives. Currently in that academic field we find somewhat to dislike but nothing to despair. To put a proactive spin on it, we have in our kit three tools that we hope the rest of our profession may find as useful as we have.

In short, we believe our terms can help us English teachers and scholars escape from a corner into which we have painted ourselves. This disciplinary cul-de-sac or malaise can be exposed in two ways, diachronic and synchronic, and we will attempt both. As for the history, it seems that the discipline's engagement with the conceptual adventure called postmodernism has come to an end, and did so perhaps a decade or so ago. (We do not like the term "postmodern," but feel stuck with it, which is part of the malaise.)

At the core of the postmodern apparatus was an attack on foundations of every guise. This maneuver took two basic tacks. One was deconstruction, roughly earlier and especially favored in literary studies. Deconstructionists problematized and critiqued positivism in science, truth in philosophy, intention in authorship, transparency in language, ideology in politics, essentialisms and totalizings everywhere; they championed indeterminacy, intertextuality, representation, interpretation, and critique itself. The other tack was social constructivism, roughly later and especially favored in composition studies.

---

1. Had we space in this book, hospitality and technology would have joined potentiality and singularity to form a quadrilogy on authoring. Hospitality is the cultural and social vehicle for authoring, the relational customs and conventions that mediate and bring together the potentials and singularities of the writer and reader (see J. Haswell, R. Haswell, and Blalock 2009, and the last section of this book, "Envoi: Hospitality and Alice Sheldon"). Technology is the material means of authoring that exercise their own mediations and allowances, including the latest conferencing tools like Blackboard or Wimba and social networking sites like MySpace or Bebo.

Constructivists problematized and critiqued individualism in politics, liberalism or humanism in ethics, expressionism in discourse, self in psychology, originality in authorship, authority in scholarship, individuality in gender and ethnicity, social independences and personal isolatoes everywhere; they championed social identity, collaboration, consensus, diversity, dialogism, performance, spectacle, and again critique itself. The deconstructionist and constructivist sides of postmodernism, of course, were flanks of the same attack.

The malaise with postmodernism also has two varieties, both stemming from its core position on foundationalism. One is the sense that postmodernists engaged in a fundamental logical contradiction (some of the earliest counterattacks on postmodernism came from the philosophers). How can one pry foundations loose without operating from a foundation of one's own? How can one deconstruct truth claims with truth claims? What is the social construction of the exposé of social constructions? There is the suspicion that postmodernism, at least the radical or uncompromising part of it, was an elitist operation, a critique of others that declined to extend the critique to itself. The other variety of the malaise, of course, is the sense that while the postmodernists investigated certain foundations, they forgot others necessary for decent and fruitful human interaction, including interactions among teachers, students, and written texts. It is the second side of the malaise that has largely motivated this essay for the discipline of English. In particular, we feel that postmodernism left authoring outside its box.[2]

Our critique of historical postmodernism is made with a high respect for it. Both of us earned our degrees and taught during the years of high postmodernism, and the dismantling of foundations and the analysis of social constructions lie in our bones. What postmodernism taught about critique itself should never be forgotten or left untaught to students. Part of our dislike of the term postmodern is the "post-," with its suggestion of an after without a continuity.[3] We agree with Neil

---

2. Note that we distinguish author*ing* from author*ship*. Authoring includes the physical act of generating discourse and the author's phenomenological sense of that act. Authorship is the way authoring plays out in history materially, socially, and culturally. Naturally, the two overlap in a tangle of ways.

3. The problem we sense with various proposals for a post-postmodernism—such as neo-realism in literature and embodied materiality or post-process in composition—starts when they assume that something old, disembodied or pre- must be abandoned. We are not making up the term "post-postmodernism" (see Eshelman 2000).

Brooks and Josh Toth that "the ghost of postmodernism is essential to the future of our critical discourse. Postmodernism might be dead, but it still has much work to do" (2007, 11). Throughout this book we lament postmodernist and constructivist theory, but only the radical edge of it, not its commonsense core. But it should not be forgotten that the pronouncement of the "death of postmodernism," albeit widespread, comes from the meta scholars. In the primary scholarship and classroom practice, postmodernisms and constructivisms of the most marginal sort can operate in ways hardly ghostlike, and more with the vigor of a person in the prime of life. Radical deconstructive and constructive strategies of interpretation and composing thrive still largely uncontested in English department courses.[4]

Hence the synchronic approach to the problem, which makes up the bulk of our essay. Can our new terms—potentiality, singularity, authoring—help with current practice? Without a doubt, they disturb a lexicon that put and still puts the emphasis elsewhere. English faculty are much more likely to talk of *textuality* than authoring, of *performance* than potentiality, of *community* than singularity. These are the terms in the know, the foyer where current literary and compositional studies prefer to start. To most members of English departments, they lead to offices with a very comfortable, lived-in feel.

	Current Emphasis	Current in Literature	Current in Composition	Our Emphasis
Discursive Ground	Textuality	Literary Work	Composing	Authoring
Discursive End	Performance	Interpretation	Outcomes	Potentiality
Academic Self	Community or Group Identity	Canon	Disciplinary Standards	Singularity

Textuality and performance, performance and outcomes, canon and standards, etc.—each cell opens readily into the other but uneasily into our strange compartments.

Take *performance*, for instance. Discursive performance uses language to construct an identity that will survive within a group or

4. Klaus Stierstorfer (2003) charts the rise and decline of postmodernism in literary and cultural studies and estimates its peak in the early 1990's. Some critics have suggested that the death blow to postmodernism's attack on foundationalism happened on September 11, 2001.

a community. Performance, "twice-behaved behavior" (Stern and Henderson 1993, 9), succeeds by iterating previous language. Just as actors on stage are handed and perform a script to be replaced by the characters imagined by the audience, offstage a person shapes or manipulates stock language into an identity, a performance that displays or impersonates characteristics already scripted by a particular group, during which "who you are, and are taken to be" becomes indistinguishable (Cameron 1996, 47). In English departments, the stress falls on the "taken to be." For students the rewards are in the script (input) and the performance (output) rather than in the cryptic in-between. Accountability will lie with mastery of the performed word, whether it be mastery of a literary canon or a standardized disciplinary style. Judgment will lie with interpretation of privileged scripts or with outcomes of exercise in privileged rhetorical modes. It seems the route performance takes departs farther and farther from our terms. Potentiality is only outcomes in a nascent state, and singularity is the antonym of "twice-behaved behavior."

Or take *community*. Open the panels of the black box of community, and there the members move around, identities known and accepted through the performance of their roles. Community is a shared collectivity, self-selected or not, where new members are embraced on the basis of previously agreed-upon behavior, iterated language, and displayed beliefs. There are communities within communities, of course. Within the academic community lies the community of the English department, for acceptance into which a student must appreciate an established canon of literary works appropriate to legitimized cultural groups (input), and write an established style appropriate to legitimized disciplinary fields (output). All of this rarely leads to notions of potentiality or singularity. Community is nervous with the "autonomous" self or the enterprising "self-made" individual who might be so foolish as to think that singular ideas exist and will be allowed free play. According to the community paradigm, the principle of "difference" is vital, but only to distinguish one community from another and to identify outsiders, not to legitimize insiders.

Or start with *identity*. Identity is the kind of person that a community recognizes you to be through your performance. James Paul Gee isolates four primary operations of identity, mutually inclusive. Nature-identity says we are what we are because of a given "state" that we did not select and cannot change (age, sex, genetic makeup, for example).

Institution-identity says we are what we are because of positions we occupy or functions we serve in society (receptionist, soldier, student, for example). Discourse-identity says we are what we are because of language accomplishments in interacting with other people (raconteur, mediator, plagiarist, for example). Affinity-identity says we are what we are because of habits, experiences, and practices that we display within an affiliated group (Methodist, health club member, psychology major, for example). In an English department, the identity of students—beyond that inscribed by virtue of enrolling in classes—officially depends on their literacy, that is, their demonstrated capability to handle assigned readings and discourse genres (input) and produce texts subject to evaluation (output). Although Gee says that a person can be actively or passively engaged in identity formation, clearly the outcome swings on what the person cannot control, the extant "interpretive system" that underwrites identity's recognition. In the current identity box, there seems to be no sanctioned space where the potentiality of students can form a singular self that resists identification (2002, 99-107).

Above all, or perhaps we should say surrounding all, operates the god-term *textuality*. Whether the focus is on the scribal processes that generate text types (compositional input) or on the interpretive glosses that texts generate (literary output), textuality steadfastly diverts attention from the only operation that can possibly connect the two, authoring.

We are not arguing that the current black boxes of English studies are any darker than our proposed ones. Nor are we arguing that our black boxes should replace the current ones. Although in the chapters that follow we will take our licks at various posts still more or less erect, we aim to carry on rather than start over. Basically, we feel boxed in by the going terms in English studies and English instruction, whatever their provenance, and we mean to find out where a redirection of attention may take us.

We are not suggesting, however, that all boxes are equal. At root all may be cryptic, but they vary in their usefulness in directing inquiry, prompting hypotheses, shaping diagnoses, and jumpstarting every kind of logical and moral reasoning. Different boxes—presuppositions, axioms, "self-evident truths," and the like—have very different consequences. Consider just a few implications of the textuality-performance-community paradigm. First, if discourse behavior is "performed," if every identity is constructed, produced, or practiced, then there is little reason to look for anything "authentic" or "original" in the student. Second, if self identity can exist only so far as it is recognized by others outside the self as belonging to a category or group (organized by gender, race, ethnicity, class, ideology, etc.), then the student has little reason to look inward for his or her sources of meaning. And third, if personal self is only a "subjectivity," subject to society's projection of group identity, a projection that will change over time only glacially, then students will construe learning in terms other than personal change, freedom, and creativity.

The implications of the authoring-potentiality-singularity paradigm lead in very different directions. If teaching vests authority in authoring, students will be recognized more by their promise than their performance, will be encouraged to develop personal distinction rather than group affiliations, and will be affirmed in their inner dignity rather than in an "identity" assigned by the culture at large. The township of textuality-performance-community does not ban promise, personal distinction, and inner dignity, but it lacks clear road signs pointing in those directions.

Our three terms are not old pedagogical abstractions newly named and elevated. We are talking about realities, pedagogical effects some of which are highly unpleasant, though old indeed. In 1751 James Harris observed that British teachers treat students as if knowledge could be poured into them "like water into a cistern" (1751/1968, "Preface"). Two and one-half centuries later, Mary Rose O'Reilley observed that students in the United States learn by being "insulted, bullied, turned into objects" (1993, 30). To the extent that such a pedagogical tradition continues, it is elevated in no sense of the word, and under it the experiences of students, thousands of students every working hour, are in no way abstract. Any approach that changes this tradition will be new, no matter what it is called. It is perhaps the central argument of this essay that material objectification of students tends to be supported by classrooms that privilege canon, standards, outcomes, the public performance of identity, and a communal interpretation of texts, and that it is worth proposing a change of direction toward classrooms friendly to the potential and singularity of authoring.

Whatever directions the following chapters take—they might more accurately be called explorations or divagations—each gravitates toward the actual and the practical. In Chapter 1 working authors describe their felt sense of authoring. In Chapters 2-7 the concept of potentiality leads first to a study of two student writers insisting on their potentiality, while peers and teacher insist on denying it; then to the astonishing history of William Butler Yeats's discovery of the woman's voice within him; next to a curious moment in the life of journalist William Cobbett, when he found himself preferring a sand hill to his college education; and finally to a feisty student who concluded that thirty-one English teachers and thirty-one peer students were wrong about her writing. In Chapters 8-13 the fact of human singularity and its implications for teaching and studying literature and composition are explored through investigations of individuals: a minor character in one novel by Paul Scott who talked her way into the central voice of another Scott novel; a student who is part Hispanic, part African American, and part Native American; another student who discovered that her mother's consoling fable was a lie; another who finally faced the truth that her brother had died in Vietnam thirty-four years ago. In Chapter 14 more individuals appear: a minor transit official at an obscure border crossing between Ecuador and Peru; two hundred ninth graders and first-year college students in Nueces County, Texas; and Michael Yeats, a famous son of famous parents, on a Caribbean cruise ship. And in transit, four interchapters relate the confounding life of author Alice Sheldon, whose nom-de-plume was not only a public script, but also a necessary part of her singular potential as an author.

This book is written to help further the project of college English. Partly, it is for English teachers who often work in departments that suffer jealousies, rivalries, ostracism, and other Pandoran ills. In that, English is no different from other university disciplines. With disciplinary black boxes, is one happier in the dark or in the know? It's our hope that if the authoring of texts is a conceptual box that holds all of the English department's various compartments—literature, composition, linguistics, and creative writing—then opening up that concept may help faculty relinquish some of their local spats, the squabbles that we have experienced and lament. As it is, this volume is too small to deal with all four of these factions, and we can focus on only the first two—literature and composition—subfields that the two of us have merged throughout our academic careers. We leave the topic of authoring in linguistics and creative writing for someone else's authoring.

Above all, our study is written for students in English classes. It is they who perhaps suffer the most from conflicts among their faculty, and who may wonder why they do not learn more about what it is to *be* an author when they are continually asked to study or become one.

1

AUTHORING ACCEPTED

A word on Academies: Poetry has been attacked by an ignorant &
frightened bunch of bores who don't understand how it's made, & the
trouble with these creeps is they wouldn't know Poetry if it came up
and buggered them in broad daylight.

Allen Ginsberg, "Notes for *Howl* and for Other Poems"

Writing in 1959, the poet Ginsberg was angry at the initial reaction
of literary scholars to Beat literature, especially "Howl," and both his
intemperate dismissal of their kind of knowledge and their temporary
dismissal of his kind of poetry can be chalked up to the passing historical moment. Still, Ginsberg's charge that university scholars don't
know how poetry is *made* carries some lasting weight. How much do
English teachers know about the inner workings of working authors?
In the academy, the project called English largely consists of students
taught to read creative literature by teachers who do not regularly
write creative literature, and taught to write essays by teachers who do
not regularly write essays. No wonder that authoring, as we say in the
Introduction, may be the one discursive concept from the toolkit of
their trade that teachers of writing and written discourse use least.

Not that English teachers are unaware of the distance between
them and their disciplinary subject. Sometimes they have argued that
the distance itself is necessary to their scholarly business. As we have
noted, radical postmodern scholarship brackets the act of authoring in
order to concentrate on contextual input and textual output. English
teachers may have other reasons why they tend to keep authoring
under the shelf. In many ways, the act of authoring does not fit the
shape of their teaching practice, either pragmatically, ideologically, or
temperamentally.

What if the phenomenology of authoring, the reported felt sense of
how it is made, were pulled out from under and placed on the counter,

"in broad daylight"? In the eyes of the profession, how alien would it appear? Does real-world authoring look like something English teachers and scholars could live with?

APPROACHES TO AUTHORING

The English profession approaches the act of authoring in five basic ways. On the literature side, the most familiar approach treats it as part of the biography of well-known authors. Tillie Olsen snatched what moments she could as a working-class mother, sometimes writing on the city bus, standing up if she had to. Thomas Wolfe actually preferred to write standing up, with the top of the refrigerator as his table. On the composition side, the most common approach offers teacher-sanctioned guidelines for composing. Keep your audience in mind. Make sure each paragraph has a clear and circumscribed topic. Invent first, edit last.

Two other approaches to authoring emphasize the instrumental: focus on tricks of the trade and focus on the study of authorship. With the first, composing habits are offered as literary history. By luck, novelist Kent Haruf acquired six reams of pulpy yellow paper—no longer manufactured, but a stock paraphernalia of his writing ritual. Or composing rituals are offered as advice to student writers. Set aside a time of day for writing, and write every day. With the focus on authorship, acts of composing are reduced to their social, cultural, or historical causes and effects. Literature students are told that Coleridge kept his borrowings from Schilling unacknowledged in the *Biographia Literaria* to uphold the "Romantic" notion of the writer as original and self-inspired. Composition students are told that their reader will know them not as they imagine themselves, individual "writers," but instead will construct them as "authors" according to the persona they project through their words, perhaps an image of the honest scholar or the empathetic caseworker.

The fifth approach to authoring does what these other four do not; it asks or surmises how authors *experience* authoring. Writing behavior, composing guidelines, tricks of the trade, and authorship can and usually do stand free of that felt sense, which includes drive, mood, proprioception, recollections, irritation at the barking dogs next door, and an endless wealth of inner life. Theoretically, of course, literary studies have long dismissed the phenomenology of authors as unreliable, ephemeral, even chimerical.[1] On occasion literary biography may provide some of this side of authoring, inferring it from letters, journals, anecdotes, and elsewhere. Another source is the author interview, although that genre does not register very high on the discipline's scale of prestige. A major curiosity is that the phenomenology of authoring attracts composition studies even less.

As a systematic research effort, of course, the phenomenological approach to authoring thrives in psychology, where investigative paths have been richly sustained into motivation, self-regulation, self-efficacy, self-therapy, working memory, and other aspects of the inner life of authors. The phenomenology of authoring, if we may be allowed to keep this term, is one of the mainstay approaches of this book, in part because so far the English profession has shown only piecemeal interest in it.[2]

WHAT AUTHORS SAY ABOUT AUTHORING

If composition studies of late have contributed little to the phenomenology of authoring, it may be due in part to a stubborn and—to our minds—enigmatic contradiction in the field concerning students and authors. The issue is whether students in composition classes are authors. Maybe they are just writers, or just student writers. An older position (e.g., Harste, Short, and Burke 1988) is that students are maligned and disadvantaged when their teachers do not treat them as bona fide authors. Teachers assign and treat course writings as exercise work not worthy of publication, or when they do publish students' work,

---

1. An important dissenter from this critical tradition is Francis-Noël Thomas, whose book *The Writer Writing* (1993) reaffirms author intention as a legitimate element of literary analysis. At the other extreme is Jacques Derrida, who argues that the act of inscription involves an aporia, a "secret," that no mode of analysis can explain (1995). Derrida's notion sets a limit to our use of author testimony about authoring in this chapter, since even the inscriber cannot explain the secret. But that also sets a limit to what teachers can know of student authoring, as we argue in Chapter 14.

2. Not that we will present or apply a systematic philosophical or psychological account of phenomenology. Such a project would be germane, and books could be written on the concept of potentiality in Heidegger or singularity in Husserl or authoring in Levinas. Instead, we will apply a fairly pedestrian notion of phenomenological description that involves, in compositionist Louise Phelps' words, "not only intuiting, analyzing, and describing particulars of composing in their full concreteness, but also attempting to attain insight into the essence of the experience" (Waldrep 1985, 243).

they neglect to get their students' permission.[3] This argument now runs concurrent with the opposing position that students are maligned and disadvantaged when their teachers *do* treat them as authors—when students are expected to be autonomous or original, for instance, or held to published-author standards and models they, as apprentices, are unable to meet, and the students thereby become marginalized (e.g., David Barthomolae 1986). We can appreciate efforts to explain and dissolve this contradiction over student authorship through analysis of the historical, political, and material conditions of disciplinary splits within English departments, and within the academy or society in general (e.g., Susan Miller 1993; Bruce Horner 1997). We would point out, however, that both the contradiction and these proposed resolutions tend to cut students and their teachers off from the *experience* of being an author. To our minds, the "student/author binary," as Horner calls it, cannot be resolved fairly unless we ask different questions. Do students share the inner life of working authors? Can English teachers find ways to help their students not only navigate authorship but experience real-world authoring as well?

This book says yes to both questions. In doing so, it follows in the footsteps of Donald Murray, whose contrarian composition textbook *Shoptalk* consists largely of quotations from working authors testifying about their craft. Murray believes, as we do, that of course students are authors: "My students discover that their natural responses to writing are often the same as experienced writers" (1990, xiv). He also sees that the experience of the experienced sometimes runs counter to the teaching of the teachers. "The testimony of writers often contradicts the beliefs of nonwriters and that, unfortunately, includes many teachers of writing from kindergarten through graduate school" (xiii). It bears noting that Murray worked as a writer before he worked as a teacher. He was a freelancer and journalist who won a Pulitzer for his editorials in the *Boston Herald* before he signed on with the University of New Hampshire's English department.

For our purposes, *Shoptalk* has some problems. It is dated, a commonplace book begun when Murray was in junior high in the 1930s.

---

3. Peter Elbow (1987) strongly advances this older position. Elbow argues that when teachers fail to read student writing as *readers* (rather than as teachers, evaluators, or editors), they reinforce the students' sense "that writing means doing school exercises, producing for authorities what they already know—not actually trying to say things to readers" (65). They undermine, as we would say, authoring itself.

His snippets mostly come from fiction writers who were publishing before the 1980s. Also, Murray's own interests keep the focus of the testimony largely on craft rather than on psychology, and his categories chiefly deal with writerly strategies such as audience awareness, composing habits, beginnings, endings, maintaining flow, finding form, playing with language, and revising. Our own survey of author testimony—think of it as an excursion taking off from Murray's last chapter, "The Feel of Writing"—serves more as a synopsis than a commonplace book. Our selections and categories are equally intuitive, but tap more recent writers, achieve more of a balance between fiction and nonfiction, and center on what writers say about the phenomenological experience of authoring.[4] The testimony we found, however, is not less divorced from English department pedagogy than is Murray's.

From our survey we construct a dozen most common traits of the experience of authoring according to working authors.

1. *Drivenness*. Authors cannot not write. In high school biographer and poet Muriel Rukeyser promised a friend to stop writing poems, but couldn't keep the promise because of "the pressure and the drivenness" (Sternberg 1980, 221). "There's the blank page," says Margaret Atwood, "and the thing that obsesses you" (Sternberg 1991, 156). The compulsion is so strong that sometimes it seems to come from outside: "I couldn't help myself; it was done to me, so to speak," explains Cynthia Ozick (Wachtel 1993, 13). Or else it is an internal drive so natural it can't be turned off—like a walnut tree putting forth leaf and fruit (William Saroyan), a silk worm producing silk (Doris Lessing), a baby letting out a squall (George Orwell), an adult sneezing (E. B. White), or a guerrilla never giving up the fight (Walter Mosley). Basically, writers experience writing as primal and therefore always first. Alice Hoffman tells how she put off an operation for breast cancer because she was compelled to finish a book: "More than anything, I was a writer" (Darnton 2001, 97).

2. *Pleasure*. Drivenness can be seen negatively, felt as an obsession, a subjection, a bête noire, a disease (Patrick White), a form of insanity (Charles Bukowski), a "quirk or virus" (Ken Donelson, Waldrep 1988, 53), "an addiction" (Lil Brannon, 22). But as with many addictions, the composing itself is felt positively as a pleasure. The

---

4. Along with adventitious finds, our quotations and categories emerge from a systematic reading of interviews and essays collected by Janet Sternberg (1980, 1991), Tom Waldrep (1985, 1988), Eleanor Wachtel (1993), and John Darnton (2001).

pleasure may derive from other qualities of the phenomenology of authoring described below, such as the surprise of unplanned discoveries (Alice Munro), the exhilarated feel of a creation taking shape (Seamus Heaney), the joy of mental concentration (Donald Hall), the satisfaction of achieving something difficult (Joseph Heller), or the "pleasant sense of anticipation, like starting off on a journey" (Muriel Harris; Waldrep 1988, 105). Authors also describe writing as a relief from social demands or private frustrations. "How I think about my work," explains Diane Johnson, "is indistinguishable from the way I think about my needlepoint or cooking: here is the project I'm involved in. It is play" (Sternberg 1991, 141). The experiential bedrock of pleasure, however, again seems to rest on the feeling that writing is a natural and needed exercise of the whole person. "I write," says compositionist Toby Fulwiler, "because if I don't, I cannot sleep" (Waldrep 1988, 88). In a recent interview, Irish novelist Martin Waddell put succinctly what many other authors have said about composing: "It's what I want to do and I'm happy when I'm writing and not happy when I'm not writing" (2002). Working authors, like everyone else, love having written; but they also love writing.

3. *Preparedness.* Although the writing is compulsive and pleasurable, that does not mean it is spontaneous. The consensus seems to be that writing emerges from a feeling of readiness, and readiness emerges from material, or things to say that have long been experienced, collected, internalized, and finally are poised for the saying. Novelist and literary critic Kaye Gibbons puts it in one short sentence: "I write about what I know best" (Sternberg 1991, 60). To prepare an idea, a character, a plot, an intellectual position may take years. Books "come very gradually," says Michael Ondaatje, "It's really a case of lugging something around for about five years, and leaving things behind in somebody's house and having to go back and pick them up again, building an arc situation" (Wachtel 1993, 56). Writing is a matter of waiting, with E. B. White like a surfer looking for the "perfect wave on which to ride in" (Murray 1990, 77), with Richard Ford in "galvanic repose" (Wachtel 1993, 67), with Virginia Woolf "holding myself from writing it till I have it impending in me: grown heavy in my mind like a ripe pear; pendant, gravid" (2003, 136). Writers' block is not writers unable to scribe ideas, but rather ideas that are not ready to be scribed, premature (Joyce Carol Oates), inadequately understood and in need of more research (Barbara Tuchman), not yet settled until the inessentials have been forgotten (Jonathan Raban).

4. *Concentration.* The sense of being prepared is accompanied, however, by the opposing yet complementary physical and mental state of concentration. There are many names and phrases for it, including "heart and mind open to the work" (Walter Mosley; Darnton 2001, 163), "intensity and attentiveness" (Susan Sontag; 223), centering, meditation, focus ("fierce and pointed"; Marge Piercy 1982, 17). What writers describe is not a sudden raptness of attention, such as a hunter might experience when a covey flushes, but a habitually heightened state of alertness, "a temperament that accepts concentration over the long haul" (Ward Just; Darnton 2001, 116). Donald Murray himself describes the author's concentration as one of the great gifts of life: "In the act of writing I experience a serene, quiet joy, a focus of all my energy and knowledge and craft on the task" (1990, 189).

5. *Uncontrol.* In part, the preparing and the concentration are a controlled practice with the aim of losing control. Writers associate uncontrol with different names, shapes, and feelings: dreaming, the subconscious, the unconscious, the irrational, demon, trance, disembodiment, kinesthesia, magic, the "inner teacher" (Doris Lessing; Wachtel 1993, 243).[5] But they all describe basically the same thing— the way the drafting or the drafted sometimes takes control away from the author and assumes a "Ouija board will of its own" (Diane Johnson; Darnton 2001, 113). The experience of uncontrol is not contradictory to the state of concentration. It's like the Zen art of archery, when the archer is so focused the arrow releases itself. Nor does uncontrol mean the author relinquishes the work. Jonathan Raban describes how writers, who "are in some sense secretaries to their own books," must take control over the writing that is generated. "If the book has any real life of its own, *it* begins to take control, *it* begins to demand certain things of you, which you may or may not live up to, and it imposes shapes and patterns on you; it calls forth the quality of experience it needs" (Wachtel 1993, 120).

6. *Unpredictability.* Obviously uncontrol leads in ways authors cannot predict. When authors find themselves writing things they had not set out to write, they feel surprised, delighted, self-affirmed, proud. They find they are more than they thought they were. The usual term for this authorial experience is "discovery," and Murray includes pages of testimony to it. The way writing turns out unpredictable, "a journey of discovery and exploration for the writer" (Marge Piercy;

---

5. Uncontrol is the essence of Giorgio Agamben's notion of "genius" or "daimon" (see Chapter 14) and related to William Butler Yeats's concept of daimon (see Chapter 6).

Darnton 2001, 180), is one of the most commonly reported experiences of authoring. Discovery happens so consistently that authors use it as a motive to write. Cynthia Ozick says of her plan to write an essay on Henry James' novel, *The Awkward Age*, "I don't know yet what I'm going to say, what I'm going to discover, and I will surely make discoveries" (Wachtel 1993, 15). The sense that writing is "a voyage of discovery" (Nadine Gordimer; 178) turns the usual academic assumption, that one writes out of a topic understood, on its head. "In fact," writes Amy Tan, "if anything, I write about it because I *don't* understand it" (283).

7. *Shaping*. Uncontrol and unpredictability also seem to turn on its head the standard notion of writerly craft. How can an author shape a work through materials and tools such as diction, syntax, revision, and knowledge of audience if the work takes directions of its own? In the phenomenology of authoring, however, craft plays a secondary role. Authors take craft as something they apply in response to more primary motives. But there is a felt sense of the application, one that embodies the experience of uncontrol and unpredictability. It is the sensation, almost tactile, of a body of discourse taking shape, "the actual pleasure of feeling something under your hand and growing," as Seamus Heaney put it (Clines 1983). Imagine home builders standing on the backyard deck they are in the process of constructing. Not surprisingly, the most common metaphor for shaping discourse is carpentry: "I'm just trying to make this thing fit right, the way a carpenter likes everything square and plumb, even if it won't show" (Robert B. Parker; Murray 1990, 40).

8. *Truth-finding*. Even if it won't show. Author after author describes the same experience, of forgetting about the opinion of readers and using the composing to test his or her own observations and beliefs in a search after some individual truth. They have no squeamishness or compunction about using that word, "truth." "While I'm writing," says Andre Dubus, "that's when I face the exposure, that's when the right word comes, or the temptation to use the wrong word and duck out, the temptation to skip something. That's when I always have to bear down and try to write as closely to what is the truth as I can feel with my senses and with my heart" (Wachtel 1993, 127). This kind of truth-finding necessarily proceeds with a strong sense of resistance to received notions, and sometimes with a hope to change them. "This matters, the remaking of an untenable world through the nib of a pen," insists Carol Shields, and "it matters so much I can't stop doing it" (2002, 137). Usually such truth-finding proceeds with an aware-

ness of its difficulty: "A harder truth. How to explain that?" asks Amy Hempel. "I want to say something truer than the obvious observation about a person—go deeper" (Wachtel 1993, 206).[6]

9. *Poaching*. It also proceeds with a complex, even ambivalent sense involving the author's position vis-à-vis private and public. Over and over, authors describe themselves as solitary beings who spend hours every day working alone to achieve a personal truth, yet extracting that truth from the outside world in order to direct it back toward the world outside. The feeling of both taking and giving, of transgression, transformation, and transference, comes close to Michel de Certeau's notion of "poaching" (1984), by which he means tactics of the disempowered to improve their conditions by stealing and adapting hegemonic cultural practices, perhaps thereby changing them. Joyce Carol Oates says that writing is "a species of exploration and transgression," and "to write is to invade another's space, if only," she adds, "to memorialize it" (Darnton 2001, 168-9). Conrad got it right. The author feels like a double agent. Cynthia Ozick describes half of her writer's self as "Jewish" and the other half as "a wild animal" (Wachtel 1993, 8). Doris Lessing, raised in Zimbabwe and living in England, says, "I have this double vision of absolutely belonging and absolutely not belonging, which is extremely valuable for a writer" (Wachtel 1993, 251).

10. *Potentiality*. Lessing's double vision extends to her phrase, "for a writer." She means the phrase two ways: for the accomplishment of the writing, but also for the self-protection of the writer. With her own use of the phrase "for a writer," Nadine Gordimer spells out this double meaning:

6.   Hempel's metaphor of going "deeper" is shared by most authors. They may compare truth-finding to peeling an onion to its core, or excavating an archaeological site, or digging a well into their own psyche. "When I described this as falling from layer to layer," says Nadine Gordimer, "I meant falling through layers of illusion and coming slowly, stage by stage, to certain truths" (Wachtel 1993, 178). In her book analyzing the figurative language in author interviews, *Authors on Writing: Metaphors and Intellectual Labor* (2005), Barbara Tomlinson has no truck with this inner search for truth, which she shelves along with the illusions of "the Buried Life of the Mind," a myth or mystification of writers who are deluded into thinking they possess "the special selfhood of the heroic author" (2). When authors think they are looking inward for individual truth, she explains, they are actually participating in an outward social praxis. In her analysis of mining imagery, Tomlinson says that "writing and mining both involve searching in an *external* world for something of great value" (55; our emphasis). So when novelist John Gardner describes the unpredictable discoveries authors make in the act of writing as "poking your pick into a piece of respectable earth and silver shows up in an iron-ore vein and God knows where you're heading" (which Tomlinson quotes), or as "your unconscious pushing up associations" (which she doesn't), he is getting his direction wrong.

"I have fought to retain that freedom to write what I like, how I like, and not follow any line, because I think that the first imperative duty, if one wants to use that word, for a writer is to be true, to preserve the integrity of whatever talent he or she has. This is the one thing you have that matters, and your first duty to yourself and your society is to develop it." (Wachtel 1993, 180)

Preserving the integrity or continued capacity of one's talent expresses the gist of what in this book we mean by *potentiality*. As Chapter 2 will explain, an author's potentiality is not something that is acquired and then used up like a wad of money. It is an ongoing capacity for creative work that needs to be constantly protected and nurtured. Working authors are driven not only to complete the work, but also to maintain the drivenness. They are thoroughly attuned to their potentiality, though that is rarely the word they use for it, and in our commonplace book on authoring we have more cites under *potentiality* even than under *discovery*. Gish Jen faces it directly: "I knew that I was not written out, something for which I have perhaps morbidly always watched: I have long vowed not to keep on past the point where I ought best stop" (Darnton 2001, 104). In the process of writing, authors show their awareness of their potentiality in many ways, by switching genres when blocked (Marge Piercy), deciding to lie fallow (Richard Ford), taking up writing that is more challenging or different (Amy Tan), admitting present failure to increase the chances for future success (Mary Gordon), defending the freedom to write any way on any topic (Cynthia Ozick), accepting as natural and motivational the knowledge that one does not really know how to write the next work (Wendell Barry), resisting the impulse to save material for a future work (Annie Dillard), not overdrawing one's internal battery (Norman Mailer), not spreading oneself too thin through self-imitation (Elie Wiesel). Writers are all alike, says poet and nature writer Diane Johnson, "in their sense of having the work inside them in some potential form. The analogy to gestation is very exact" (Sternberg 1991, 147). Chapters 2-7 explore this fertile ground of potentiality and authoring for English teachers.

11. *Singularity*. Potentiality, and the unpredictability of the writer's work that keeps potentiality alive, lead without fail to a trait that all authors share, the sense of themselves and their work as unique. The sense of individual singularity, that no one else is exactly like me, is a normal and healthy intuition, of course (see Chapter 8). With authors, it assumes a reason and motivation to write. Singularity empowers writers. "I felt a kind of entitlement," as Amy Hempel describes her

climb out of a personal slough of writer's despond: "I am entitled to tell this particular story in a way no one else can—which is a kind of power" (Wachtel 1993, 207-208). "To find your own characteristic way of narrating and insisting," Susan Sontag argues, "is to find your own inner freedom" (Darnton 2001, 225). Deaf to postmodernist conclusions that language is never original, working authors extend singularity from their sense of self to their sense of their work under construction, all aspects of it right down to the sentence. "My material," A. S. Byatt insists, "is my own and unrepeatably my own" (Wachtel 1993, 84). Rick Bass' experience of the covey flushing, "the thunderous explosion of wings," is his alone, he swears, and although another person might be there, "that person would not be me, would not be inside me" (Darnton 2001, 16). "A page of mine," Gail Godwin insists, "will never be mistaken for a page of Jane Austen or Elmore Leonard or Margaret Atwood, however much I admire and relish their voices" (Darnton 2001, 75). "One never puts down a sentence," writes John Cheever, "without the feeling that it has never been put down in such a way" (Murray 1990, 191). Chapters 8-13 explore how English teaching can be changed by the acceptance of this fundamental experience of the author, even the student writer, "as distinctly—exhilaratingly, uncomfortably—singular" (Gish Jen; Darnton 2001, 107).

12. *Hospitality*. Authors sometimes extend this inescapable intuition of singularity to their sense of audience, sometimes to their dismissal of audience. "My only readership is me," Graham Greene once said to an interviewer, and added that authors who write to an unknown audience are just short-order cooks (1983). More common, and it is very common, is the sense of writing to a single person or to a select group of people. Compositionist, biographer, and novelist Richard Marius says, "I write especially for my editor and for a few other good friends. I respect them and want them to respect me" (Waldrep 1988, 152). Naturally, authors are aware that their publications will also be read by strangers, not just by acquaintances. Thus, the underlying frame for the sociability of authoring is hospitality—hospitality in the traditional sense of entertaining a limited number of strangers. This authorial *experience* of audience is complex, since it involves establishing an intimacy (Maureen Howard), a sharing (Muriel Rukeyser), or an epistolary correspondence (Saul Bellow) with people one doesn't know. Authors intuit "rules for sociability, how to be a friend to a reader so the reader won't stop reading, how to be a good blind date with a total stranger" (Kurt Vonnegut Jr.; Darnton 2001, 243). What working authors never find attractive is a Benthamesque audience

calculus, writing to please the greatest number of readers, which would reduce their authoring to propaganda, demagoguery, or, as Margaret Atwood puts it, "cavorting about on the stage" (Wachtel 1993, 195).

For these twelve traits, every one of them, it is easy to find working authors who experience something quite different, sometimes almost the opposite. But taken together, the traits form a fairly dependable categorization of the authoring experience. If your ambition is to become an author, what then should you expect as the central inner experience of writing that you will share with most other authors? *You will feel compelled to write about a subject you know uniquely and fully and are ready to explore, ready to find perhaps unpopular truths and to shape them in new ways for readers who are friendly and receptive—an act of writing so intense and focused and pleasurable and full of surprises that you take care you do not spoil your desire and ability and compulsion to keep doing it.*

Is this how English teachers construct the authoring experience for their students?

THE CLASSROOM ACCEPTANCE OF AUTHORING

That question is answered with a simple comparison of these twelve authoring traits with customary college-teacher expectations of student authoring.

Author Experience of Authoring	Teacher Expectation of Student Authoring
Drivenness	Most students will not write assignments unless required to do so.
Pleasure	Students don't get pleasure from composing, but rather from the rewards of having written the assignment and receiving a good grade on it.
Preparedness	Typically, students get two or three weeks to prepare an assignment, and will put off writing it until the last day unless drafts are required; topics are better teacher-selected than student-chosen.
Concentration	Whether students focus while writing does not seem of much interest to teachers and may even seem an antiquated concern, given today's glorification of multitasking.
Uncontrol	Students are taught to take charge of all aspects of their writing; the ideal is a rational and even meta-discursive control over the composing process.

Unpredictability	Although "discovery" is sometimes offered as a purpose for writing, the academic ideal is a kind of composing in which ideas and forms are preset ("writing with a purpose").
Shaping	The essay-as-a-whole will be grasped by students as the product of set logical or generic patterns, rarely of growing organic forms.
Truth-finding	Writing is done to communicate or to learn established truths—that is, when "truth" is admitted in the English department door to begin with.
Poaching	Students are expected to rely on public knowledge, but there is only a lukewarm expectation that they will transform it into a new knowledge that they can call their own and that might be useful to the public.
Potentiality	It is assumed that completion of written assignments is good for students in that they will have learned something useful for their future, but rarely is it asked whether that task might turn them away from writing itself.
Singularity	The emphasis is upon students writing out of group identities according to widely held conventions of usage and genre in order to convey received knowledge.
Hospitality	In the end, the student addresses written assignments not to a stranger but to a known individual, a teacher who will not receive it with personal generosity but judge it by impersonal standards.

What is the message of English teachers to students about authoring? *As student writers, you will be required (however reluctantly) to take a topic teachers know well and locate received notions about it that you will turn, ready or not, into conventional academic discursive forms for strict evaluation; this will be an instructional exercise much pressured yet so imbued with opportunity for learning that you should look beyond the unpleasantness of doing it and expect more such writing throughout your college career.*

This crude comparison stands as a tempting platform on which this book could hang an injunction concerning English instruction in college: Students will learn more of what English courses in literature and composition hope to teach when the courses promote the working authors' accounts of authoring rather than the teachers' accounts. That injunction would misrepresent, however, our intentions in this book. We want to treat the comparison as a hypothesis or trial, with the traits of non-academic authoring used to critique current academic pedagogy.[7] As we say in the Introduction, we want to entertain some new terms and—for the nonce adopting the language of working authors—see if we can find in them some new truths. That we have the space to explore only two of the traits—potentiality and singularity—is a clue that we will find a good deal to support our hypothesis.

But surely not over a nearly consensus objection from English teachers. Our witnesses are working authors, to be sure, but don't they represent a small and select group? They might be called freelancers, whereas most authors earning a living are technical or professional writers. Non-freelancers write because their jobs demand it, and that conditions a different set of authoring traits. Non-freelancers aren't driven from within to write, but driven from without. They don't enjoy the act of composing any more than restaurant workers enjoy washing dishes—the only pleasure in the chore they might feel is getting it over with. For professionals, a model author of more pertinence would be Ken Donelson, editor of the *English Journal* and author of over a hundred articles in refereed journals, as well as several books (one called *Inspiring Literacy*): "I hate the act of writing. . . . I've heard more writing instructors than I care to admit tell students about the *joy* of writing, but how can anyone who writes think of writing as joy? Only people who do not write can talk with a straight face about the *joy* of writing. Writing can be, and often is, necessary or demanding, maybe even satisfying, but never joyful" (Waldrep 1988, 55-56). Doesn't Donelson's testimony fit the majority of writing done by English teachers—writing, scholarly and administrative, that is also unpleasant, pressured, conventionalized, and strictly evaluated? And doesn't it fit the kind of authoring the great majority of college students will continue doing in their technical or professional careers?

Consensus or not, this objection bears two assumptions worth reconsidering. One is the either/or fence it erects between "freelance" and "professional" writing, or between belletrist and functional, voluntary and obligatory, leisurely and workerly, or private and public. But just as the same language potential operates on both sides of the fence, so may the same phenomenology of authoring. Donelson, who said he never met a writer who enjoyed writing, might have been surprised

---

7.   By "non-academic" we mean writing not done to fulfill school or university course assignments. When English teachers author their own pieces (and comment on that authoring, as in Waldrep 1985, 1988), they join our non-academic testimony. See Footnote 9, however.

to find about half of the contributors to the anthology where he said it (Waldrep 1988), English department colleagues all, averring explicitly that they enjoy writing, or experience something much like joy. We just are not ready to concede that these authoring traits are specific to a minority of authors and would like to leave open the possibility that many of the traits (for instance, concentration, unpredictability, shaping, poaching, singularity, hospitality) might enliven the writing and the writing life of any professional, student or otherwise, where they don't do so already.

Also worth reconsidering is the assumption that the job conditions the authoring. The inner life of writers is not so passive. Who says that the act of authoring, in the right frame of mind, can't be a pleasure to do under work obligations? Or that the compulsion to write can't fall on both sides of the belletrist/professional fence? The students whom teachers have required to write their research paper may still be driven within to author other kinds of writing. Look at text messaging and twittering. So it is not a question of will or capability. They are the same people whom teachers have to test in order to get them to read Shakespeare, yet, as Chapter 14 will show, who follow their own compulsion to read other kinds of literature. How much of our authoring phenomenology is not experienced by technical/professional writers because they have been taught a limited, purely academic image of authoring from the first grade through graduate school?[8] Perhaps authoring itself is amenable to instruction—another hypothesis this book intends to test out. As it is, the book will skip the more obviously controversial of the real-world authoring traits, such as drivenness or pleasure, and work with the two that may be the most universal and least understood, potentiality and singularity.

---

8.   It is worth noting that many of the authors we surveyed have been primarily non-fiction authors, and the ones who write both fiction and nonfiction often deny any essential difference in authoring the two modes. "I don't think they are two kinds of writing. I think they're one. I don't think one changes hats," writes Jonathan Raban (Wachtel 1993, 116). "I write both fiction and nonfiction," avers Richard Marius. "The process is somewhat different for each, but there are probably more similarities in the two than differences" (Waldrep 1988, 148). When an author testifies that "There is in writing the constant joy of sudden discovery," we shouldn't assume this is a writer of fiction. In fact, the declaration comes from H. L. Mencken (1917, 27), who camped about as far from fiction as he could. How differently a selection of technical writers would describe their authoring shouldn't be presumed until we hear from them.

English teachers will raise four other objections that may tempt them to reject out of hand our hypothesis that the experience of non-academic authoring provides a useful critique of English pedagogy. In due course, this book will cover all four objections fully, so here we will merely ask for a little forbearance. First, don't English teachers everywhere find ways to transport the non-academic model of authoring into their instructional model? They find readers for student writing other than themselves, for instance, or they allow students to choose the literary pieces they will interpret and write about. How much do such teaching strategies alter, though, the basic classroom presumption about the core experience of authoring, that rather than a self-compelled pleasure, it is an other-imposed exercise (no pain, no gain)? How much more of that instructional core can teachers change?

The second objection is that, however appealing and convincing, the non-academic experience of authors simply cannot fit into the material ways of the academy. Any teacher would like to imagine first-year students postponing English courses until they had the experience and the knowledge that would give them the preparation and drive to poach fruitfully. But the first-year composition requirement cannot be postponed, nor core courses in literature delayed until students have senior-level knowledge. Our answer to this objection is that the academy, as an institute of *learning*, is not built with brick, stone, and concrete. Maybe it is time to reinstate the senior thesis as a graduation requirement (some schools have never abandoned it). Maybe it is time to rid the first two undergraduate years of mandatory writing courses (some schools already do that). Maybe it is time writing assignments were shaped to encourage discourse genres less antipathetic to non-academic ways of authoring.[9] And even if the present curriculum is written in something akin to brick, stone, and concrete, there is wisdom in knowing the exact ways it walls out non-academic realities.

---

9. In 1998, thirty-two winners of the Braddock Award, given every year for the best article published in *College Composition and Communication,* were offered the opportunity to write a commentary on their article. Only two describe the act and feel of composing the piece. Both describe exploratory essays that broke with academic conventions. Nancy Sommers said of her piece, "This was a new kind of writing for me, and I found it liberating, engaging, and surprisingly fun" (Ede 1999, 320). Ellen Cushman said that hers was written with a "recklessness" that "took shape from a deep seated need to do something with my scholarship, to go beyond the university classroom, to remember where I've come from" (Ede 1999, 388-389). So genre, profession, and attitudes toward authoring are entwined.

Third, literature teachers will point out that the realities of working authors pertain more to composition courses than to literature courses, which study published works in terms of history and critical interpretation. But how would knowledge of a famous writer's authoring change a student's interpretation? As Francis-Noël Thomas and other literary critics have been arguing for over a decade, authors are personally responsible for their own works, and that "authorial agency" imbues their texts with particular meanings. The text is a result of their actions, and those actions—much like our authors describe them—are essentially open and unpredictable, and cannot be totally explained by non-authorial agencies such as culture, language, and institutions (1993, 4). Thomas points out that Achebe wrote *Things Fall Apart* as a compulsive act of personal atonement and Shaw wrote *Saint Joan* as a poaching act of political reform, and knowing this should shape how we read the works.

The last objection is at once the most uncompromising and the most problematical. This contends that our traits describe a phenomenology of successful and experienced authors. Teachers, almost by definition, teach amateur and inexperienced authors. The kind of writing expected of students by teachers seems more like practicing or exercising than authoring because that is what it has to be. But does a novice or an amateur experience the act of writing much differently than does an expert or a professional? According to the language, all writers "practice" or "exercise" their arts and skills, and the ambivalence of the terms may point to an essential equivalence. It seems a little hasty to assume that a grade-three pianist experiences none of the phenomenology of playing experienced by the virtuoso.

Differences of opinion often stem from differences in the point where lines of argument start. Begin with the way teachers observe their students writing, and it seems reasonable to argue that real-world authoring doesn't fit, and therefore the students are not real authors yet and should not be treated as such. Begin with testimony of real-world authoring, and it seems reasonable—at least we are so inclined—to argue that since it doesn't fit our current academic conditions and objectives, the academy therefore is keeping students from experiencing real authoring. Or begin with the ways authoring is currently taught in college composition and literature courses, and it is hard not to end with the ways students don't muster. Begin with the experience of authoring that students do have, and it is hard not to end—at least this is where we end, in Chapter 14—with the ways much of it is denied by the academy.

So we begin with traits of authoring as experienced by successful, working authors. As we say, we select two experiences that strike us as universal dynamics of any act of writing, outside or inside the academy: potentiality and singularity. If they are accepted as legitimate for college-student writers, even as student-author rights, if you will, how might the teaching of English courses be revisioned?

POTENTIALITY AND ALICE SHELDON

*Two spirits were working in her, love and anonymity. Yet they were so
"haunted" of each other that separation was impossible.*

Djuna Barnes, *Nightwood*

It is customary to speak of young aspiring authors as having potential,
and of old successful authors as having realized their potential. But for
serious writers, potential is something they can't imagine as first having
and then using up. For them, as we will see in the next chapter, potentiality is as needful to ongoing authoring as perception, words, or readers. It is a personal condition that bridges the most disparate parts of
their life—past, current, and future. No one can illustrate this fact better than the author Alice Bradley Sheldon.

At three in the morning of May 19, 1986, as Alice's husband
Huntington (Ting) lay asleep in bed, she shot him twice in the head.
She then made two telephone calls, one to her lawyer and one to her
son, telling them what she had done and asking that they not call the
police right away. She wanted time to complete the suicide pact she had
with Ting. When the police reached the apartment, they found she had
lived up—though that is not the right expression—to her word. Alli was
dead, lying beside Ting, holding his hand. Her suicide note was dated
seven years earlier.

Nineteen years earlier, in 1967, when Alli was 51 years old, she wrote
what some people might consider another suicide note. In submitting
two stories to science fiction magazines, the first fiction she had written
in decades, she signed herself not Alice Sheldon or even Alice Bradley
(her maiden name) but James Tiptree Jr. Tiptree was a label she and
Ting had seen on a jar of preserves one day in the grocery store.
Laughing, she had added the James and Ting had added the Junior.
But it was a serious act. And although in a sense she was killing off her
real name, it was not a suicide, not even a suicide pact made with herself. It was an act of preservation. She was keeping alive her potential
as an author.

During the next years, known to the science fiction world only as James Tiptree Jr., Alice published more than 40 short stories and novellas. Tiptree won a Nebula award for short story and a Nebula and a Hugo award for novella. Her pseudonym was not an open or genteel pose, as many pen names are. More accurately, it might be called an anonym. No one, not even her editors, knew that James Tiptree Jr. was an alias, much less for a woman. Alice even maintained her disguise in correspondence with fans and with sympathetic authors such as Joanna Russ and Ursula Le Guin, to whom she signed herself as "Tip." Everyone was shocked and amazed when, in 1976, her identity was ferreted out by ardent fans.

No one, however, was as shocked as Alice herself. "My secret world had been invaded," she wrote later (Phillips 2006, 3). Although she continued to write and publish, it was with growing dissatisfaction and shrinking productivity. There is evidence that the loss of her anonymity played a crucial role in her diminishing sense of herself as a viable author and maybe as a viable person. A few weeks after the disclosure in 1976, she wrote an editor that "When Tiptree dies for good, I will too" (361). Three years later, she wrote her suicide note. Seven years later, less than twenty-four hours before her actual suicide, she wrote to Ursula Le Guin that "Life here is on the way down and out," and signed herself "Tip/Alli" (391).[1]

To some degree, our tale of Alice Sheldon's anonym, outing, and crippling of her potential to author is speculation. But for this book it stands as a lesson for teachers about student authoring. As teachers, what do we know of the secret energies that maintain a student's potential as a writer? What do we unknowingly do to block those energies? A student raises a hand during the first meeting of a class in writing about literature and asks the teacher if papers may be submitted under pen names. What does the teacher say? If the teacher is operating within

---

1. Before Alice's identity was revealed, she had won a third Nebula for a novella published under another pen name, Raccoona Sheldon. She said she published as "Raccoona" when she "felt the need to say some things impossible to a male persona" (*Contemporary Authors*, 444). But why not, then, as "Alice Sheldon"? For her, pseudonymity or anonymity was a way of living and writing. Over her life, she published as Alice Bradley Davey (in *Mademoiselle*), Alice Bradley (in the *New Yorker*), Ann Terry (early story), Mrs. H. D. Smith (letter to the editor), Mrs. Huntington D. Sheldon (letters on feminism), Dr. Alice B. Sheldon (her dissertation), Alice B. Sheldon (*Journal of Comparative and Physiological Psychology*), and, her staple science fiction noms de plume, James Tiptree Jr. and Raccoona Sheldon. Only posthumously was anything of hers published as "Alice Sheldon."

the current textuality paradigm that we describe in the Introduction, the response will be automatic: No, because we do group work and peer evaluation in this class and students are openly answerable for their work. The teacher might assume that the student is embarrassed to hand over work to public gaze, or the teacher might not wish to repeat the patriarchal history that has forced pseudonyms on women writers. But what if the student's question emerged simply from self-knowledge? Maybe the student writes better when composing under a pen name. If anonymity was necessary for Alice Sheldon's continued potential as a writer, why might it not also be for some student authors?

Pseudonymity or anonymity is only one of many energies of writing potential that are withheld from students in English classrooms. In a revision of English department instruction, potentiality is a good place to start.

2
POTENTIALITY AND THE TEACHING OF ENGLISH

A life is full of isolated events, but these events, if they are to form a coherent narrative, require odd pieces of language to cement them together, little chips of grammar (mostly adverbs or prepositions) that are hard to define, since they are abstractions of location or relative position, words like therefore, else, other, also, thereof, theretofore, instead, otherwise, despite, already, and not yet.

Carol Shields, *Unless*

Fiction writer Carol Shields notes that the adverb *not yet* is one of the "odd pieces of language" that lends coherence to people's understanding of their own lives, or, as we will say in Chapter 10, to the kind of authoring known as lifestory. Our noun for *not yet* is potentiality. And our question concerning *not yet* and potentiality is why the notion plays such a conflicted part in the teaching of English courses.

THE CURIOUS CASE OF POTENTIALITY

We start with a riddle. In the filing cabinet of every English teacher lies a manuscript on authoring. Each of ours, single-spaced, measures more than an inch thick. They are stored in manila folders bearing the label "letters of recommendation." The riddle is why teachers' letters of recommendation assign value to a criterion that makes scant appearance in their scholarly articles about teaching.

It's not that scholarship and letters of recommendation don't compare. Scholarly articles are published, but in a sense so are letters of recommendation. The pieces in the filing cabinet were once printed, distributed, and read by hiring-committee members who believed they were looking at a product of a scholar's careful attention. So there is an equivalency. Yet in professional letters of recommendation English teachers appraise students and their writing differently than they do in professional articles on the teaching of writing. The main difference lies in potentiality.

As an estimate of the candidate's promise, potentiality appears explicitly as a topic in letters of recommendation about a fourth of the time.[1] Ideally, it should underpin all of them, at least tacitly. A letter that merely recites a student's past performance without hazarding a prediction about the student's future performance hardly merits the name "recommendation." But is potentiality equally a central value in articles about the English classroom? Does potentiality compete with other pedagogical concepts that have shaped English pedagogy— concepts such as culture, audience, canon, critique, quality, invention? Hardly. Or, as this book surmises, *not yet*.

The disjunct between recommendation practice and teaching/scholarship practice suggests that unspoken boundary interdicts are in place. One of the boundaries lies inside English departments, dividing literature and composition. Author potentiality has much more explanatory force on the literature side. We have noted that the adoption of a pen name may have helped maintain Alice Sheldon's energies as a writer. In Chapter 6 we will see how some automatic writing of W. B. Yeats' wife opened up new avenues in his poems and plays. It seems that the interdict has to do with treating novice famous-author writing and novice student-writing in the same way. As we observe in Chapter 1 and will see over and over in this book (especially in Chapter 14), student writers are not allowed the full rights of authorship, which include respect for the work they have *not yet* produced.

This departmental boundary between literature and composition, however, is cut across by another divide. This is the line most English teachers draw between admissible and inadmissible evidence for learning within a course. Potentiality is not allowed, for instance, as a factor in grading. There are two main reasons. First, potentiality is internal, lacking the external or "objective" proof teachers feel is needed for summative evaluation. In this it is similar to the criterion of motivation. No teacher wants to be swayed by students who beg credit for "the hours I put into this assignment." Much less would a teacher be persuaded by a student who pleads, "I'll have this figured out after the course is over, so give me credit now."

---

1. Susan Bell, Suzanne Cole, and Liliane Floge (1992) provide a sophisticated analysis of letters of recommendation and a good review of the literature. Among other effects, they discovered that male recommenders were more likely to comment on "career potential" than were female—an interaction between gender and potentiality that points to our next chapter.

The second reason follows from the first. Potentiality is constrained by time. Teachers do not grade on potentiality because they are obligated first and foremost to reward only learning that is evidenced during the course. That's all they are responsible and paid for. How can student work be proven truly potential until its potentiality is actualized? For teachers, that would mean work that appears *en actualité* as the French say, or *actualmente* as the Spanish say, that is, appears today, right now. It matters not that the slow growth of verbal skill means some taught skills may first surface long after the semester is over.

In short, for teachers potentiality has problems with evidentiality. The problems are easy to show. Consider the sequence of grades earned by two students during a course:

| Student 1 | A | A | A | A | A | A | A | A |
| Student 2 | F | D | D | C | C | B | B | B |

Who should receive the higher grade for the course? The argument from potentiality is that Student 2 should, since Student 2 has demonstrated an ability to adapt to a new learning situation and Student 1 has not, and so in the long run Student 2 is more likely to become a better writer or reader of literature than Student 1. But few teachers will credit that argument, although few teachers will find it easy to discredit.

We are two instructors of literature and composition, however, who believe that potentiality should not be excluded from the teaching of English. The case for potentiality as a legitimate pedagogical concern won't be easy, but we believe it needs to be made. The way to begin is to recognize that potentiality, far from being cast outside our discipline, has always been irrevocably inside.

THE ACTUALITY OF POTENTIALITY

Let's begin—we are aware of the contradiction—with some concrete evidence for potentiality. Scholars both outside and inside English departments have argued that potentiality is a constituent element or inherent dimension in four areas central to English instruction: brain behavior, language functioning, group discourse, and author intentions. Here we will render a library row of scholarship down to seven paragraphs.

For decades now, brain specialists have abandoned the pigeon-hole model of the brain as a storehouse of images and memories with routines to access them. In this remodeling of brain functioning, no one has better led the way than Gerald Edelman. In a series of studies and books, most of them written after he earned a Nobel Prize for his work in immunology in 1972, Edelman explores a central question: How does the brain help us act upon new experience? How does the brain register, for instance, the novel situations awaiting the English student in the long run, after the course is over? Not through the accessing of exact electromagnetic traces of old experiences, argues Edelman, since new experience is never the same as old. What is stored is not a capacity to replicate, but rather a capacity to generalize. The brain does not scan single or discrete memory nodes, but rather scans patterns, combinations or associations of node activation. It is through the dynamic and transformed pattern, the "generalization," that subsequent behavior can be shaped or "recategorized." In a piece of brain-studies jargon that English-studies people may find attractive, the whole process is called "retranscription." Sensory input, traveling along neural pathways in the brain, with no guarantee that it will activate any particular response, is called "potentials"—a piece of jargon we certainly find attractive. In the way the human brain deals with experience, potentiality does not wait like a secret inheritance and pop out when some unexpected novel situation calls for it. It operates every second of our lives: for instance, in the morning when we reach for the bedside light switch, which is never exactly in the same place because on awakening our hand is never precisely in the same place.[9]

It is still operating at the end of the day when we pick up our bedtime book. Language is also a "potential" that constantly has to be "retranscribed" to function. Comparable to models of the brain, language models can be artificially reduced to a pigeonhole or storehouse form, as with dictionaries, word-frequency lists, grammar rules, or style manuals. But as we use language day in and day out, it operates in no way as a catalog that we choose from. Rather, it functions as brain patterns do, through generalizations and transformations—discursive, grammatical, lexical, and semantic frames that are activated to meet novel language situations, to make sense of what we are newly hearing and reading, or to discover what we are newly saying or writing. The functionality of language frames can be demonstrated in many

---

2. We summarize here Edelman's work in brain function as discussed in *Neural Darwinism* (1987), and later in the more popularized *Bright Air, Brilliant Fire* (1992) and *Wider than the Sky* (2004).

ways—pausal studies that show writers activating a syntactic, logical, argumentative, or genre frame before deciding the lexical and ideational choices that will instantiate it, or priming studies that show readers recalling or guessing a word more quickly when a word preceding it creates an intellectual or experiential frame for it. Language as retranscriptive potentiality follows Chomsky's venerable insight that language has to be generative or "transformational," or else there is no way to explain how children can learn to use it so fast to process novel utterances, both comprehending them and creating them. Obviously, both neurological patterns and language frames themselves have the potential to grow, and they constantly undergo restructuring through experience, age, and social context.

Indeed the social plays a major role in helping generate, reshape, and constrain brain and language potentialities. If part of Edelman's contribution has been his scientific exploration of the way the brain changes chemically in response to experience, a great deal of that experience is social and cultural in nature. Consider these two sentence starts:

(a) The broker persuaded the investor to sell . . .

(b) The broker persuaded to sell the stock . . .

Syntactically, both are legitimate beginnings in English, but English speakers feel that the second has a different potential than the first, with the rest of the sentence less predictable. That feeling is supported with electroencephalogram studies. Lee Osterhout and Phillip J. Holcomb (1993) show that readers process these two sentence beginnings with different electrical activities, "event-related brain potentials" (ERPs). As we say, such electrical activities are called brain "potentials" because they are not absolutely determined. Sometimes the external language event does not produce the electromagnetic pattern, and sometimes an absence of the external event produces it. With these two sentence starts differences in potentials clearly have social origins, since the brain's activation matches the relative frequency of past encounters with the syntactic structures. Readers and listeners meet much more often the subject-verb-object pattern of (a) than the post-nominal, adjective clause with "that" elided of (b).

So brain and language potentiality is not a potency constrained only by brain-structure or language-structure limits. It is given bounds also by the social and the cultural. Cultural semanticist Terry Reiger (1996) calls these bounds "the human semantic potential." By "potential" he means capacity or creativity within social constraints. He illustrates with the different ways various cultures represent space through language. Instead of using the relative "left" and "right," the desert-dwelling Australians speaking Guugu Yimithirr use the absolute cardinal directions. They will say, "Place the knife to the north of the plate." For another example, instead of "over" and "under," the agricultural cultures of Mexico speaking Mixtec schematize the table as an upright four-legged animal and will say that an eater's hand is located "spine-table" or "belly-table." It is possible for native English speakers to use these expressions (as we have just done), but for us their semantic potential is much more constrained.

It should not be surprising, then, that potentiality extends its presence to the rhetoric of small groups. The dynamics are too complex for any short summary, but as a start the following account fits a good deal of the inquiry and data. For a group to remain vital it must change, and this change is supported by rhetorical practices within the group that allow individual members the room and the right to explore and further their own growth. The potential of the group for long-term survival will be achieved only by allowing members, even members whom the majority of the group consider fringe, to exercise their own singular potentials. Toward this end, rhetorical practices of groups include tolerating language differences, promoting conversational and oratorical turn-taking (as with the classical Greek *skeptron*), facilitating access to uncensored language records, and creating spaces for private expression (especially spaces where subgroups can nurture resistance to the majority). In *Situating the Self* (1992), political scientist Seyla Benhabib identifies "negotiation" as the central capacity or "potential" that allows groups to anticipate the standpoint of outlier members of the group.

These group practices, including negotiation, sound idealistic but also can be very real. Compositionist Nancy Welch (1996) details some of them in a summer K-12 teacher workshop, a literacy project in which participants wrote their lifestories, interviewed an acquaintance, kept a weekly journal shared with one other participant, read drafts in small groups, shared passages from their personal reading, offered issues for town meetings, and produced a workshop newsletter. Welch theorizes the success of the workshop by means of psychologist D. W. Winnicott's notion of "potential space," a form of developmental play in which individuals create private space in order to absorb and re-create social events (the eleven-year-old reading under the covers with a flashlight, for instance). Paraphrasing Winnicott, Welch says that in potential space, "individuals, in relationships of trust and dependability, discover their potential to participate in the *reconstruction* of shared reality, rather than merely comply, adapt, fit in" (67). Her italicized word connects with the *retranscription* of brain functioning and the *restructuring* of language processing.

A negative example of potential space is explored by Giorgio Agamben, the contemporary philosopher of language, art, and politics whose synthesis of community, growth, potentiality, and singularity will inform this book in many places. Agamben's most telling example is the camp—work camps, death camps, prisoner of war camps—where usually every opportunity is taken to eradicate the potential for personal growth, where individual prisoners contribute to the group as a whole only through non-individualized labor, and where Welch's "reconstructive" rhetoric is often banned to the point that personal names are converted to numbers and guards and prisoners are not allowed to speak to one another. In *Remnants of Auschwitz* (1999c), Agamben finds in the Nazi World War II death-camp *Musselmänner* an absolute limit to the human sense of potentiality. *Musselmänner* are prisoners beaten down by shock, forced labor, and starvation to a mute zombie state. Their rhetorical resources have been reduced to one last testimony, their "extreme potentiality to suffer" (78). However extreme, the death camp, Agamben argues in *Homo Sacer* (1995a), is a paradigm for the contemporary political state in its denial of potentiality to its subjects and its appropriation of potentiality exclusively to its own constituting sovereignty (44-48). In *The Coming Community* (1993) Agamben imagines the positive inverse, a human group held together only by their willingness to make room for the open communication of each other's singular potentialities, a community whose ethos is continually in progress, not shaped by any unspoken constituting identity. That would be a community, says Agamben, to whose peaceable presence current governments would respond by rolling out the tanks (86).[3]

Finally, potentiality functions as a necessary part of written discourse production. This is true on either side of the authoring/reading divide. As we have seen working authors themselves declare (Chapter 1), writers could hardly be moved to write if they did not think of their product as having potential to move readers. It is a construction of authoring

---

3. Chapter 12 expands many of these ideas of Agamben's in connection with the post-modernist loss of self.

that easily fits Aristotle's rhetorical ethics. Through the dynamics of formal causation, as Craig R. Smith (1970) has shown, Aristotle argues that the good writer's potentiality initiates a chain reaction where each actuality perpetuates potentiality instead of squelching it. The shaping energies of the soul (entelechy) produce ideas that have the potential to become good language—good, because the language has the potential for good persuasion, and because the persuasion has the potential to cause a good act. Readers, then, continue the chain of potentiality that writers initiate. Being an author entails the understanding that the potentiality of writing products is what readers may make of them. Being a reader entails the assumption of this potentiality. Together, reader and writer construct an exchange. Their interaction is fueled, in Michael Halliday's gisty phrase, with the "functional potential of language" (1978, 160).

All this is a hasty preview, to be filled out as this book progresses. The point is that English professionals can't limit potentiality. It can't be confined to letters of recommendation, where predictions of a candidate's future are safe because they are rarely challenged later; nor can it be banned from the classroom, where teachers might hope to limit their accountability to the fifteen weeks of the semester. Potentiality is omnipresent. It is as current as the phrase that lies just to the right of the cursor, as implicated as the momentary puzzlement of American readers when they glance at the spine of a book published in Europe and open it up to find themselves staring at the last page upside down, as real as the mutual heightening of attention during a class enactment of a play, as concrete as the averted look during a writing center tutorial, as forceful as the inner fire that sets a writer to writing and a reader to reading. It should be used by teachers as readily as any other attribute that students "have": motivation, proficiency, maturity, experience, ethnicity, foreknowledge. It is a part of every iota of work done in an English classroom, and a primary constituent of thought, language, group productivity, and the act and construction of authoring itself.

A USABLE CONCEPT OF POTENTIALITY

Few words in the English language have been more probed and debauched than "potentiality." On the one hand, the philosophers—Parmenides, Aristotle, Plotinus, Aquinas, Leibniz, Nietzsche, Whitehead, Agamben—have carried on a tireless debate over the distinction between and status of potentiality and actuality. On the other hand, everyday folk have squandered the coinage until there is hardly any value left. A Chamber of Commerce advertises that an entire city is "beginning to show its potential," a political action group lays historical claim to having helped three generations of Mexican American students "fulfill their potential," a musical composition with no notes is declared "rife with potentiality," a registrar calls the entire range of people who could apply to the university "potential students"—not to speak of the common trick of using "potential" merely to upgrade the word "possibility" (that is, "There is good potential that condo fees can be reduced"). It is tempting to simply abandon a word that has become so polyvalent, slippery, and sometimes just vacuous.

We will resist the temptation, and from this soup of usage fish out three distinct notions underlying the concept of potentiality, in order to be left with a fourth for this book. We distinguish all four by their essential need. What in a particular situation is required to maintain the condition of potentiality? All have application to English instruction.

1. *Genetic potentiality*—an entity (an event, machine, person, organization of people) is already set to actualize, merely lacking time for that to happen. Police defuse a time bomb "with the potential to level a city block." The term "genetic" suggests an innate mechanism, like DNA, that will inevitably run its course, as with cell division. In philosophy, one classic image for potentiality is explicitly genetic: the example in Aristotle's *Metaphysics* of the acorn that contains the future oak tree. In English classrooms, the concept of genetic potentiality underlies older notions of innate talent ("gifted students") and some newer notions of cultural and ethnic background ("advantaged students").

2. *Quiescent potentiality*—an entity is prepared to actualize and is capable, but lacks the trigger or switch to initiate its course of actualization. The police find explosives and other ingredients to make a bomb "with the potential to level a city block," but the terrorists were waiting for the go-ahead from superiors to assemble it. The tacit notion of quiescent potentiality underlies much English teacher practice, such as searching for works of literature that will "wake up" students, or trying out new writing topics with the hope that one will "catch fire."

3. *Constrained potentiality*—an entity is capable, even eager, even struggling to act, but actualization is being held back by human forces. Students in a "big-city ghetto" are "quelled, silenced, placed in

rigid psychic isolation" and consequently are being "deprived of potential." The lines are from George B. Leonard's second chapter, "The Human Potential," of *Education and Ecstasy* (1968). In its day Leonard's book was a best seller that critiqued education through the ideas of Abraham Maslow, Carl Rogers, Rollo May, and other post-WWII existential psychologists who saw the human self as cabined and suffocated by social rules and conventions and in dire need of release, of "freedom to learn." As we will see, the notion of constrained potentiality continues to speak powerfully to many educators today, who may ridicule Rogers' vision of "self-actualization" yet still talk of students' "rights to possibility," or of classrooms as "sites of potential transformation." For example, critical pedagogy holds dear Freire's vision of oppression and rebellion and has little compunction in calling itself "liberatory."

4. *Maintained potentiality*—an entity constitutes or furthers a framework for creative work that needs room and encouragement to keep healthy and growing. Such is this book's particular notion of potentiality. We will refer to it as *phenomenological potentiality* when we focus on its inner personal workings and *systemic potentiality* when we look at its functioning in society (where one aspect of it is environmental sustainability). Maintained potentiality is not defined by any particular outcome or actualization, as with genetic or quiescent potentiality, nor is it defined by forces that try to hold it back, as with constrained potentiality. Rather, it is defined by its ongoing creation of actualizations, and by its ability to absorb and transform outside forces. It is our term for the capacity of Edelman's human brain that grows as it "recategorizes" itself in ever-new response to an ever-changing world of experience, for the functioning of languages and literary genres whose structural and evolving frames allow a constant output of sin-gular utterances, or for the activity of human groups whose elastic inner organizations promote individual action leading to new group response to novel contingencies. For the English teacher, the idea of maintained potentiality recommends a pedagogy of patience, nurturance, resistance, and tolerance that is the main plea of this book.

This notion of phenomenological or systemic potentiality is not easy to grasp. Here are four handles for teachers, much indebted to Agamben:

1. *Currency*. Potentiality points to the future, but it exists now. It's easy to imagine that potentiality has only a post-hoc reality, and that its pres-

ence appears only with the actualization of whatever it was preparing. How can teachers work with something that by definition has not yet achieved material status, that indeed lies in a blank area of the screen just to the right of the cursor, or, to use another of Aristotle's metaphors for potentiality, lies in the unmarked wax tablet? Note, however, that Aristotle's wax-tablet image was of the human mind, the entelechy, a metaphor of its power to imagine and shape things, including language, into effective form. That mind is current. Even with the oak tree, it may no longer be an acorn—but acorns, as acorns, exist, and their genetic potentiality to become an oak tree can be nurtured, maintained, or destroyed (hence the term "epigenetic" preferred by developmentalists and cell biologists). Mental creativity does not wait passively until acted upon, but rather actively interacts with the environment, as psychologist Liane Gabora says, "in a state of potentiality that can unfold different ways" (2005).[4] The English student is given a task—to read a work or to write a paper—and the potential of the student to do it is as present and active as his or her desire to do it, or as the surrounding cultural, ecological allowances to do it.

2. *Teachability*. Unlike genetic potentiality, maintained potentiality is not predetermined, but teachable. Part of ecological allowances can be the teacher. Ongoing potentiality, open to change, is open to instruction. The best-known version of this is Vygotsky's zone of proximal development, that particular area of instruction in which more adept people help advance less adept people. Aristotle formulates it more abstractly, explaining that potential existence is actualized through the agency of existence already actual (*Generation of animals*, Part II, Chapter 1).

3. *Continuity*. The true end of potentiality is potentiality. Aristotle's formulation leaves open the possibility that the actualization can exhaust the potential. As agent, a teacher may concentrate on the student's production without seeing that its effect may destroy the

---

4. Gabora's full sentence reads, "Rather than viewing the mind as a hotbed of competing memes or ideas that get selected amongst, it is more parsimonious to view it as existing in a state of potentiality that can unfold different ways depending on how it interacts with the contexts it encounters." In her novel *Feather Crowns*, Bobbie Ann Mason has an image better than Aristotle's acorn for the way this quality of potentiality combines with the singularity of a person's lifestory (see Chapter 10). Mason's hero, Christie, a 19th-century farm woman, looks back on her life and says, "I was always busy a-doing something and trying to find out something that nobody else would think to fool with. Partly, it's just keeping ahold of your real self there inside, the same way you need to save out a little bit of sourdough for the next raising" (1993, 446).

student's desire to produce similar work in the future. Potentiality throws a distinct light on educational acts that are self-contradicting because counter-productive. A pedagogy of maintained potentiality would say that the only skill a teacher should promote in a student is one that will sustain itself, not a skill that will use itself up in completing certain assignments for the teacher. Agamben's exegesis of Aristotle brilliantly distinguishes this pedagogical skill. Agamben finds in Aristotle two modes through which potentiality is articulated. The first, "mere potentiality to be" (*energeia* or actualization), has as its end a particular product or actuality. The second, "effective potentiality to not-be" (*dynamos* or potentiality itself), has as its end potentiality (1993, 34). The second has the power to not actualize as well as to actualize, and it will refuse to actualize in order always to "conserve" itself, always to "set aside its own potential" (1995a, 46). This is not philosophic quibbling. Agamben points out that "The architect retains his potential to build even when he does not actualize it" and will not build if building "jeopardizes his potential to build" (1999b, 245). Obviously, in the classroom the skill that will sustain itself and the skill that will suffocate are sometimes inadvertently confounded.[5]

4. *Free will*. Maintained potentiality is more than preparedness or readiness. The student can be prepared, taught the potential, to pass a test. The student can be trained to be ready to pass the test. But these capacities of preparedness and readiness are merely quiescent potentiality if the student does pass the test but subsequently discards the skills or knowledge needed to pass a similar test in the future. Conversely, the capacities are maintained potentiality if they are preserved even if the student does not take the test. Such potentiality, potentiality to not-be, among other things maintains the student's ability to decide not to take the test. Consider the pedagogical import of two students who refuse to take a test, one unable to pass it and one able to pass it. In either case the refusal may be a legitimate critique of the test but the critique is more persuasive in the second case. Say it really is a stupid test. As teachers we would rather teach the potentiality of the student who refuses to take it than the potentiality of the student who takes it. The potentiality to not-be is ultimately the ground of free will, a quality that, as Agamben says, makes potentiality "the most proper mode of human existence" (1993, 43).[6] Teachers

---

5. Examples from physical exercise are especially clear. Smart exercisers won't start a new exercise in a way that will destroy their desire or ability to continue it. Smart runners won't attempt a marathon until they are sure running it won't destroy their desire or ability to run it again.

6. Agamben returns again and again to the question of potentiality. An early exegesis

should always be open to the needs of students to preserve their potential, even needs that run counter to the teacher's plans.

5. *Preferring not to.* Sometimes potentiality is damping itself to protect itself. It's worth emphasizing that the negation that defines potentiality—the capability to refuse to actualize—is a positive part of its force. This potential of students may show up in ways that can be mistaken for ignorance or deficit. Students may not only refuse to take an exam, they may also take it but deliberately do poorly on it. Or they may write on an unassigned topic, may leave the last half of the Austen novel unread, may skip class that they think will be boring.

---

of Aristotle is the genesis, a 1986 lecture published in *Potentialities* (1999) in which he reinterprets some very cryptic remarks in the *Metaphysics*, such as: "All potentiality is impotentiality of the same and with respect to the same"; "What is potential can both be and not be, for the same is potential both to be and not to be"; and, most cryptic, "A thing is said to be potential if, when the act of which it is said to be potential is realized, there will be nothing impotential." In these remarks Agamben locates a definition of human freedom as the capability to not act or the capability to be one's own impotentiality. In 1993, he explored the assertion of Melville's Bartleby, "I would prefer not to," as the ultimate formula of pure potentiality and therefore of essential human freedom—a formula that connects potentiality with Leibniz's modality of the contingent (as opposed to the possible, the impossible, and the necessary), which "can or can not be and which coincides with the domain of human freedom" (1999b, 261). *The Coming Community* (1993) posits effective potentiality as the mode of human existence most central to ethical action and most in need of social protection. In *The Man Without Content* (1999), Agamben uses this notion of effective potentiality to qualify art; the twentieth-century reproducible artwork is activated by mere potentiality (*energia*), since the original potentiality that created it (*dynamos*) is abandoned. In *Homo Sacer: Sovereign Power and Bare Life* (1995), Agamben argues that the modern political state has appropriated effective potentiality as its "paradigm of sovereignty" (1995a, 46), maintaining itself in relation to actuality through its ability to ban or exclude from normal law some of its own human subjects, retaining an original "constituting power" indefinitely as a mode of pure potentiality. In *Remnants of Auschwitz* (1999), and especially in the astonishing chapter "The Musselmann," Agamben argues that the death camps denied prisoners their last potential, the possibility of authentically experiencing a "proper" death—that is, the possibility of living with and toward a death that is one's own and not owned by others; ironically, the "death camp" was the very place where death was banned, at least a true or dignified death, and where mere corpses were produced. The Musselmann testifies to the human denied all potential and therefore the human undistinguished from the inhuman, and as such stands as the extreme opposite of Bartleby, although superficially their catatonic-like states might be confused. Between the student who cannot and the student who cannot not and the student who *can* not—all perhaps with zombie-like behavior—the teacher had better be able to distinguish, since the three are occupying radically difference modalities of agency: incapacity, necessity, and potentiality. For some central passages reflecting Agamben's fertile synthesis of community, Aristotelian potential, human growth, and human singularity, see *Idea of Prose* (1995b) 95-98; *The Man Without Content* (1999a) 59-67, 98-103; *The Coming Community* (1993) 16-19, 22-24, 62-65; *Potentialities* (1999b) 177-184, 214-219; and *Homo Sacer* (1995a) 39-48.

They may choose these and a hundred other refusals and resistances not out of inability but in order to conserve and even further their potentialities. If teachers are going to teach to potentiality, they are going to have to respect impotentiality as well, because, as Aristotle says in the *Metaphysics*, potentiality and impotentiality are the same. Teachers will have to treat Bartleby's "I would prefer not to" as a worthy pedagogical outcome.

Let us express the teacher's obligation most stringently. Faced with a given learning task, a student will choose to take it up or not take it up under four different conditions: with the potential to make good potential of it, with the potential to decline to make good potential of it, with the potential but not the time or opportunity to make good potential of it, or without the potential to make good potential of it. A teacher who has disallowed these conditions may be imposing a task, but in essence it is not a learning task.

POTENTIALITY AND TEACHING

These five qualities of maintained potentiality sit uneasily within familiar instructional notions of student potential, such as 1960s models of John Dixon growth or Carl Rogers facilitation, or later zones of proximal development, sites of possibility, or transfer of skills. The light that maintained potentiality throws on teaching practices is radical. Nonetheless, it can provide English teachers with questions that will help them choose what and how to teach. Say the curriculum calls for a Samuel Beckett play. First, do students already have the potential to read that particular play productively? If so, why teach it? Second, if students lack the potential, can the teacher help build it so they can read the play productively? If not, why teach it? Third, will reading the play, with or without the teacher's help, conserve the students' potential to read Beckett in the future (or modernistic drama in the future)? If not, is it ethical to teach it? Fourth, will assigning the play give the students the opportunity to productively refuse to read it? If not, on what ethical grounds can the teacher proscribe the refusal?

Admittedly, these sound like the kind of questions that can unpin current modes of college instruction entirely. But maintained potentiality, phenomenological and systemic, is not incompatible with the academy. To begin with, a teacher can help students discover and start using a potentiality that they did not know they had. An appealing illustration is provided by Barbara Harrell Carson (1996, 15). Carson talked to students who had graduated from Rollins College about thirty years earlier and asked them about their teachers. Which teachers and instructional events had lasted? Carson says that a common memory, a positive one, was of "incidents in which the professor acknowledges the student's academic or intellectual potency." One student recounted a moment during an audition when a drama teacher had asked her if she could dance and she had said no. "He responded by joining me in a waltz to prove me wrong. I carry that attitude with me today." The student added at the end of her survey, "Did I mention what a great dancer I am?" Substitute reading or writing for dancing and you have a central narrative paradigm for the English teaching moment when potentiality is both elicited and furthered. The diabolical inversion of the paradigm, of course, tells of the teacher who cuts the potentiality of students off at the root, of which inversion there are many tales.

These kinds of questions concerning maintained potentiality will occupy us for the rest of this book. In the next chapters, we will take up riddles of students and authoring that English teachers wrestle with every day: allowances of gender, parameters of response, exercising of voice, preparation for career, limits to interpretation, and diagnosis of error. Eventually we will show how potentiality, as a phenomenological and systemic ground of literacy, links with the sense of self-singularity to produce a pedagogically fruitful concept of authoring. Potentiality grounds authoring in every way.

3

POTENTIALITY AND GENDERSHIP

There are few human beings who receive the truth, complete and stag-gering, by instant illumination. Most of them acquire it fragment by fragment, on a small scale by successive developments, all wearily, like a laborious mosaic.

Anais Nin, *The Diary, 1934-1937*

When she was 18 and in Jan's first-year composition course, Victoria wrote an impromptu essay on the topic of "your search for truth." After the course was over she let us use her piece for an experiment. We were interested in instructional response to student writing—in particular, response as it interacts with the reader's perception of the sex of the writer. We had Victoria's essay read by thirty-two English teachers and thirty-two peer students, who looked for good and bad qualities, recommended revision work, and surmised about the unnamed writer's sex. It's hard to say who was more shocked by the outcomes, Victoria or us.

The piece and its author received a pummeling. Many of the readers assumed that the essay was composed by a male and suffered from liabilities in expression and thinking typical of male writers. In a post-experiment debriefing, we passed the response of the readers on to Victoria, who was a sophomore by then. As we will see, the debriefing proved a critical moment for her. Three years later—she had just graduated—we sent her a draft of our research report and asked her to reflect on the experience, in a way giving her a second chance to discuss her "search for truth." We heard from a changed writer.

Victoria said that as a sophomore she had not been cowed by the sixty-four responses—in fact, just the opposite. "Apparently," she wrote, "my writing style had unique qualities that caused a variety of reactions from teachers and fellow students. The assumptions and comments they made stimulated my fighting spirit. How dare they label me or judge my work based on gender, real or implied?" She said she had turned their misreadings into gain. "For the first time I became conscious of my own 'voice' as a writer and as I gained control of this concept my proficiency in the medium grew. Imagine my sense of power once I realized I had something nearly as individual as a fingerprint that was flexible enough to control each reader's perceptions and response." As this chapter would put it, her potential to exercise gendership in her writing was stimulated by her encounter with sixty-four antagonist-critics. Victoria is the hero of this chapter.[1]

Its topic is the interaction of potentiality with gender and the way that interaction shapes the response of readers. If, as we assume in Chapter 1, potentiality is no different than other human capacities such as reasoning, drive, curiosity, affect, or sense of humor, then it will intermix, as do those capacities, with cultural givens such as gender, ethnicity, age, social class, and regional heritage. Separating potentiality from its surround is like seining a shoal of fish from its reef.

This commingling of student-writing potential with sociocultural givens and teacher response has been investigated by writing specialists Keith Gilyard and Elaine Richardson (2001). Their experiment is relevant because it operated under the assumptions of what we call constrained potentiality. Gilyard and Richardson taught features of African American Vernacular English (AAVE) to African American students in basic writing classes—features such as proverbs, sermonic tone, call and response, and signifying or use of indirection to make points. They found that essays showing more AAVE features tended to receive higher rates from English teachers (who were unaware of the experimental conditions). Gilyard and Richardson conclude that familiarizing African American students with AAVE gives them their right to possibility, that such teaching results ("potentially at least—in better political possibilities"), that is, in release of potential for the students and the larger community. Gilyard and Richardson's study of ethnic style, writer potentiality, and teacher evaluation runs parallel to our own experiment in gendership, writer potentiality, and teacher response, from which Victoria so unexpectedly made profit and to which this chapter will quickly turn.

Victoria herself connected our experiment with potentiality. In her letter to us she said, "I feel that it is vitally important to involve students in research applications because the potential for learning is expanded beyond what is set forth in the typical curriculum." Notice

---

1. Victoria's first-year composition essay is reproduced at the end of this chapter. Her letter to us three years later is reproduced in Chapter 7.

she wrote that student potential is "expanded," and not "discovered" or "applied." She must have shared our sense of maintained systemic potentiality, or something close to it, as an ongoing, dynamic, creative capability intimately connected with maturation and cultural givens, individual as a fingerprint (to use her metaphor), and reaching beyond the classroom door. "The more I understood about the results of the study, the more I paid attention to my own writing and that of others. I had confidence in my writing ability and my style matured. Writing gained significance beyond the completion of an assignment. Suddenly aspects of cultural doctrine, gender, and human nature were thrown into the mix. I can honestly say I never looked at my homework the same way again."

She begins her letter with the quotation from Anais Nin that we have borrowed for our epigraph. Victoria says her understanding of gender and voice did not come in Nin's "instant illumination" but neither was it gained piecemeal, "all wearily, like a laborious mosaic." Her message to us is our message as well, that when student "potential for learning is expanded," learning can be extended, sometimes in rapid growth spurts of literacy that all of us have probably experienced and most of us have probably forgotten.

POTENTIALITY AND GENDERSHIP

How are gender and potentiality connected? If one accepts the now standard distinction between "sex" and "gender," then one accepts the connection of gender and potentiality. Sex is biological and, in terms of potentiality, hardly rises beyond the *genetic* in our hierarchy of definitions. Gender, however, is a personal and social construct and therefore is open to the full resources of *maintained* potentiality. Gender can be nurtured, configured, expanded, and withheld at will, as is demonstrated by posture, play, fashion, conversation, and a hundred other creativities of the human involving not just sex but sexual projections and sex roles. Gender has both systemic potentiality in its social affordances and phenomenological potentiality in the way persons imagine and transform their own sexualities.

Therefore, all the more does potentiality entail gender*ship*. We had to coin the word "gendership" to describe the dynamics of classroom response uncovered by our study. As we define it, gendership is a rhetorical strategy that creates the image of the writer's sex interpretable from text. It is the gender dimension to the authorial personality intended by the writer or the gender dimension of the implied author imagined by the reader.[2] Better, it is a joint creation of writer, reader, text, context, and culture. The "ship" in gendership reflects the same etymology (Old English *scipe* or *sceap*, to create or shape) as in words such as friendship, courtship, or stewardship.

Or author*ship*. As authorship is not the flesh-and-blood author, but rather a discourse figment, gendership is not simply the biological sex of the writer. It is the author's projection and the reader's imagination of the author's sex. Some of the projected and imagined ways that writers try to gender shape the reader's image of their authorial personality are well known. It is a ploy of male as well as female authors. Just as Alice Sheldon published her first short stories as written by "James Tiptree Jr.," Edward L. Stratemeyer launched his first Nancy Drew mysteries as written by "Carolyn Keene." Sheldon and Stratemeyer gender-marked their pen names to shape how readers valued their fiction, the first perhaps to avoid presuppositions about the unsuitability of women as authors of science fiction, the second perhaps to help build a female readership. In short, the *a priori* gender identity[3] of writers and the *a posteriori* gendership that they help create through their texts are not always the same or meant to be the same. This authorial terrain has been much explored by literary scholars. But the way student writers in college employ gendership has been little discussed. Even less discussed are the ways teachers can deny students gendership potentiality—that precious ground of free choice for students in constructing, expressing, engaging, and expanding, shaping and reshaping their gendered selves in and through the act of writing.

Gendership is no minor part of a college writing student's potential. Although we had designed our study to elicit effects of gender on the evaluation of student writing, we were astonished at the amount, variety, and complexity of those effects.[4] In brief, we conducted one-on-one interviews with the sixty-four participants and taped their responses to

---

2. For "authorial personality," see Louis D. Rubin (1967). For "implied author," see Wayne Booth (1961). Gendership, then, is an aspect of the author's *persona*—a perennially useful concept from literary criticism that we explore further in Chapter 5.

3. "Gender identity" is defined as one's self-image based on sexual history, status, and role. One's gender identity (called "gender typing" by socio-psychologists) is continually being developed throughout life.

4. For our initial interpretation of major findings, see "Gendership and Miswriting Students" (J. Haswell and R. Haswell 1995). For design, methodology, and full data, see our "Gender Bias and the Critique of Student Writing" (R. Haswell and J. Haswell 1996).

two essays, Victoria's and another written by her classmate Kevin. With each essay, the readers were asked first to read and evaluate, offering suggestions for revision and summarizing the good and bad qualities of the writing, and then second to identify clues to the sex of the author, discussing whether they felt knowledge of a student writer's sex should influence a teacher's evaluation of the writing. Readers did not know the sex of the first essay's author and had to infer it, but they were told the correct sex of the second essay's author—a feature of the research design that revealed some of the more unsettling fate of gendership in the college writing classroom.

It's not an exaggeration to say that their response was steeped in gendership. The participants' readings of Victoria's and Kevin's brief impromptu classroom essays on the innocent topic of "your search for truth" were awash with it. It didn't matter whether the reader was male or female, first-year student or teacher of first-year students, versed or not in feminist and gender theory. Gender of the author, the reader, and the interviewer proved operative in every sort of ordinary teacherly act that our design covered: in the kind and agency of student author-ship envisioned, in the good or bad writing features detected, in the relative amount of positive and negative commentary offered, in the kind of revisions suggested, in the grade or point value assigned.

Consider only the way readers read gender into the authoring of these two texts. When knowledge of the sex of the author was withheld from readers, 65 percent of the time they formed a gendered image of the writer anyway; in this inference they were wrong about half the time. Their picturing of the writer as male or female was spontane-ous, even though at the same time they were hiding it from the inter-viewer—an odd but characteristic human behavior reported in other studies of reading. Readers avoided "she" and even the universal "he" when referring to the writer, choosing instead the sex-neutral "they" or the agentless "text" or "essay." Even when they had been told the sex of the writer, they still avoided gendered pronouns. Yet when readers were asked how they determined their assignment of sex to the author, they pointed to an astonishing panoply of textual features. More than half of the text of the two essays was cited by one reader or another as gender marked. For instance from Victoria's essay, among the phrases identified as male were "it's up to me to figure out" and "I don't like to be proven wrong." From Kevin's essay, among the phrases identi-fied as female language were "I get most of my information from other people" and "I want to believe it is real." Some passages were used as clues to both male and female authorship.

Victoria's response to the gender marking of her own essay is interesting. During the debriefing, when we told her that many readers thought the piece was written by a man, she conceded that the stance of personal independence might be taken as masculine. But she noted that there are phrases that bear the mark of her feminine personality, such as "conflict with the law," "gut instinct," and "load of bull"—those very phrases that many readers read as masculine. (Victoria's essay at the end of this chapter shows all this sex-identified language.)

Moreover, to infer the sex of the author from the text, our readers used the creakiest of knowledge frames. We were amazed to see how much their response was built on gender stereotypes and supported by shaky biological, psychological and social presuppositions. Here is a truncated list of assumptions taken verbatim from the thirty-two teachers—all of whom, we might add, had been formally trained in composition pedagogy.

Females	Males
• find it easier to organize ideas	• are redundant
• write more elaborately	• are circular
• write with honesty	• are repetitive
• write with careful observation	• use business terms and slang
• tend to be better writers	• tend to blow off assignments
• are more verbal	• don't have a point of view
• use passives	• need to rationalize or split hairs
• use concessions	• are skeptical of advice
• let emotion get in the way of logic	• get right to the point
• value emotion	• use short sentences
• are more convinced that what they think is true	• are argumentative, aggressive, and Cartesian in their thinking
• focus on values	• are emotionless and analytic
• are hesitant	• are self-reliant
• use complex sentences	• have a vigorous style
• don't use action verbs	• weigh information logically

We hardly need point out that most of these distinctions between male and female writing have no empirical foundation, and the few that do record only slight differences, typically with 85 to 90 percent of males and females performing in the same range.

The threat to Victoria's and Kevin's gendership is clear, as is to their potential as authors. A more blatant instance of constrained potentiality is hard to find. Whether a reader knows the sex of the author or infers it through "blind reading" (aptly named, and beloved of large-scale writing assessment), gender stereotypes reshape the gendership of the text and thus reshape the author regardless of the author's intentions. All this cannot be attributed solely to experimental effects. Even among enlightened English professionals, assumptions about gender can be stereotyped, bipolar, and static. This is just as true now as in the days of June Cleaver, when a woman's place was so notoriously limned and delimited. Gender stereotypes are perpetuated by everybody, including feminists themselves. Even supposedly objective researchers, such we have tried to be on this occasion, are not immune. "Research on gender and language, despite intentions to the contrary, has polarized, essentialized and stereotyped differences between men and women," writes social psychologist Ann Weatherall (1998). And teachers, largely unaware, impose their fantasies upon their students.

Readers everywhere, of course, apply interpretive frames that authors did not anticipate and might not like. That is the reader's constitutional right as reader—a freedom constitutive to print communication. But a teacher is a special kind of reader, one with the authority and power to force idiosyncratic interpretations back on the writer. This chapter imagines how the gender frames applied by college readers can put the gendership potential of writing students in jeopardy. The image of herself that Victoria may have wanted to project—say, independent woman or independent person—was distorted by many of her readers. What would she have done had one of these readers been her teacher and she had taken the teacher seriously? Change the way she presented herself in terms of gender? Change the way she conceived of herself in terms of gender? Sincere and well-intentioned as these readers were, they threatened part of her potentiality as a writer. In one sense, the opposite of human potentiality is unacknowledged self-censorship. Victoria's readers were sending her the message that a part of her developing creativity and productivity of writing should be turned off, closeted, maybe forgotten. Many young authors less strong-willed than Victoria might have done just that and, worse, not know that they had done it.

* * *

VICTORIA'S FIRST YEAR COMPOSITION ESSAY

Writing prompt: When Plato describes a person's "search for truth," he uses the Allegory of the Cave. How would you describe your "search for truth" and the process you use to pursue it?

Time limit: 20 minutes.

Our editing: Except for italicizing and underlining, Victoria's essay is the original in-class text. We have italicized parts of the essay readers used to argue that the author is female, and underscored parts used to argue that the author is male.

* * *

The process by which I search for "truth" is dependent upon what kind of an answer I am looking for.

For example, if I were looking for the answer to *a question of morality, I would look within myself*. I believe that *only I can know if what I am doing or what I am saying is "good" or "bad"*. *I use myself and my own personal values to determine the difference between right and wrong.* I use the beliefs I hold strongly to act as a kind of guide to help me through some more complex *moral decisions*. For instance, *I believe in obeying the law* but I realize that the law is only as perfect as those who made it. Thus, *if an occasion arises where someone is in danger or is hurt and helping them would conflict with* the law, I would tend to ignore that specific law.

If I were searching for an answer to *a question involving knowledge, I would first look to myself* and see how much I know about the particular subject or question I am contemplating. I then will take what knowledge I have and *compare it to what other people (or other sources) know. This process also involves a* gut instinct, for *I'm the only one who can decide if a source or a person* is giving me a qualified answer. In other words, it's up to me to figure out *if sombody/source* is feeding me a load of bull. Once I have the chance to gather as much information that I can, I will try *to make as accurate an answer as possible*. It should be noted that on some occasions I choose not to use other people/sources *to find the truth*. Sometimes I am able to *find* the answers without the help of anyone else.

In conclusion I would like to say that, while these methods for finding my own kind of truth seem to work *fairly* well, I realize that *there are drawbacks. One involves emotion. Sometimes, in cases where there is a lot of emotion going on, I am apt to make decisions that are* too hasty. *Another drawback* is the amount of time I have to make these decisions. In cases such as these, *I just go with what I know definitely and my instinct*. Also, like any other person, <u>I don't like to be proven wrong</u>, but *I guess* it's something I've learned to live with.

4

POTENTIALITY, GENDERSHIP, AND TEACHER RESPONSE

How do you propose to express yourself?
An anonymous teacher to an unknown student

The threat to a healthy writing potentiality of student writers like Victoria and Kevin, however, does not stop with the production of gendership. Because they sit in a *writing* course, not only do they have to turn their gendership over to the interpretive vagaries of readers, but afterward they have to reshape it. This happens when teachers ask them, as composition teachers are wont to do nowadays, to revise their first drafts. We assume that in legitimate writing-course response, that is, in criticism devoted to the improvement of student writing rather than just to the evaluation of it, teachers will require only revisions for which a student writer potentially has the capability. What educational benefit in demanding a task the student can't see and do?

Revision, then, is an arena where teachers should gauge potentiality. In our study, however, teachers and peer students seemed more bent on constraining Kevin's and Victoria's potential than—to use her word—expanding it. Consider some more findings of the study.

Before our readers suggested revisions, they decided on a point value for the essay under review. That rating turned out to be heavily associated with gender. Overall, the association showed a pro-female bias. Readers tended to assume that women were better writers than men. Within this general pattern, though, readers also expressed same-sex depreciation. That is, male readers rated the text they knew to be male-authored lower than female readers rated the same text; female readers rated the text they knew to be female-authored lower than male readers rated the same text. The most negative reaction, however, surfaced when the author appeared "cross-dressed"—when readers thought that the female writer sounded like a man, or the male writer sounded like a woman. Negative ratings associated with cross-dressing were present both when the reader had been told the writer's sex and when the reader inferred it. Not surprisingly, but surely more significantly for the gendership of the two authors, all three of these patterns—pro-female bias, same-sex depreciation, and negativity associated with cross-dressing—also surfaced in the degree of praise offered in the readers' commentary.[1]

How the readers' ratings and praise converted into recommendations for revision involves two new and interesting gendership dynamics. The first dynamic berates a public sin, and the second commits it; in our interviews, both operated simultaneously. On the one hand, our readers lamented gender bias, which in teachers' evaluation of student writing they took to be preconceptions about gender unwanted by the writer or unwarranted by the text. The readers believed that a critic of writing should deactivate gender bias by not using sexist language and not falling prey to stereotypical, discriminatory, and demeaning attitudes toward one sex or the other. We call this belief gender neutrality. Our readers disagreed on how much gender might be part of the text, but they all agreed adamantly that gender should never be a factor in evaluation of the text. Their professional competence and training insisted it shouldn't matter whether the writer is male or female. The quality of the writing is what is being judged.

Yet the interview transcripts reveal that in their practice of response, cryptically, the same readers often exhibited gender bias. Other researchers have documented the same dynamic. The very readers who profess a position of gender neutrality conduct gender attacks on

---

1. Within this variation, we also saw the status of the reader (whether he or she was a teacher or a student) and the sex of the interviewer as significant variables. Since our original study, we have asked our own students in a variety of classes and on very different campuses to undertake the same protocol with the same two essays, and we consistently see patterns similar to our original findings. It is worth pointing out that these gender differences reported here and in other studies are differences in *evaluation* of performance. When one looks at *performance* itself, the closer one gets to an objective measurement of it, the closer males and females appear. Janet K. Swim and others (1989) reviewed over one hundred studies that compare gender performance and found that the average difference accounted for less than one percent of variance, and the majority of studies recorded differences that were statistically nonsignificant—a contemporary confirmation of Montaigne's venerable intuition that "les masles et femelles sont jettez en mesme moule: sauf l'institution et l'usage, la diference n'y est pas grande" ("males and females are cast in the same mould; take away education and custom and the difference is not great" (1958, 5). The new findings and the old intuition do not question the extent of gender stereotyping or sexual inequalities, of course, but rather underscore the extent of their fabrication.

the writer, usually attacks more subtle than discriminatory or politically incorrect remarks. Perhaps the most hidden bias—hidden to the readers themselves—surfaced in their advice on revision, where gendership potentiality of the student author is most at stake.

In recommendations for revision, such attacks on the writer followed two basic routes. The first we call gender neutering. Sometimes readers removed gender from the human doing the revision: "They [not he or she] should simplify this sentence." Sometimes readers erased the agent entirely: "This sentence should be simplified." Gender neutering was the norm in the transcripts. It prevailed not because the readers lacked knowledge of the author's sex. Knowledge of the sex of the writer was withheld from readers only half of the time, yet nearly three-quarters of all their commentary was genderless or agentless. Nor can it be argued that gender neutering protects the writer from gender discrimination. For instance, one of our readers refused to guess the sex of the author, insisting that, in so doing, a teacher would be unfair to the student writer. Later in the interview, however, the reader volunteered that she was fairly sure the writer was African American and "probably not used to looking at abstractions." An extreme instance of racism in the guise of gender sensitivity, certainly; but consider that, across all transcripts, four out of five comments couched in genderless or agentless terms were negative, compared to three out of five for "she" and "he" comments. Gender neutering seems to abet the detection and expression of faults in the writing.

For the health of a student writer's gendership potential, it is important to see that gender neutering marks a dire turn of critical dynamics. To note that potentiality can be maintained, as we do in Chapter 2, is to note that it can be undermined. With gendership *neutrality*, readers merely suppress their own sense of the student author's sex, an act that lies within anyone's rights who is reading a text. But with gender *neutering*, teacher-critics exclude sex from someone else's authoring of a text. The unconscious switch is in locus of agency—from a decision about their own agency in reading to a directive about the student author's agency in revising. The first constrains present gendership in the text, and the second constrains potential gendership in the rewriting of the text.

A second form of gender bias in recommendations for revision was gender tailoring. Here readers resorted to cultural pattern books for gender fashions. Their most common strategy was to rely on stereotypes to locate and appraise gendered qualities of the text, and then use the stereotypes as the basis of their advice for revision. When an essay was known or assumed to be written by a male, readers might describe it as repetitious, wordy, abstract, or overly rational, and therefore in need of concision, fluidity, details, or personal feelings. The same essay, when thought to be female-authored, was found to be passive, illogical, hesitant, and personal, and in need of clarity, directness, reasoning, and critical thinking (see Chapter 14 for actual examples of this strategy). Another strategy was for readers to shape revision out of a sense of solidarity with their own gender group. Female readers encouraged the writer they knew or believed to be female to work toward "feminine" strengths of connection and empathy with others. Males advised her to work away from "masculine" strengths of logic and abstract thinking. Female readers encouraged the writer thought to be male to be more impassioned and use the first person pronoun. Male readers encouraged the "male" writer to be more logical and to think on a global, abstract level beyond the personal.

Same writer, same text, sometimes radically different advice for revision. In the advice student authors receive for revising, they are trapped in a kind of critical colonizing that enforces locked home-protectorate gender positions. Again, the writer most at risk from gender tailoring is the cross-dresser, the male who creates a female gendership or the female who creates a male one. The perception of cross-dressing evoked especially harsh responses from our readers, most often from female teachers who had little sympathy but many rewriting directives for a female writer who dared to write logically and to say "load of bull." The woman who wants to reason philosophically and the man who wants to write about family take grave risks.

However Victoria may have intuited or construed the gendership of her own essay, it had to have suffered damage, because the readers' evaluation of her authoring was so contradictory. When believed or known to be female, Victoria was described one way. She thinks in terms of social context and "more about people." She would defy the law in order to protect the people she cares about. She clearly values moral issues. She is open to emotion and relies on her own instinct. Although she can be hasty at times, she is comfortable with looking inside herself for answers. Her essay is mature, well organized, and contains few grammatical and syntactic flaws: "She's very fluent for a 101 student." Her lapses are emotional departures from logic and from formal style, using slang like "gut instinct" and "load of bull" and qualifying her attitude about the process she uses to search for truth with the admission that there are drawbacks and that sometimes she makes mistakes.

But when believed to be male, Victoria becomes a very different writer. He is decisive, logical, and linear in his thinking—maybe too much so: "This is set out in just an organized way, and without a lot of lively things but just basic facts and organization, logic." He hates to be proven wrong. He is competitive, self-reliant, and independent, "aware that the question asks for *his* search for truth." He will weigh evidence from other sources, albeit grudgingly: "sort of picking things up individually and holding them up and pretty consciously saying, 'No, that's not it.'" He is assured except when it comes to emotions. He has a vigorous style that is straightforward and aggressive, made evident by phrases like "gut instinct" and "load of bull."[2]

These readings seem to describe diametrically different acts of authoring, yet they are in fact talking about the same author and the same text. What purported to be gender-neutral critical commentary often didn't emerge so much from Victoria's complex response to the in-class prompt but rather from the simplistic, bipolar expectations of gender and gendered writing that readers, teachers and students alike, brought with them into the interview, unconsciously detected and judged in the essays and then unconsciously used to shape directives for revision and mould Victoria into the simplistic, bifurcated man or woman of their imagination. It is as educationist Jane Roland Martin

---

2. Kevin met with a similar fate. Kevin seen as male was accused of being "repetitious," "wordy," and "abstract." "He repeats himself to the point of distorting or annoying the reader," one participant said. "He writes the way he talks," noted another. Readers also found that the male Kevin lacked focus and stylistic grace; that he is rebellious, self-confident, and emotionless; that he acts independently of the opinions of others and validates truth within himself. "It seemed to be kind of empiricist, scientific, male-oriented kind of thinking . . . . He's saying, I'm getting this data from my family and friends and cannot live without data. I cannot think without data, I have to judge it." Some readers assumed that the essay was dashed off just to fulfill the required assignment, typical of "scared student writing." But when readers presumed the author of Kevin's essay to be female, they tended to see her writing as stylistically fluid, with complex sentences and detailed observation. She is caring, honest, and sincere: "The way the paper sounds to me is friendly, I mean I have a sense of voice in the paper." She is comfortable with personal relationships and willing to engage in dialogue with others, "very much in a social network . . . in a web of relationships." Her essay displays a willingness to "analyze in depth" elements "that she obviously values."

warns: "An educational philosophy that tries to ignore gender in the name of equality is self-defeating. Implicitly reinforcing the very stereotypes and unequal practices it claims to abhor, it makes invisible the very problems it should be addressing" (1985, 195).

What damage are English teachers doing to a student's potentiality as a writer, indeed to a person's potentiality as a man or a woman, when they enter the writer-reader relationship in such a way? If potentiality is teachable, as we say in Chapter 2, then teachers are responsible. While we understand that readers perforce write a text anew, we believe that teachers have a special obligation to respect the gender identities of a student author because they will be directing that student to compose in particular ways in the future. Surely, when teachers take on this authority, they should do so openly and not pretend that they dislike bad writing when what they really dislike is hearing a man speak about caring or a woman write with logic.

Our study recommends a different dialectic in writer-reader engagement. Victoria showed us that gender lived by each person and shaped into text by each writer—in a word, gendership—is dynamic, complex, versatile, and not sex-specific. Victoria's indignation over her encounter with sixty-four readers is not only righteous, but right: "Apparently, my writing style had unique qualities that caused a variety of reactions from teacher and fellow students. The assumptions and comments they made stimulated my fighting spirit. How dare they label me or judge my work based on gender, real or implied." This book agrees with Victoria. In this life, gendership is one facet of the singular potentiality of each person, who in this country should have the license to craft her or his way of dressing, of speaking, of writing, of "being" a woman or a man. And shouldn't that license be extended to student writers, who are perhaps the most vulnerable in having their gendership constrained?

By and large, English teachers are conscientious and passionate defenders of student rights. Their main goal is improved writing, and carefully designed formal studies usually show they achieve that goal. But as our own formal study shows, English teachers are as susceptible as anyone else to invisible gender influences and to an educational doctrine that ends up, as Martin says, "implicitly reinforcing the very stereotypes and unequal practices it claims to abhor" (195). Against these forces, the awareness of potentiality can act as a safeguard for teachers. It advocates a particular kind of audience for the Victoria in the classroom, one that accepts her work and her authority over her work not within the narrow confines of an institutional, ideological, or historical agenda, but rather within the generous discourse and gender parameters that any author enjoys in a hospitable society.

Our notion of gendership emerged only at the end point of our study, in part because it defined itself for us by its *absence* in the explicit commentary of the readers. There was one exception, a teacher who said he would ask the author of Victoria's essay the question, "How do you propose to express yourself?" It is the kind of simple query, deceptively simple, that rhetorical gendership recommends for English teachers. It is a question that would have helped defend Victoria in her struggle against the commentary that sabotaged her full authority in making authorial decisions—decisions, for instance, on how to reason out her ideas, how to organize her essay, or how to present her voices.

5

POTENTIALITY, GENDERSHIP, TEACHER RESPONSE, AND STUDENT VOICES

I write not because I am male, female, both, or neither, but simply because I am myself.

Jan Morris, "Traveling Writer"

The voice is all me.

Victoria

We say "voices" advisedly.

Today among English teachers, the term "voice" has a hair trigger. This small word holds an arsenal of conflicting meanings, each defending critical and ideological positions in which people are often deeply invested. Stylists hear in voice the timbre of a literary persona successfully projected. Expressivists take voice as a sign that the student writer is speaking out of authentic experience. Developmentalists read voice as evidence that the young adult has matured to some point of self-autonomy. Critical pedagogues champion voice as a means to resist political oppression ("voicing dissent"). Early feminists found in voice a vehicle for women's independence ("the feminine voice"), while later feminists distrust voice as a ploy of patriarchal individualism ("the feminine voice"). Poststructuralists deconstruct the notion of voice, with its assumption of personal discursive origins. Social constructivists dismiss voice, with its trust in the myth of the autonomous individual or the isolated author. Analysts of discourse sites disconnect voice entirely from the human larynx and attribute it, if anywhere, to an organizational complex and its disembodied electronic communication network. As a critical term, "voice" is in worse shape than "potentiality." The temptation is just to abandon it to the sea of depleted terminology.

As we did with "potentiality," however, we will stick with "voice." One reason is that for student writers in college the term still has appeal and use. They know what they mean by it, and they often resort to it in defending their ground from teacher encroachments: "I turned down your suggestion for revising just because I thought it took away some of my personal voice."[1] Victoria, it will be remembered, thought that the notion of "voice" helped advance her writing after first-year composition: "For the first time I became conscious of my own 'voice' as a writer and as I gained control of this concept my proficiency in the medium grew." The term especially helps students gain confidence that they can handle different styles to operate within social and institutional contexts that they are gradually beginning to recognize as distinct and powerful. Victoria continues, "Imagine my sense of power once I realized I had something [voice] nearly as individual as a fingerprint that was flexible enough to control each reader's perceptions and response." In a word, from the perspective of students and their sense of authoring, voice carries potential.

Let us see if our own perspective on potentiality may help maintain "voice" as a viable critical term.[2] The readers in our study affirmed that textual gendership is partly achieved through voice. To more than half of them, for instance, Victoria's essay *sounded* like a man. Through what socio-semantic "potentials" this interpretation was channeled is impossible to tell, of course, and we are not about to argue that the teachers were resorting to a simplistic sense of voice produced solely by human vocal chords. As voice functions as a vehicle for gendership, it operates out of both systemic and phenomenological potentiality. Like gendership, it can serve authorial ethos, however mediated by institution or culture, intended or not by the writer; or it can help generate the implied author, however mediated by institution or culture, imagined or not by the reader. It also carries the authors' sense of their own

---

1. Quoted by Peter Elbow in "Voice in Writing Again" (1987, 170). Elbow, along with other compositionists, recognizes the polyvalence of the term "voice" but argues that at times it is still useful for writers and critics to see texts through "the lens of voice and the lens of not-voice" (185).

2. In *For More Than One Voice*, philosopher Adriana Cavarero (2005) argues that the corporeal voice allows expression of the uniqueness of the person, and that the "devocalization" of our print culture has helped erase singularity as a political reality. In *The Gutenberg Elegies*, Sven Birkerts extends the same line of reasoning to digital technologies, arguing that as individuals we each have "a unique presence that is only manifest on site, in our immediate space-time location," a presence that before the megaphone and the telephone was conveyed by the human voice that could carry no further than "the distance of a shout," and a presence largely eradicated by the popularity of electronic forms of communication such as "voice mail" (1994, 226-227). Voice, then, unites potentiality with singularity as explored in the second half of this book (see Chapters 8-13).

possibilities of self-projection, and, like gendership, it may be taken as a capability that furthers an ongoing framework for creative work. For teachers the potentiality of voice, as every kind of human potential, has currency, teachability, continuity, and rejectability. Just as students ought to be allowed a full range of gendership, they ought to be allowed a full range of voices.

None of this necessarily defends the treacherous concepts of authentic voice, personal voice, or individual voice, concepts that many teachers today reject on quite reasonable grounds. What it does defend is the concept of voices, or the need for students to keep exercising their creative production and shaping of tone, emotion, register, and other elements of style that compose the particular speaking voice in a piece of writing in a particular discursive situation. The danger comes not from teachers denying or affirming those disputatious concepts of voice (authentic, personal, individual) but from their starving of this writerly potential. And the method of starvation may not take so much the form of an open prohibition of certain voices (feminine, masculine, colloquial, African American vernacular, undisciplinary, etc.) as the promotion of one voice to the exclusion of all others. The starvation may take an even more devious route wherein the notion of voice, and of companion notions such as "style," "diction," and "tone," are tacitly displaced by a toolkit of formal skills such as mechanics, exemplification, arrangement, argumentation, and sentence construction—skills that without saying so generate a particular voice. In correcting and recommending revisions, teachers replace pronouns, reposition thesis statements, remove or add hedges, request more specifics, insert counterarguments—all in the stated interest of "clarity," "correctness," "logic," or "persuasiveness." But sub rosa, they are promoting a particular academic or disciplinary voice. Even when they are open about the style they are promoting, they may not explain the range of voices that are viable within an academic or disciplinary discourse. What teachers may unteach, without knowing it, is the sense of the potentiality and manipulability of voices, which, as we will see, can be so liberating for students.

A harsh supposition, but one supported by evidence from the readers' protocols from our study. The most comprehensive way of showing this is to look at commentary where participants discussed the good and bad qualities of the essay and recommended revision. When their commentary is rendered down to discrete propositions and each of these 850 propositions classified according to discursive centers of value, the distribution is as follows:

expressive   5%   success in expressing psychological constructs of the author, such as openness, sincerity, or anger

mimetic   6%   success of the writer in conveying objective reality truthfully or logically

rhetorical   23%   success in conveying the writer's purpose and in handling the pragmatic situation that prompted the writing

formalist   61%   success in creating a conventionally correct or stylistically approved text[3]

In sum, nearly two-thirds of the commentary addressed itself to the conventional values of form (*formalist*) and only a twentieth to the inner values of the author (*expressive*).

What does this mean for the future of voice? Deep down there is a political agenda here to which feminists and others alert us. Formalist criticism of student writing tacitly says that academic writing is the only acceptable discourse in academia. Of course, that particular discourse has its distinctive voice, typified by indulgent correctness, stuffy register, suppressed emotion, timid metaphor, up-front organization, reverential ideas, cautious point-making, dutiful exemplification, and cheerful supplying of detail. Students must master this voice or they will not succeed, either here or, it is implied, in the world beyond the academy. Derek Owens (1993) characterizes the voice as "Eurocentric and patrifocal," for the way it narrows response to writing despite discipline-wide theorizing about diversity, audience awareness, and multicultural rhetorics. Whatever lip service we pay to voices, teachers are constraining voices by habitually imposing a single, formalist standard in evaluating and re-authoring student writing.

The way our readers limited Kevin's and Victoria's voices, as well as their genderships, can also be seen through bottom-up analysis of their commentary. When readers spoke of "voice," "tone," or "style," usually they were directing the author toward the academic register. "Usage (such as 'gut instinct') should be checked to make the tone as lofty as the question's." "I have a sense of voice that isn't distant." "The style

---

3. Five percent of the commentary judged the writing in a free-floating way that did not attach itself to any value center (for instance, "Not a bad effort"). The value centers, or "axiologies," are taken from Richard Fulkerson (1990).

is too conversational." More disturbing, readers used the actual words "voice," "tone," or "style" in their protocols rarely. Each occurred just five times. Contrast that pittance with the flood of toolkit terms that teachers habitually wield to further the academic voice: "organization" 62 times, "point" 82 times, "example" 89 times, "sentence" 91 times, and "ideas" 117 times. Thus has the discipline of English erased voice as a viable critical tool not only for understanding working authors but also for advising authoring students. The most complete erasure in the commentary, however, is a sense of potentiality with these two students, a sense that their essays were temporal emanations of ongoing, evolving, lifelong, creative capabilities. Out of 850 comments, only one, from a student commenter referring to Victoria, attributed "potential" to the writer.

Our study is hardly alone in these findings. The academic voice has been heavily promoted by teachers in their response across decades, educational levels, and nations. In 1986, high school teachers in New South Wales were devoting 16 percent of their paper comments on "what the pupil is trying to say," 54 percent to "manner of expression," leaving 30 percent of the papers to be returned with no comment other than the marking of mechanical mistakes (Watson 1981). In 1993, of 3,000 college papers from across the United States, only 6 percent displayed teacher comments that concerned "anything about audience considerations such as tone or voice." And only 8 percent "dealt with the writer's work as a developing system," or gave "longitudinal commentary" that might have touched upon the writer's potentiality as writers (Connors and Lunsford, 1993).[4]

Are teachers aware how much these patterns of response to student writing look like self-interest? In his call for reform in English studies, Robert Scholes (1998) recounts the student experience of Louis Althusser, who learned that success in academia entailed imitating the "voice" and manners of his professors in order to mirror back their own image of themselves, "their own nostalgias and hopes," self-images that they had unconsciously projected on him (60-61). Theoretically, English teachers have long argued that such "tricks of the trade" (Scholes' term) involve precisely the tools, including the proper aca-

---

4. Currently the scholarship in college composition records more than 500 data-supported studies of teacher commenting on student writing. We're willing to bet that none of them found teachers spending anything close to the space on authoring that they spent on textual features.

demic voice, that students need to succeed in higher education. But the narcissistic circularity of that argument is easy to spot: I (a teacher) am teaching you this to save you from someone else (a teacher). Althusser, and Scholes himself, believe that the circularity rotates around a void in higher education, "a fraudulent space in which artifice not only can but must work" (64). Academic success is not the only goal set for students that happens to fit the teachers' own interests. Compositionist Linda Brodkey (1989) studied letters exchanged between lower-class adult basic writers and their middle-class teachers and found evidence of what she labels "discursive hegemony," by which "the teachers frenetically protected educational discourse from [social] class." Under the banner of gender, class, cultural literacy, or racial neutrality, teachers forced students to "articulate themselves as the subjects teachers represent, or not at all" (139-140).

Scholes and Brodkey are studying a slippage between the theory English teachers profess in the discipline and the standards they promote in the classroom. In theory, the trust in a single voice (academic or otherwise) has long come under fire. The attack is part of the radical postmodernist agenda discrediting the notion of the unified self. Because a writer is capable of multiple subject positions, and in fact is a convergence of multiple selves, he or she will manifest multiple voices. In book after book and article after article the profession has used this philosophical position on multiple voices to question the "myth" of the single, isolated, personal voice. Yet in classroom after classroom teachers have used the "reality" of the single, isolated, academic voice to reduce multiple voices in student writing down to one.[5]

The ambivalence may be due in part to the fact that, for English teachers of both literature and composition, the idea of multiple selves itself comes freighted with ambivalence. On the one hand, it bears the stamp of elite theory and the promise of new pedagogies. One of the more informed articulations of the individual as multiple-selves comes from Derek Owens, who applies the idea to voice in the composition classroom. Owens' primary argument is that there is no

---

5. Of course, as they progress from their first year in college, students hear and are required to match a variety of academic voices. And the idea of disciplinary styles is now deeply entrenched and energetically studied in the English field. But to what extent do the idea and the findings shape writing assignments and teacher response in individual classrooms? Usually it is the student, perilously moving from a course in one field to a course in another, who becomes the most sensitive to changes in voice, at least judging from ethnographic studies of students and teachers.

such thing as an authentic, personal voice, whether the authoring be of creative narrative or mundane nonfiction. Every act of oral or written communication is no more than a mask, "only one fictive guise in an immense spread of other (also fictive) voices" (1993, 160). For support Owens turns to James Hillman, the maverick Jungian who lays the foundation for a contemporary understanding of the mask in his discussion of the human personality. In *Re-visioning Psychology* (1975), Hillman argues that the self is composed of multiple personae, no one of which is more or less real than another. If the self is a spiral of "splintered psyches" and not "a single, autonomous unifying entity," then it is futile for psychologists to determine if actions or fantasies "really mean" something or if they approximate the "real self." While there may be a favorite, comfortable, or "momentarily fixed version" of the self, that persona is only one image among a myriad of images, each masking the others. Owens sees all this as opportunity for the discursive imagination. To write "is to fashion not so much our identities," he argues, "but bridges that connect various facets of our experience within an incomprehensibly dense and unmapped personal landscape" (165). As Hillman would put it, attempts to interpret and reinterpret human identity are never ending, and the purpose of communication is not to solve or resolve these fictions, but rather to offer them to others via the active imagination.[6]

On the other hand, it should not be forgotten that the concept of multiple selves originated during a time that also feared multiplicity As Marta Caminero-Santangelo (1996) reminds us, multiple selves or faces became a focus of mental health professionals in the 1950s and 1960s, years when deviation from cultural norms was often judged to be politically and culturally threatening. Multiple personalities was seen as a sign of dramatic dysfunction wherein confusing and contradictory aspects of the patient (often female) were subjected to manipulation and control on the part of the psychologist (usually male). It is no accident that most multiple personality patients were women; their symptoms were similar to forms of female "madness" such as

---

6. Quotes from Hillman are from pages 26, 33, 38, and 51. In many ways the thinking of Owens and Hillman rejuvenates the notion of the "persona" in works of fiction as an aesthetic artifact, fictive in nature, distinct from the real, authentic, unvarying self. Hillman and Owens straddle that old dichotomy, their persona being both an imaginative construction and a real projection of the self in its multitudinous forms. Even less than "voice" does "persona" appear as a working critical term in the response of our readers to Victoria and Kevin—not even any of the teachers used the word.

hysteria or anorexia nervosa. In short, a woman with Owens' multiple selves was a woman out of control. Notably, the same adjectives used positively to describe postmodern subjectivity were applied in diagnosing such personality disorders: "multiple," "fragmented," "shifting," and "decentered."[7]

We suspect that the situation today with English teachers is pretty schizophrenic itself. How much of the current run of teachers retains a legacy of this old fear of multiple selves, and how much do they actually buy into the new valorization of constructed identities? In later chapters we will return to these issues of the constructed or multiple self and the possibility of singularity in student writing, since we feel the ideas are central to authoring as a normal and sane human activity. Here, we just want to emphasize that the attitude of students, too, may appear divided. The great majority of them live with the inner, phenomenological sense of having a stable self distinct from everybody else's, yet they take readily to the projection of that self through a train of rhetorical masks. The student's position, however, is a reasonable one and easily justified in terms of what we have called phenomenological potentiality or, more traditionally, of inner and outer representation, or of appearance and reality. The teacher's position is harder to justify when he or she professes the value of multiple styles, and maybe even multiple selves, yet represses the expression of them in classroom writing. Teachers encounter multiple voices in the classroom, either in terms of a collective chorus of diverse voices from many writers or a variety of voices from the same writer, yet they seem uncomfortable, unwilling, or unprepared to encourage those voices. In our gendership experiment, we may have caught a glimpse of "verbal hygiene," or the policing of language and acceptance of only a very narrow swath of it as within normal, preferable range.[8]

When verbal hygiene follows two contradictory patterns—discounting the notion of a writer's singular voice and maintaining the profes-

---

7. Caminero-Santangelo (63, 70). During the same years, R. D. Laing and other psychiatrists were explaining schizophrenia as the effort to communicate by an individual whose ontological sense of a unitary self had been denied or fragmented by family and society. Chapter 12 discusses *The Saturated Self* (1991) by Kenneth Gergen, a contemporary psychologist who sees the postmodern multi-voiced and multi-selved self in a positive light.
8. "Verbal hygiene" is linguist Deborah Cameron's term, which she defines as the labeling of certain usages or registers as "functionally, aesthetically or morally preferable to others" (1996, 36).

sion's obsession with regimented, formalist evaluation—students may be caught in terrible binds. Compare three writers:

Writer 1: A first-year voice student who writes an essay after attending a concert featuring Brahms, Tchaikovsky, and her favorite, Haydn. Because she had visited Haydn's home in Burgenland, she writes an imaginative, almost lyrical description of the composer's life and music, which she characterizes as "sparkling with singular good humor and unspoiled straight forwardness." She has a stunning ability to identify and capture the mystery of this music that speaks to her so deeply.

Writer 2: A re-entry student hoping to enjoy academic life after many years. In her first semester back, she struggles with in-class testing situations. Despite the fact that she keeps up with the readings on a daily basis, she has a difficult time writing a timed, organized essay in the approved academic voice—nit-picking yet deferential—that insists on separating elements perceived as important from others perceived as incidental. When she receives a "D" on her first test, she leaves the classroom crying.

Writer 3: Assigned to a group project, this student elects to write the script for a presentation on the Holocaust. After weeks of research, she rejects an analytic or historical approach. Instead, she interweaves firsthand narratives of ghetto victims, Auschwitz survivors, footage from *Schindler's List,* and even speeches from Adolf Hitler, all into a moving and artistic drama. Each presenter reads the words of one of the victims—voices out of history—and passes a burning candle down the line to the last member of the group, who acts as the voice of Hitler and snuffs out the candle. At first the class has a difficult time catching on, but they quickly realize that they have entered into a non-conventional but important ritual to honor twelve million dead.

In these three snapshots, the potential for the students does not look promising. Writer 1 may encounter academic disaster if teachers won't buy her lyricism about Haydn and instead want to see an objective argument supported by concrete details and correct citations from the concert program. Writer 2 simply may not survive in college if her teachers don't understand her difficulty in executing an essay under pressure in an academic style. And Writer 3 is also courting disaster, considering that her script for the group presentation did not meet her teacher's assignment, which was to "identify a current events problem, research historical background, and offer solutions." If the other students can't even take notes, then what's the academic value? The odds are not good for these three students, in the light of studies such as ours that show teachers censoring forms of gendership and voice on the basis of narrow, uncontextualized rhetorical standards. Instead of relishing a "constellation of voices" (as Gesa Kirsch [1999] and other writing specialists have urged), teachers are more likely to force these three authors into one mold.

Or, we should say, these three voices. For instead of three different authors, each with a different voice, we have described three of the voices belonging to a single writer. Her name was Becky. Becky was the re-entry woman student, majoring in music, devoted to Haydn, with a poetic soul, political sensibility, keen mind, and dramatic presence. How ironic that she was also taking voice lessons. Certainly, her range of voices is as complex and varied as postmodernists would wish. No one would want a student with such potential excluded from college.

So who is at fault in making her so liable? It may be that both theory and practice share some blame.

As has been often noted, radical postmodernist theory offers few safeguards against the struggle for control of authority over student authoring. Linda Brodkey (1989, 1996) was one of the first to point out that the postmodernist "subject position" bows to raw power in the writing classroom, in large part by disregarding or denying students' agency. Within this framework, Becky is discursively fragmented because she is largely constructed by cultural and social forces beyond her control. She has voices, but no say over them. True, in English studies some postmodernists trust that by helping students become aware of the forces that shape them, they can be freed by that awareness. But how can the theory exempt "awareness" itself from those same forces? If students are not free agents when they walk in, if they are not somebody but rather some subject, then theoretically can they act otherwise than iterate gender, race, class, and classroom positions, mouthing the voices of others?

Most English teachers vocally resist this radical and now largely discredited form of postmodernism, this strong version of cultural determinism. But they still seem attracted to its code words (subject position, hegemony, transcription, function, performance, episteme, and rhizome, for example), as if they find something comforting or self-affirming there. Perhaps that is the point, or better, the ideology, behind postmodern theory in the English classroom—to perpetuate the status quo by rendering Becky down to her social, political, or economic function, or her subject, author, mother, student position. It certainly makes it easier for us teachers to sing to the one voice our discourse community finds familiar and comfortable, the voice that we can manipulate because we have mastered it, the voice that protects us from seeming to be apprentices of different discourses ourselves. As we have said, even when teachers discount the old postmodernist creed, often in their teaching they further its conservative leanings.

The concept of potentiality and its relationship to authoring resist this furthering, in part by penetrating or skirting its deadlock of theory and practice. From the point of view of authoring, voice is just one of those concepts at which postmodernists long scoffed, for which teachers now show little or mixed regard, and in which productive authors all along have continued and perhaps needed to believe. From the viewpoint of potentiality, voice falls victim to teaching that is little conscious of the need to maintain creativity, continuity, choice, and a sense of elbow room in student writers. Teach students the academic style so they can succeed in college; so goes probably the most common defense of first-year composition, in which it is decidedly uncommon to ask what that will do to the students' potential to continue writing after college.

The trick is to return authoring and the potentiality essential to authoring back into the English classroom.

For Becky, yes, that might mean helping her develop strategies to master the conventional academic voice. (Becky, sorry about that "D.") But it also might mean encouraging her to practice other discourses that she is drawn to, including non-Western rhetorics, creative formats, and lyrical styles. For teachers, though, it means to be more critical of the voices of theories that speak about "allowing" students to write out of multiple discourses, as if the authority and the capability lie in us, not in them. It means, yes, pushing students toward a consciousness of the way the authority of social, political, cultural, and institutional voices try to replace our own voices, but also pushing them toward the kind of self-authorizing consciousness that Victoria achieved: "For the first time I became conscious of my own 'voice' as a writer and as I gained control of this concept my proficiency in the medium grew. Imagine my sense of power once I realized I had something nearly as individual as a fingerprint that was flexible enough to control each reader's perceptions and response."

As we have said, voice is a rhetorical concept that most college students believe in and make use of. During our debriefing with Victoria, we listened as she evaluated her own essay. After rereading it, she pronounced, "It's me, it's me!" She was pleased with the lasting validity of her response to the prompt. "It says everything I stand for." The writing was stronger than she remembered, and although she would revise various sentences, she would not change the style: "The voice is all me."

On occasion, we English teachers hear passages in student writing that touch us with a sense of the power Victoria describes. It is a refreshing experience—perhaps even necessary if we hope to maintain honest, engaged response to stacks of student papers. That voice we hear may be like a hand to a drowning swimmer, who cares little whether "personal" is or is not the right name for it. What counts is that the voice is distinctive and promising, that the authorial presence that separates itself from the stack of essays may be one of a repertoire of voices of which this student writer could be capable. One mistake is in doubting that this presence reflects a singular person and a singular voice (see Chapter 8), but another is believing that students do not have the potential for such a repertoire. Perhaps what counts most is imagining on the other end of every piece of writing, however voiced, not something functioning or some subject positioning, but rather someone alive.

6
POTENTIALITY, READING, AND GEORGE YEATS

Personality, no matter how habitual, is a constantly renewed choice.
William Butler Yeats, *A Vision*

Speaking of voices!

It is the evening of April 6, 1919, around ten o'clock, in the parlor of a house on the outskirts of Dundrum, then a hamlet separate from Dublin. William Butler Yeats and his young wife George, married for less than a year and a half, are engaged in intense talk. Their dialogue might as well be called authoring, because she is writing down both his questions and her answers. And their dialogue might as well be called publishing, because they would like to believe that her voice is not hers but the voice of spirits.

"Is daimon of opposite sex to ego?" he suddenly inquires.

"Yes," responds George, or the entity she is broadcasting.

With good reason, this exchange can be taken as fanciful, nonsensical, or ludicrous. But for Yeats in 1919, already a well-established writer and public lecturer, it proved formative. For English teachers today the exchange, understood in the context of Yeats's life-course and especially of the automatic writing, can alter the way they read and teach some of his most famous poems and plays.

The point of this chapter, however, is not that biographical information will newly explicate some literary classics. Certainly, the little-known story of Yeats's curiosity about the sex of the daimon is fascinating in its own right, and we will not apologize for recovering it from the three thick volumes of the Yeats automatic script and retelling it in some detail. The stranger-than-fiction history will illustrate our previous positions on authoring, potentiality, gendership, and voice and allow us to extend them from novice-student writing to famous-author writing. For our purposes, Yeats's odd tale finally applies not only to reading his works but also to reading anything, including student authoring. The 1919 answer from the spirit guides, according to our interpretation, has to do with the potentiality of reading. And Yeats's wife George, who was the voice of the spirit guides, has much to teach us about the way teachers can maintain and expand the potentiality of their students.

Up to this point we have been looking at authoring in the classroom largely from the angle of student production. The same emphasis can be put on reception, not only how teachers might read student texts better, but also how students might better read their own texts in process and the works of others already published. As we will see, approaching the act of reading from the angle of potentiality will help collapse the distinction between students as mere "writers" and published writers as actual "authors" that we questioned in Chapter 1.

Like writing, reading also survives by maintaining potentiality. Like writing, reading is a capacity that can stall or burn out if it lacks an ongoing frame for creative work and room and encouragement to keep fit. Every literature teacher who is reading "The Second Coming" for the twenty-second time knows this. But not every student knows it. Weird as it sounds, George Yeats's automatically uttered reply can generate a chain reaction of potentiality, from the potential for success of her marriage, to the potential of the gendering of her husband's daimon, to the potential for gendership in his literary output, to the potential for interpretation in his readers, to the potential for students to continue reading—and authoring—all their lives.

YEATS, GENDERSHIP, AND HIS READERS, PART 1

Let's begin *in medias res* in this chain of potentiality. Gendership in Yeats's writing is a good example of the way potentiality in reading can be stalled. Everyone knows that he sometimes wrote in the voice or, as he would say, with the mask of a woman. The motives of Yeats and other male authors in doing so, however, has not met with universal approval. For instance, in a 1994 collection of essays called *Men Writing the Feminine: Literature, Theory and the Question of Genders* (Morgan 1994), the editor and contributors accuse "cross-gendering" male authors the likes of Wordsworth, Lawrence, Verlaine, and Faulkner of assuming "the false identity of a woman," of probing "repressed and evaded aspects" of their own gender identity through ambiguous "bisexual poetry," of "ventriloquistic illusion" or "female impersonation" that is narcissistic and voyeuristic at heart. The common thread is an assumption that male authoring in the voice of a woman is a kind of fictional-ization laced with duplicity, like some rhetorical sleight of hand has taken place.[1] "Cross-gendering" dubiously lines up with other terms of hybridity such as "cross-pollination" or "cross-breeding."

In applying the term "cross-gendered" to Yeats, literary critics have implied that he also transgressed some biological or moral boundary. Most notably, literary historian Elizabeth Cullingford (1993) allows Yeats the license to dramatize a female's experience and concedes that he does so effectively, but she detects inherent limitations in his efforts. In reference to "Her Triumph" from the sequence "A Woman Young and Old," Cullingford says that "The limits of this poem lie not in Yeats's writing of the female body, but in his inability to imagine a love without tyrants and slaves, even if those tyrants and slaves frequently exchange positions" (203). It seems that Cullingford discerns in Yeats's "cross-gendered composition" (5), disguised as the diction and gestures of an imagined woman, the mind and body of a man with masculine drives toward repressive power. Cullingford appears to harbor underly-ing assumptions about male poets who use female voices. With Yeats's poem "The People," she allows that "A male poet cannot produce an 'authentic' female voice, but he can adopt a female subject position which contests and in this case defeats his own prejudices" (223-224). Ultimately Cullingford suspects that Yeats's woman-voiced poems stem from discomfort with his own sexual identity: "Yeats had considerable trouble becoming a man" (1991, 21).

Note two omissions. First, there is no counterargument that a healthy and balanced male might want to speak in the voice of a woman for artistic or any other purposes. Second, there is no examina-tion of Yeats's own reasons for doing so. License and success aside, what was Yeats's motive or rationale for projecting the voice of a woman? In a phrase, what was the "authorial agency" (Thomas 1993, 4) that pro-duced Yeats's feminine voices? As with most of Yeats's work, we must seek the answer behind his multiple masks, behind that public person-ality he called "a constantly renewed choice." In this case, remarkably, the best evidence is revealed in his occult writings.

THE STORY OF GEORGE, W. B., AND W. B.'S FEMALE DAIMON

The trouble that literary critics have with Yeats's cross-dressed verse feels like the distrust of cross-dressed student writing that we found

---

1. The quotes are from Morgan, pages 7, 14, 90, 123-128, and 193.

in our teachers' and students' responses to Victoria and Kevin, here writ large in formal literary criticism. At work is a more subtle form of essentialism but perhaps the same gender stereotypes, an assumption that, while imaginatively males can separate gender and sex (male poets such as Yeats may dramatize a female subject position), biologically they cannot produce "authentic" feminine voices. In Chapter 3 we argued that student authors should be free to shape their own gendered presence in texts, just as Alice Sheldon was free to do so.

Why they might is a different question, one that is not always easy for teachers to answer unless the student is unusually self-reflective and forthcoming. Published authors often divulge more about their motivations to write. But unless the writer is accepted as a singular person with every right to gendership, even famous authors will be superficially read by scholars, no differently than Victoria and Kevin were superficially read by teachers and peers. Only when we accept maintained potentiality as a vital faculty of Yeats, only when we stretch our own potential as readers, will we be able to interpret his "cross-gendered" poetry in its eccentricity, richness, and power. Then we might prefer a different name for such poetry, "double-voiced." It is a term validated in April 1919 through the automatic authoring of George, her husband, and the spirits.

Yeats knew quite a lot about daimons before George informed him of their sexual nature in 1919. Following Plato, Plotinus, and Plutarch, he regarded daimons as spirit beings inhabiting human beings. Departing from these classic thinkers, he further believed the daimon to be a discarnate soul engaged in its own post-temporal purging, an activity sensed by the human host through the psyche. Yeats's daimon was a personal one, more controlling even than the guiding spirit of Plotinus or Plutarch, that can directly interfere in human action and use its host as a vehicle to fulfill its own designs.[2]

---

2. In Plato daimons roam the inner and outer spheres and serve a unitive function by preventing the universe "from falling into two separate halves" (1951, 81). Each person has a daimon, "that kind of soul which is housed in the top of our body" (1926, 245). Plotinus' "Guiding Spirit" is appointed to aid the soul in its efforts to accomplish its destiny (Ritvo 1975, 45). In Plutarch the daimon is again a kind of guardian angel, guiding the human "in all the actions of his life . . . presiding over and by divine instinct directing his intentions" (1871, 388). Yeats's daimons reflect the influence of Plato (daimon as bridge between spiritual and temporal realms), Plotinus (daimon as destiny), and Plutarch (daimon as guardian and reincarnation).

Four years earlier, in his 1915 essay "Per Amica Silentia Lunae," Yeats had described the relationship between person and daimon as one of conflict and love.

> When I think of life as a struggle with the Daimon who would ever set us to the hardest work among those not impossible, I understand why there is a deep enmity between a man and his destiny, and why a man loves nothing but his destiny. I am persuaded that the Daimon delivers and deceives us and that he wove that netting from the stars and threw the net from his shoulder.

Yeats goes on to describe this love/hate relationship as analogous to the relationship between man and sweetheart, so that sexual love "is an image of the warfare of man and Daimon." But in "Per Amica Silentia Lunae" the daimon is a universal "he" (1959, 319-369). Yeats does not yet align gender with the identity of the Daimon nor with the dynamics of the poetic mask.

That all changed when George informed W. B. that the daimon is opposite in sex to the person inhabited.[3] Perhaps it had to be a wife to tell her husband that the being inside him with whom he was so ambivalently at war was female. But it could only be George, the remarkable person W. B. had married, to lead him through one of the most extraordinary co-authorings in British or any other literature, a labor of love that would generate the philosophy he would later expound in *A Vision* (1925) and, among other things, alter so radically his notion of mask or creative persona. The collaboration started on their honeymoon, when George, a woman twenty-six years his junior, resurrected her ability to mediate automatic writing. Biographers have suggested that she needed to distract a brooding husband who feared that he may have betrayed three people by marrying: Maud Gonne, W. B.'s first love who had married someone else; her daughter Iseult, to whom he had rashly proposed; and George herself. Distraction or not, the automatic writing quickly turned into an enthusiasm, and for the next four years, 1917-1921, George witnessed the enormous potential of the dialogues for W. B. She became not just his medium and recorder, but his inspiration, collaborator, and teacher. In a number of ways, but espe-

---

3. A note on naming. From this point on it is not fair to refer to William Butler as Yeats since George had also become a Yeats. She was born Bertha Georgie Hyde Lees, but was affectionately called "George" by her husband and others. His friends called him "W. B." to distinguish him from "J. B.," his father, John Butler Yeats (the painter).

cially in the way she defended the writing potentiality of her husband, George is the hero of this chapter.

We will never know the extent to which George deliberately manipulated her husband's interest in the occult. Nor can we be sure of W. B.'s motives in keeping hidden for so long his wife's formative role in the vision system, her insistence on secrecy notwithstanding. At some point, he must have taken the words of the discarnate guides literally: "You can say it is a sequence & your original thought—that is to a degree true" (*YVP1* 123).[4] What we do know is that *The Automatic Script* was actively shaped by two carnate individuals, as directly by George as by W. B. The Script is a genuine dialogue of at least two authorial voices, voices that reflect the ever-curious personality of W. B., with his skepticism, assurance, and rapacious appetite for knowledge, and the ever-present personality of George—intelligent, knowledgeable, imaginative, uncertain, directive, even irascible when necessary. Our argument is that the nature of the mutual production of the automatic writings, the information it generated about daimons in particular, and the material part George played in the authoring, all inform the female voices in W. B. Yeats's poetry and drama and, in giving a unique cast to those voices, ask readers to enlarge the way they read and appreciate them.[5] We also will argue that in her dynamic shaping of the Automatic

---

4. Here and elsewhere we abbreviate the volumes of the 1992 edition of *The Automatic Script*, that is, George and W. B.'s transcriptions during their automatic writing sessions. *YVP1* refers to *Yeats's VISION Papers, Vol. I*; *YVP2* to *Vol. II* (a third volume is the post-session notes of W. B.). George's presence is muted throughout the Script, yet so undeniable that Margaret Mills Harper labels the material "unremittingly gender-coded" in purpose, content, and expression (*YVP1*, 36-37). Not until the publication in 1987 of George Mills Harper's two-volume history of the automatic writing experiments did it become clear how important and active was George Yeats's role in the scripting sessions. With the release of the complete *Automatic Script* in 1992, the full mystery is revealed behind Yeats's veiled confession: "the whole system is the creation of my wife's Daimon and of mine" (1925, 22).

5. The spirits of George and W. B. make some Yeats scholars uneasy, not knowing how seriously to treat W. B.'s mystical life. Harold Bloom, for instance, refers to W. B.'s "spooks" (1970, 140). George herself was reported as saying that her first efforts at automatic writing with W. B. were "fake," but later she disowned the word (Saddlemyer 2002, 103). It should be noted that W. B. initially perceived the *Automatic Script* as creative in nature rather than as systematic in philosophical truth: "even my simplest poems will be the better for it" (1986, 781). Everyone is familiar with the poems that resulted from this mystical exploration, including "The Second Coming" and "Leda and the Swan," along with perhaps his finest plays, *The Only Jealousy of Emer* and *The Death of Cuchulain*. For detailed interpretation of the connections between the script and Yeats's art, see Janis Haswell, *Pressed Against Divinity: W. B. Yeats's Feminine Masks* (1997), especially Chapter 20.

Script, George Yeats emerges as a model for English teachers who want to protect and nurture the potentiality of their students.

Throughout the sessions W. B. assumed the role of inquisitor and pupil, an apprentice of the spirit realm at the knee of spirit guides. George's role was not as mere secretary, although the bulk of the Script is in her handwriting. Nor was she merely the medium or interpreter through which the spirits instructed the poet. W. B. would ask, George would answer. For over four years, she responded to more than 9,000 questions during 450 sittings that take up 3,600 manuscript pages. So factor in spirits as you will, George Yeats's accomplishment in the Script is enormous and multifaceted.[6] As we will see, she shaped the content of Yeats's symbol system in major ways, including the complex design of the daimon in human life.

But she also served as a monitor over her and W. B.'s authoring of the Script, in effect protecting both his and her writing potentiality. Her concerns show in the format and scheduling of the writing sessions. W. B.'s energy and obsessive interest were all-consuming and George soon set limits to the number and duration of the sessions. As early as November 1917, she advises, "The fatigue is the safeguard against excess" (*YVP1* 64). At times the fatigue made work impossible: "you are both too flat to go on," the spirits warn (69). At other times George would limit the number of questions: "I will answer 3 questions now—no more till tomorrow" (110), or simply beg off: "I

---

6. There is a wide range of critical opinion on the collaboration. For example, Richard Ellmann insists that despite George Yeats's participation, "the Yeatsian system is . . . not merely a pot-pourri like Theosophy." Although he credits "the influence of the unconscious mind of Mrs. Yeats in building up images" to be "almost as important" as W. B. Yeats's efforts to unify "the fragmentary theoretical revelations," Ellmann concludes that "in the end everything is stamped with his personality and brought into line with his work" (1979, 230, 231). In his general introduction to *The Automatic Script*, George Mills Harper seems awed and confounded by George's contribution: "George's bewildering ingenuity was remarkable" (*YVP1* 34). Harper's daughter, Margaret Mills Harper, puts a different light on it, arguing that progressively the sessions "were being weaned away from the model of a male source of power and female receptivity with which they began: Yeats asking questions, the spirits answering, and George passively relaying information between them, her own words effaced. No longer even in procedural details would she be an empty vessel for a male text, a female body bearing the offspring of male minds" (*YVP1* 47). Virginia Moore rejects accusations that George deceived her husband or that W. B. wanted to be duped, justifiably concluding, "I think one must salute so tireless a seeker: a great poet who fought for a world-conception, and whose ideas about God and man's salvation show . . . a remarkable consistency" (1954, 447). For a sympathetic and skeptical account ("George had played her trump card"; 104) and all the biographical details, see Ann Saddlemyer (2002).

am sorry—I am too tired" (195). Eventually the spirits start scheduling set times: "Tomorrow I want to come at 5:30" (321); or refuse
daily communication: "I do not wish to write for 3 days" (343). A
year into the writing sessions, the voices insist that "script is bad for
medium especially if she refuses to rest" (*YVP2* 124). Sometimes her
needs are touchingly transparent: "Let medium take a hot bath then
write" (270).

George equally looked after her husband's needs. On occasion she
may be concerned for his health: "you will be better now [if] you drink
more & you should take more exercise . . . this is to the man not the
medium" (*YVP1* 80). Typically, though, George uses her function as
medium to nurture the health of W. B. as a writer. She urges him to
simplify his life and limit public appearances (208) and recommends a
diversified schedule of writing poetry, reading, contacting the spirits,
working on the symbol system, and exercising (*YVP1* 208, 159, 443;
YVP2 123). In particular, she presses her husband to spend his days
in original composition and not simply in codifying ideas from the
Script. As early as February 1919, the spirits are clear: "I do not want
you to write on system[.] I would like you to write something through
which I can give you ideas" (*YVP1* 197). A month later the command
is repeated: "you must begin writing" (223). By August the spirits are
adamant: "you must write poetry" (387). Occasionally George Yeats
even resorts to threats: "For every public speech or lecture you give
after tomorrow during the next 6 months I shall stop script one month"
(*YVP2* 222). It would seem that George sensed early that her husband's
process of composing would not only help order, internalize, and uti-
lize their metaphysical discoveries, but also mark a significant achievement in his artistic development.

Her interest in W. B.'s productivity can also be seen in her insistence
on secrecy. She displayed reluctance to engage the spirits if there was a
visitor in the house and refused to let anyone else participate in their
sessions: "I said alone was better" (*YVP2* 49, 476; *YVP1* 242). Fairly
early, in March of 1918, the spirits explain their demand for secrecy:
"because [if] you speak to unbelievers you destroy our help . . . I do
not wish the spirit source revealed" (*YVP1* 369). Was George protecting a means of intimacy with her husband, or was she protecting W.
B.'s art? She knew well that he was in continual correspondence with
friends such as John Quinn and Lady Gregory, who did not approve
of such experimentation (*YVP1* 13). The more exclusive the dialogues,

the more George was assured of her husband's undivided attention. She also knew that if outsiders would question the authenticity of the experiments, they might undermine a source with great potential for W. B.'s poetry; and she was very aware of his vacillation, shown throughout the dialogues, between doubt about the entire process and yearning to validate the universality of the arcane information. At one point in April 1919 the spirits divulge a shrewd resolution to this quandary. They make it clear that the occult system indeed exists, but not apart from W. B. and George (and—a maternal touch—their daughter Anne, who had been born a month earlier).

> it is developed and created by us & by you two or you three now from a preexisting psychology—all the bones are in the world—we only select and our selection is subordinate to you both therefore we are dependent on you & you influence our ability to develop & create by every small detail of your joint life. (*YVP2* 240)

For W. B., this explanation clarified why other philosophers and poets had not happened upon the same answers in their search for transcendental truth, and it affirmed that the content of the Script could not be generated in the same way with different individuals (say, W. B. with any other woman).

Thus George shepherds the automatic scripting onward with an irresistibly appealing blend of the facilitative and the connubial. She can be gentle when the metaphysics get especially thick ("Wait a little longer for medium—great difficulty—your mind is away"; *YVP2* 148), cautionary when W. B. seems too passive ("you are not critical enough of this script"; 415), and irritated at his hurry to acquire information, his meandering questions, his fixation on the personal rather than the archetypal, his lack of preparation for sessions, and his lapses in understanding ("do please think"; 251). Sometimes we hear her reach the end of some internal rope. When W. B. asks about the possibility of lies being generated through automatic writing, there comes this response: "Perfectly fruitless and very useless—I am upset by this stupid subject" (*YVP1* 238). Yet George always insisted on their psychic partnership, although it sometimes demanded that he acquiesce to her lead. "Take up the line she offers—be subservient to that opening" (328), advise the spirits. And they advise him with words that guarantee not only a successful script but a happy marriage: "The more you keep this medium emotionally and intellectually happy the more will script be possible now" (*YVP2* 119).

And sexually happy as well. The concern of the spirits with W. B. and George's sex life connects directly with the daimon and with W. B.'s double-voiced literary works. When the poet asks what kind of fatigue his wife should avoid, the answer is "mental." "Sexually?" he wonders. "That is part of mental fatigue," comes the response, but the spirit adds that the sexual activity should be limited "only when otherwise tired." (*YVP1* 209). George is vigilant to assure that her husband did not neglect his marital duty. In the dialogue of July 31, 1919, she warns him that infrequency might lead to "declining power." Her husband observes, "I have been under the impression that we have been too irregular lately." The reply: "*Yes certainly*" (emphasis in original). But George hastens to assure him, "your power will always be amply sufficient" (*YVP2* 349). As Victoria and Kevin's reader transcripts, the Automatic Script is awash with sexuality, but it is the genuine sexual engagement of an intimate couple (curiously made public through the spiritual medium), not the gendered manipulation of cultural stereotyping.

There are literally hundreds of pages that explore W. B.'s sexual experiences, for instance, directly in reference to Maud Gonne or masked in the bizarre exploration of the life of Anne Hyde, Countess of Ossory (who historically died in childbirth in 1681 but appears as a spiritual voice in the sessions requesting that W. B. father a child with her). But the historical, fictional, and domestic sex is inseparable from W. B.'s drive for metaphysical truths, especially his long-standing interest in the "universal masculine & feminine in soul." All led to the crucial issue of the sex of the daimon in spring of 1919. Earlier in the writing sessions, W. B. wanted to know "what makes a soul incarnate as a man or woman," but for nearly all of 1918 the spirits keep postponing answers (*YVP1* 250, 271, 283). Then in April of the next year comes George's fateful answer to W. B.'s deceptively simple question, "Is daimon of opposite sex to ego." "Yes." (*YVP2* 235).

As a working writer for W. B., the implications must have been staggering. Twelve days earlier he had been assured that the daimon and himself were unseverable ("Is my daimon part of me? Yes"; 211). So when he learned that the daimon's identity is contrasexual, he had to reconceive his theory of the mask, or the way artists create fictional persons different than themselves. He had to shift from a concept of his "self" (ego) and "anti-self" (daimon) locked in conflict, to one

of himself as male poet and female daimon knitted together in common pursuits. The literary mask must be a psychodrama as well as an
aesthetic construct. His art takes on an entirely new potential, that of
dynamic action—or daimonic action—expressing his multi-gendered
self. In short, the female voice is not inauthentic or foreign to Yeats, but
comes from "the woman in me."[7]

George and W. B. kept exploring the idea of the opposite-sexed
daimon to the end of their automatic-writing sessions in 1921.
The ramifications are astonishing. During male-female sexual intercourse, the two daimons exchange information of which their hosts
can become conscious. Daimons also manipulate their hosts during
Initiatory Moments, when the self is "lured" by someone of the opposite sex from abstract dreaming and inaction to objective emotion and
action, leading up to Critical Moments when one's life is significantly
changed through events—even one's next life if these daimonic conflicts are not resolved in this one. All this microcosmic sexual drama
repeats on macrocosmic levels. The "universal masculine & feminine"
appears in a variety of archetypal manifestations, primary and anti-
thetical, objective and subjective, solar and lunar. Their relative mix
explains everything in the temporal order, from the history of cultures
to the life-course of personality types. George Yeats is creating with W.
B. Yeats a metaphysical system that through sexuality emphasizes the
here and now, yet opens up human spiritual consciousness.

7. This definitive phrase comes from a revealing 1936 letter to poet Dorothy Wellesley:
"My dear, my dear—when you crossed the room with that boyish movement, it was no
man who looked at you, it was the woman in me. It seems that I can make a woman
express herself as never before. I have looked out of her eyes. I have shared her
desire" (Yeats 1964, 108). George and W. B.'s androgynous psyche is nothing new,
of course. According to Jung, "No man is so entirely masculine that he has nothing
feminine in him" (the anima), just as women have their own unconscious masculinity
(the animus) (1953/1983, 297, 678). In *A Room of One's Own*, Virginia Woolf speaks of
a spot at the back of a man's head, about the size of a shilling, which only a woman
can see. "It is one of the good offices that sex can discharge for sex," she tells us, "A
true picture of man as a whole can never be painted until a woman has described that
spot" (1957, 94). Apparently Woolf held the belief—rarely noted by scholars—that
the reverse is true for women. "A woman also must have intercourse with the man in
her. . . . A mind that is purely masculine cannot create, any more than a mind that is
purely feminine" (102). Sandra Bem's Sex-Role Inventory (1993) typically categorizes
around half of respondents as neither masculine nor feminine, but rather androgynous (showing strong preference for both masculine and feminine roles) or undiffer-
entiated (showing little preference for either masculine or feminine roles). Lifespan
psychologist Gisela Labouvie-Vief (1994) argues that as people mature they tend to
move toward positions typical of the opposite sex, despite the efforts of the culture to
curb that tendency.

We will resist the temptation to explore further the unorthodox authoring of this fascinating psychological, historical, cosmological, and mystical system (well, not entirely resist, since Chapter 14 returns to one of its more outré moments, when George and W. B. suspect that their daimons are conniving to make their child the New Avatar of the world). We are in enough of a position to answer our original question. If, united to his daimon, Yeats is never solely male, for he has passionate and ceaseless contact with the feminine embedded within his own being; if, for the sake of his destiny in this life and moral purification in the next, he must allow the feminine part of himself free and formative play; if it is through women, such as his wife, that he is morally and spiritually led, then should readers modify their interpretation of his "double-voiced" verse? And is there a lesson here for the teaching of reading in English courses?

YEATS, GENDERSHIP, AND HIS READERS, PART 2

In "Her Triumph," composed by Yeats a few years after the end of the automatic writing sessions, a woman speaks, comparing herself to Andromeda rescued from the sea dragon and to the princess Sabra rescued from the land dragon. The man addressed by the speaker had come like a hero, Perseus or St. George, and destroyed her conventional view of love "as a casual / Improvisation, or a settled game." Now, released from convention, the two "stare astonished at the sea, / And a miraculous strange bird shrieks at us." Elizabeth Cullingford argues that "The limits of this poem lie not in Yeats's writing of the female body, but in his inability to imagine a love without tyrants and slaves" (1993, 203). But what if, in tune with the Automatic Script, Yeats is not writing of the female body, but rather of his own body? What if both dragon and female victim, tyrant and slave if you will, lie within him? Whether the rescuer comes from within or without is moot (since microcosm and macrocosm interact), but either way Yeats has imagined "a love without tyrants and slaves" since he is speaking from a position of self-release. Then the title would refer to the success of the female daimon (or anima) in tricking the male self into a greater and less self-binding acceptance of himself?

Or take a simpler example, the famous last stanza from "Crazy Jane Talks with the Bishop," also a post-Script poem:

> A woman can be proud and stiff
> When on love intent;
> But Love has pitched his mansion in
> The place of excrement;
> For nothing can be sole or whole
> That has not been rent.

Speaking as Jane rejecting the Bishop's plea for her to forget the earthly and embrace the spiritual, Yeats might be projecting a chauvinistic picture of women as submissive and inevitably tied to their biology. Feminist critics have so charged. But what if Jane is Yeats's daimon speaking? Yeats then is imaging a part of himself that has striven and will continue to strive to balance that other part of himself which overly yearns for the abstract, immaterial, moral, or spiritual.

Daimonic readings, both, which take the poems not as cross-gendered but as double-voiced. At the opening of this chapter we noted the resistance of some readers to double-voiced literature. The contributors to *Men Writing the Feminine* (Morgan 1994) ask what are the consequences of a male writer trying to speak like a woman? What is in it for him? What will women lose because of it? None of them defends a male writer's license to speak as a woman, or appears convinced that cross-gendering might enrich the text and enlarge our understanding of gender itself. The male feminine voice is pronounced "fictional" but not so the "purely female" or "authentic" female feminine voice, equally fictional. Little differently than Victoria and Kevin's readers, contributors to *Men Writing the Feminine* label specific behaviors, emotions, and attitudes as masculine or feminine according to jaded stereotypes, pursuing reading strategies just as jaded. Certainly the contributors do not consider the benefits of people—authors or readers—in expanding their countrasexual potential.

Fortunately, the bipolar gender theory of *Men Writing the Feminine* has a helpful alternative in *The Routledge Anthology of Cross-Gendered Verse* (Parker and Willhardt 1996). The editors argue that "cross-gendered" poems should be understood as gendered acts, or gender in performance, and thus stand between the dramatic lyric and the masked lyric. The dramatic "I" of each poem expresses but also differs from the poet's own subjectivity, making possible a "third term," a speaker who is neither purely male nor purely female. Parker and Willhardt challenge assumptions of biological essentialism, subvert literary conventions, and affirm the authority of any poet to cross or dissolve gender boundaries. In a sense they subvert the title of their own book.

This collection is a step in the right direction, alerting scholars to the extent of valid literary works that do not voice good-housekeeping-approved polarized sexuality, then reshaping reading strategies accordingly. Yet in a sense the approach is still not radical enough for Yeats. What term of sexual orientation—gay, bisexual, transgendered, cisgendered?—fits his singular sexual history, involving spiritualism, wife-as-medium-instructor, daimons, universal masculinity and femininity, historical gyres and shuttles, and images from the Anima Mundi, "Lion and woman and the Lord knows what"? It is not that the readings in these two collections are wrong. Reading, as reading experts have been demonstrating for decades, is like writing in that it is individually creative. At base readers, no differently than writers, are ethically free. Nor are we arguing that our application of the newly published Automatic Script material makes our interpretation of these two poems more accurate, since Yeats could have rejected any of that material when authoring his poems—as indeed he surely cast aside a good deal of it late in life in writing lines like the one above from "The Circus Animals Desertion."

We are arguing first that readers need to be free and creative for the health of their continued reading, and that part of the freedom and creativity entails admitting and looking for the same in writers. Let readers trust in phenomenological potentiality and do what they can to make it systemic. The same, or more so, for English teachers. As readers of Yeats, and therefore also as teachers of readers of Yeats, we have to start by owning his right to speak in the voice of a woman. It is true that without the background of the Automatic Script we probably could not guess at the idiosyncratic view of the self and the world that might have motivated him to choose the persona of woman in "A Woman Young and Old" or the Crazy Jane poems. But even so, we must start our reading with the basic allowance that it is within Yeats's authority as author to speak in those voices—or within Virginia Woolf's authority to speak in the voice of Septimus Smith, or Alice Sheldon's to write under the pen name of James Tiptree Jr., or Victoria's right to reason linearly.

Second, and perhaps more controversially, we are arguing that the capacity to read must always entertain alternate, non-standardized interpretations in order to stay alive. W. B. and George's daimonized voices may be as odd as authoring gets, but to some degree all authoring is odd—as we will take pains to demonstrate in Chapters 8-13. To maintain itself, a healthy reading capability must always look toward the eccentric and the singular in writers. So our caution is the danger of reading habits limited and ultimately deadened by reliance on set frames, such as gender stereotypes (men don't understand non-hierarchical, sympathetic caring, and women do), literary received truths (Yeats had ambivalent feelings toward women), or modish literacy theories (culture dictates one's subject position). These ready-made frames simply do not entirely fit individual authors and their singular lives. And individual readers cannot sustain their potential for open and rewarding engagement with new texts if they read only in the light of these frames and not in the expectation of writers breaking them. An English teacher who instructs students in their reading to only match certain expected interpretations and not to search for singular, unexpected ones is putting one more nail in the coffin of all those potential readers departing college dead to reading[8]. As Yeats said about the personality, reading is "a constantly renewed choice" and should be taught as such.

THE MODEL OF GEORGE YEATS

George and W. B.'s automatic scripting sessions ended on June 4, 1921. In the closing days the spirits describe the toll of the four-year experiment upon the medium: "used up—nothing else—intellectually tired" (*YVP2* 499). The spirits were prophetic. It seems obvious that the Automatic Script is an extraordinary dialogue involving joint authors in whose text it is impossible to distinguish between the finger and the clay, and that the subsequent philosophy of history and corresponding insight into individual personalities disclosed in *A Vision* cannot be understood as wholly William Butler Yeats's own. Yet George Yeats evaded all claims of authoring during her life. She never sought credit for her role and actively resisted publicity during the years she managed the Yeats industry, from his death in January 1939 until her death in 1968. Scholars such as Margaret Mills Harper and Ann Saddlemyer are restoring the credit to her. To it, however, we would like to add an accomplishment no one yet has praised. That is the model George gives us in the Automatic Script of the ideal teacher-reader: mediative, companionable, persistent, directive, self-effacing, attuned to the

---

8. For findings of a study on the way English instruction in the schools and colleges may vitiate reading potential, see Chapter 14.

physical exigencies of composing, translator of the voices of outsiders (the spirits), remover of him or herself from the final authoring, caretaker and part shaper of the potential of the still-learning writer.

Much has been made of midwifery, or maieusis, in English teaching. The metaphor appeals because it draws a simple emblem of this ungraspable, multi-voiced, overdetermined discipline of ours: just two people, one lending a hand to help the other create. Into the next chapter we will transport the picture George Yeats gives us during that 1919 evening in the isolated house on the outskirts of Dundrum, Ireland, morphing it into the picture of a model English teacher teaching, hunched over a text both public and private, co-authoring yet not co-authoring it with a student author whose life-course may be altered by it.

7
POTENTIALITY, LIFE-COURSE, ACADEMIC COURSE, AND UNPREDICTABILITY

Narrative is the meaning of the cipher left by a life.
                    Peter Brooks, *Reading for the Plot*

Friday September 27, 1822, on the heath or commons between Tilford and Farnham in Hampshire, England, in a small dale called the Bourne. Two men are on horseback, and the horses are stock still. It is not a heroic pose. One of the men certainly should have considered himself a hero. Rural born, self-educated, he had made himself England's best-known independent journalist. But at the moment, within a few months of his sixtieth year alive, William Cobbett is reminiscing.

He is in the middle of a surprising four-year journey. Who could have predicted it? Riding mainly alone through the lanes and byways of rural England, Cobbett is appraising, firsthand, the "real conditions of the land." At this particular point, he had invited one of his sons to travel around the countryside in which he grew up as a boy and had been searching for, and to his delight he had found a particular sand-hill. A half-century ago Cobbett and his two kid brothers had been wont to roll each other merrily down from the top of it "like a barrel or a log of wood." In terms of his life-course, a half-century later Cobbett attaches a serious import to those childhood romps.

> This was the spot where I was receiving my *education*; and this was the sort of education; and I am perfectly satisfied that if I had not received such an education, or something very much like it, that, if I had been brought up a milksop, with a nursery-maid everlastingly at my heels, I should have been at this day as great a fool, as inefficient a writer, as any of those frivolous idiots that are turned out from Winchester and Westminster School, or from any of those dens of dunces called colleges and universities. It is impossible to say how much I owe to that sand-hill. (1912, 99-101)

When Cobbett says he may partly owe to the sand-hill his efficiency as a writer, he is referring to his career as a journalist loved by the British people and feared by British politicians. "I went to return it my thanks for the ability which it probably gave me to be one of the greatest terrors to one of the greatest and most powerful bodies of knaves and fools that ever were permitted to afflict this or any other country" (99-101).[1]

Consider the perspective his renewed encounter with the sand-hill takes on education. It is a sane and natural perspective, which we will call the life-course view, distinguishing it from the academic-course view. Cobbett's mode of learning has three driving traits. It is fructifying: the sand-hill experiences keep operating within him after they are physically over. It is long lasting: Cobbett still is indebted to those experiences five decades later, and though emerged from childhood play they became integrated into adult work. And it is generational: Cobbett wants to pass his learning on to his son ("I had often told my sons of this while they were very little, and I now took one of them to see the spot"). In a word, Cobbett's return to the sand-hill enacts a mode of learning and teaching fully compatible with this book's take on potentiality.

The scene is almost heraldic. Two people, expert and novice, together contemplate a public spot where one of them had learned something important. The scene compares to the emblem of English teaching that George Yeats bequeathed us, but with a new emphasis. On the teaching moment, Cobbett brings to bear the history of his life. His emblem casts a judgment on the teaching of college English in the United States: our current "dens of dunces" are just not set up for a life-course approach to teaching.

English departments, it has been argued, have promoted three different heraldic scenes. At least they have proved much more central to the teaching of composition during the last forty years. Imagine

---

1. As a sample of Cobbett's narrative verve that makes *Rural Rides* an enduring read, here is his sketch of the way he "received the rudiments of my education" on the Bourne sand-hill: "Our diversion was this: we used to go to the top of the hill, which was steeper than the roof of a house; one used to draw his arms out of the sleeves of his smock-frock, and lay himself down with his arms by his sides; and then the others, one at head and the other at feet, sent him rolling down the hill like a barrel or a log of wood. By the time he got to the bottom, his hair, eyes, ears, nose, and mouth were all full of this loose sand; then the others took their turn, and at every roll there was a monstrous spell of laughter. I had often told my sons of this while they were very little, and I now took one of them to see the spot" (101).

nineteenth-century *tableaux vivants*. The first scene, entitled "Product," is a teacher, alone at a desk, responding to a student paper and seeming to ask, what do I do with this essay? The second, called "Process," is a student, alone at a desk, composing a paper and seeming to ask, what do I do with this essay? The third, called "Society and Culture," is a class, students and teacher, contemplating some writing and seeming to ask, where did this piece of discourse come from and what is it used for?[2] Like all emblems, these representations of teaching pedagogies are caricature, but historically they point to widespread and very real differences in the way composition has been taught. Just walk by a composition classroom to view some *tableaux actuels*. Today the teacher is no longer lecturing out of McCrimmon's *Writing With a Purpose* or Hughes and Duhamel's *Rhetoric: Principles and Usage* and students are no longer bent over their desks intently scribbling freewrites. More likely, students and teacher are peering into their computer screens figuring out the discursive, cultural, or political implications of a website or a blog.

As we say, Cobbett's *tableau vivant* is two people, mentor and novice, contemplating a public spot where one of them has learned something that lasted. It is called "Life-Course." Translated to the English curriculum, it seems to be asking a different question: Student or teacher, what do you want this writing to do in your life? Not a common inquiry. In our experiment with 64 students and teachers, 63 neglected to follow it. The one possible exception was the reader who suggested asking the author of Victoria's essay, "How do you propose to express yourself?" This variant and other variants of the life-course question would change the typical English classroom in ways this book has been and will be trying to discover, ways connected not only with gender, response, voice, and interpretation, but also literary appreciation (Chapter 9), writing assignment (Chapter 10), feminism (Chapter 11), self (Chapter 12), and diagnostics (Chapter 13).

Certainly the classroom oriented toward the life-course of students would not be fixated on product, where the teacher does all the work;

---

2. It's fashionable to call this third approach "Post-process," a label that we will not use in this book for reasons we give in the Introduction (see Footnote 2 to that chapter and Footnote 3 to this one). John Trimbur, one of the first to apply the term, explains that it refers to the "social turn" in writing studies, "theory and pedagogy that represent literacy as an ideological arena and composing as a cultural activity by which writers position and reposition themselves in relation to their own and others' subjectivities, discourses, practices, and institutions" (1994, 109). Why not call the approach "social" or "cultural"?

or fixated on process, where the student works alone; or fixated on audience, where student and teacher absorb themselves with or into society and culture. It would be a classroom that encourages the kind of language work we have already seen promoted by a respect for the maintained potentiality of learners: provision of elbow room, tolerance of resistance, allowance of unmodish voices, enticement to join in teacher work. Most centrally, it would be a classroom that encourages learning not ending with the course.[3]

A pedagogy easier thought than effected. In some ways life-course is synonymous with potentiality. As Agamben has often shown, a life without potentiality is hardly a life at all and desired only by dictators, slave-owners, and prison camp commanders—and for others, not for themselves. Chapter 2 notes how the academic course does not readily embrace potentiality either, since the notion upsets the traditional functioning of syllabus, grading, assignment, and other practices that depend on course-stopped learning. How can an English course, which has to fit inside ten or fifteen weeks, be shaped to fit the future lives of students? It is a riddle like the one that begins Chapter 2.

Some answers are suggested by common assumptions that English teachers already have about human life change. For instance, we all know that the mastering of technical stylistic conventions is gradual

---

3. We do not see our life-course classroom as a logical or historical subsequence or successor to the product, process, and sociocultural approaches, just as we do not take these three teaching orientations as forming a progressive development in which later invalidates earlier. If the approaches look sequential, it is because they are attached historically to political turns of the last half century; the product approach, for example, marching shoulder to shoulder with the activism of the 1960s and 1970s, and the sociocultural approach marching arm-in-arm with the Reaganite conservatism of the 1980s and 1990s. Advocates of one or another who assume logical or ethical progression, "post" boasters, may be falling prey to Nancy K. Miller's "generational fallacy," which assumes that "later theory is therefore better theory, and that the best theory of all is the position from which we happen at the moment to be speaking" (1997, 63). At least they seem to have forgotten some history. (Those who think the process movement of the 1960s marked the dawn of a new pedagogical age should read Alfred Hitchcock's 1927 *Bread Loaf Talks on Teaching Composition*, and those who think the sociocultural movement in the 1980s marked the dawn of a new discursive age should read Holland Roberts, Walter Kaulfers, and Grayson Kefauver's 1943 *English for Social Living*.) These so-called "movements" are just shifts in emphasis, or better are recrudescences of central modes of language teaching that have existed as long as writing has: editing drafts (product), directing exercises (process), and coaching for public address (sociocultural). If the life-course approach marks any recrudescence, it is of the master-apprentice system of writing instruction, a system in fact that has never gone out of style in workplace environments such as newspapers or technical-writing groups.

and dependent upon the student's entry into technical or disciplinary fields, so why not teach acquisition instead of mastery? Or many of us have experienced the enhancement of motivation to write that comes with a new job, so why not teach ways to handle motivation? Or if we believe that socialization into a new community requires new discourse, why not teach language socialization instead of some particular new discourse? Neo-Marxist notions of radical liberation through social critique of discourse, personal maturation models of self-actualization through interaction with others, sociological theories of demarginalization and acculturation, learning theory of the shift from novice to expert, life span developmentalist conceptions of adult growth— from these and other conceptions of language and life-course change English teachers and their students are not exempt, and from them can be extracted any number of academic-course practices. In particular, studies of lifestory, with emphasis on the creative and the singular, strike us as so rich with implications for the teaching of authoring in English courses that we will return to them in depth in Chapter 10.

Two things are sure and inevitable. First, students will always be enrolled in a life-course (tuition is free). Singular and owned only by themselves, it will be more important to them than any academic course—certainly more important than the trappings of any course, including assigned readings, assigned papers, or assigned style. Second, in the act of authoring, student writers cannot but articulate their life-course. In doing so they partially reshape, creatively use, and stubbornly resist the models of speaking and writing that surround them. Teachers should not presume "to fix what expressions of a language will mean," as Deborah Cameron rightly observes," because meanings cannot be fixed, and interpretation will be dependent not on the authority of some vast internal dictionary, but on the creative and ultimately idiosyncratic use of past experience and present context" (1985, 143).[4]

---

4. What teachers *can* do, Cameron points out, is make it possible for our students to assume responsibility for their relationship to the world and for their behavior, "in its way an act of the greatest political importance" (1985, 172). Sociolinguist Barbara Johnstone argues similarly and provides a wealth of linguistic evidence that the act and the responsibility constitute perfectly normal language behavior. "Ways of acting and talking provided by regional, ethnic, vocational, and gender models (among others) can be adopted or resisted, used predictably or creatively as can ways of acting and talking, provided by certain audiences, situations, or topics" (1996, 155).

There is another thing that is sure, but it is not inevitable. That is the vast lack of information teachers have about their past students' present lives. Scholars have provided only the least smatter of knowledge. All the existing studies of what individual composition and literature students do with writing and reading after college could fit inside a manila envelope. More telling, by habit teachers don't much look to acquire such information themselves. One of the saddest signs of course-stopped learning and its control of higher education is the way the English teacher and the English student, once the grade is submitted, diverge from the course of each other's lives.

VICTORIA'S UNPREDICTABLE SAND-HILL

This is one reason why Victoria turned out so important to us. She shows that the divergence is not inevitable, and that when the contact between teacher and student outlasts the course, both can learn. When we sat down with Victoria and contemplated our experimental hill of data, we re-enacted Cobbett's heraldic scene—experts and novices staring at a public spot where at least one of them had learned something fructifying. What Victoria learned she later put in a letter to us. Between you, reader, and the two of us, we publicly set the letter, whose influence on us has lasted more than a decade.

> Anais Nin once wrote, "There are few human beings who receive the truth, complete and staggering, by instant illumination. Most of them acquire it fragment by fragment, on a small scale by successive developments, all wearily, like a laborious mosaic." Many years ago I was asked to write an essay on my own search for truth. So here I am, come full circle, talking truth once again.
>
> As a student participant in academic research, I was given the wonderful opportunity to become a small "fragment" in the "mosaic" that is our search for knowledge. I feel that it is vitally important to involve students in research applications because the potential for learning is expanded beyond what is set forth in the typical curriculum. Not only are we able to visualize the learning process, but through our involvement we connect on a personal level.
>
> For example, when I wrote my essay, I was operating in a single dimension—the completion of an assignment for freshmen level composition. It was somewhat personal because it involved my system of beliefs. Later, as I talked with Jan and Rich Haswell about their research project, I saw my essay in a much richer context. Apparently, my writing style had unique

qualities that caused a variety of reactions from teacher and fellow students. The assumptions and comments they made stimulated my fighting spirit. How dare they label me or judge my work based on gender, real or implied? For the first time I became conscious of my own "voice" as a writer and as I gained control of this concept my proficiency in the medium grew. Imagine my sense of power once I realized I had something nearly as individual as a fingerprint that was flexible enough to control each reader's perceptions and response. The upshot of this was that the more I understood about the results of the study, the more I paid attention to my own writing and that of others. I had confidence in my writing ability and my style matured. Writing gained significance beyond the completion of an assignment. Suddenly aspects of cultural doctrine, gender, and human nature were thrown into the mix. I can honestly say I never looked at my homework the same way again.

By participating in academic research I don't feel as if anything was taken from me except my picture and that was gladly given. Nor do I feel used, slighted, or misunderstood. On the contrary, I am honored to have been a small contributor to the "illumination" otherwise known as learning.

And here are three of the pictures of Victoria "gladly given."

Victoria's letter describes certain dynamics of life-course learning that run contrary to the typical academic course. Victoria revisited her first-year essay after a lapse of two years, allowing her to "come full circle" and evaluate an old performance in a new light. The academic course cuts a linear path, rarely allowing the student to reconsider old work, and then only after a few days or weeks. Victoria participated in real work. The work in an academic course is, well, academic, where students deal with model essays, illustrations, cases, simulations, and other second-hand experience. Victoria was able to "visualize" her old learning from a perspective separate from that academy learning, the viewpoint of formal research. The perspective academic courses usually provide originates from inside the course, and even the "outside visitor" often is another teacher from the same institution.

More differences. Victoria entered a "richer context" when she saw her essay judged by a variety of readers on a variety of dimensions such as voice and gender. The boxed-in environment of a single-teacher classroom and itemized course objectives means students usually are "operating in a single dimension." Victoria was judged by people outside the course, making her more "conscious" of her own powers, giving her a reason and vantage to fight back, and leading to a burst of confidence. Academic courses usually have one judge, the teacher, affording students fewer opportunities for self-appraisal, fewer openings for resistance, and less chance of gain in confidence. Victoria saw the long-term effects of her own work, making her aware of a world beyond "homework" and leading to a moment of insight or "illumination." Academic courses rarely break free of their own homework.

Of course, academics have always been aware of the hermetic nature of the ten-to-fifteen-week, single-teacher academic course and the limits it sets to learning. They have fought against that nature with course sequences, team teaching, pen pal assignments, outside readers, community visitors, senior seminars, service learning, and field-based programs. On the other hand, experts in human life-course, such as life-span psychologists and life-history sociologists, have long documented the fact that the features of the learning described by Victoria—revisionary, extracurricular, multi-perspectival, multi-dimensional, contextual, resistant, and illuminatory—typically require long breaks in time and the age and experience of people who have lived past the college years. We are back at our question: How can a college teacher write life-course learning, such as Victoria's, into an academic course?

A different—and unexpected—answer is suggested by another quality of Victoria's account. That is its unpredictability. Could anyone have guessed that the first-year student who so dutifully completed her twenty-minute in-class essay on searching for truth would, only two years later, put that effort down as "operating on a single dimension," or predict that the woman of eighteen years so eager to defer to others ("I don't like to be proven wrong, but I guess it's something I've learned to live with") would so fiercely defend herself at twenty ("How dare they label me or judge my work")? The photographs show a stunning, dramatic, confident junior with the moxie to take on thirty-two English teachers and thirty-two peers, but few who knew her as an entering freshman could have imagined those future poses. And who could have guessed that Victoria's simple decision to let her impromptu first-year essay become part of a scholarly experiment would lead her to a sand-hill experience?[5]

Victoria is certainly a distinctive student, easily written off as atypical. But as it turns out, the unpredictability of her life-course is rather predictable. Social psychologists who have conducted extensive longitudinal cohort studies find that most people demonstrate major changes in personality traits over the course of their lives.[6] The few longitudinal studies of English students record shifts that might astonish their teachers. "Jacob" writes creatively in high school, once making up a book and then reviewing it for a book review assignment, and continues writing novels on his own as a freshman in college; then as a junior he selects physics for a major and as a masters student switches to a degree in computer science (Herrington and Curtis 2000, 134-215). As a freshman in college "Lawrence" insists in writing personal essays

---

5. Victoria is now a mother of two and a fine poet. We regret that we cannot follow up with Kevin as we can Victoria. As we have noted (Chapter 4, footnote 2), many readers disliked his essay all the more when they perceived it as cross-dressed. When told during our debriefing that some thought his text was written by a female, he admitted that his response to the topic wasn't typically male. Only part of him touted the self-sufficient masculine pose. He called it "macho stuff." The other part had no need to do so: "I don't feel that way myself." But after the debriefing we lost touch with him. In that sense he typifies the way students disappear from the lives of teachers and vice versa.

6. With almost 800 participants, Mumford, Wesley, and Shaffer (1987) studied personality "crystallization," the point in a human's development when he or she has formed "a niche or adaptive style," "a predictable and self-propagating pattern of environmental transactions" (294), and found that less than half had crystallized before college and that just after college the percentage had increased only to 62 percent for men and 68 percent for women. Caspi and Roberts (1999) reviewed the developmental research and found that rank-order consistency of personality traits achieves the most stability around age fifty. For thirty-year-olds estimates of personality-trait ranking from childhood ranking is only about .5, a figure that indicates about 75 percent unpredictability. For the typical entering college student the stability of traits would be even less.

that English teachers dismiss as "expressivist" and "confessional," but as a senior composes papers for his gender studies major in the impersonal jargon of social constructivism (Sternglass 1997, 265-289). As a senior in high school, "Lynn" is a participant in one of composition studies most famous investigations into the composing process and becomes an eponym for the classic impulsive, self-assured, well-off adolescent writer: spending only seconds thinking over a topic given to her before starting to write, never using an outline, finishing in one draft, providing titles only under duress, and revising only when teachers require it (Emig 1971, 45-73). Two decades later, "Lynn" is interviewed by another researcher and it turns out that during her life after high school she learned to feel insecure about her writing only from her college and law school teachers, became a social activist, and now as a top immigration lawyer plans and outlines her writings in depth (Nelms 1992).

One reason such accounts are rare is that the students may often be unaware of their own changes. In her first year at university, a British student saw little value in an experimental module that combined writing and choreography, where among other activities she had to dance verbal transitions. Three years later a researcher had to remind her of that exercise and only then ("funny you should say that") did she make the connection with a moment the day before when she was reading aloud a draft for her tutor and noticed "quite a few places where something was missing, you know, like a linking sentence" (Mitchell, et al. 2000, 95). Would the discouraged teacher of the dance module have predicted this outcome?[7] Teachers usually discover similar stories about their own students only by accident. Only through a chance encounter did one of us learn that a previous student, who had expressed such an antipathy to writing and who had composed such tattered and beggarly pieces of his own that he barely passed first-year composition, three years later sought and won a summer internship with the Coast Guard, in which he distinguished himself by his ability to turn the night-sea jottings of patrol logs into clear and impeccable

---

7. The British student's forgetting of her first-year course is typical. When first interviewed by Gerald Nelms, "Lynn" had forgotten that she had participated in Janet Emig's high-school experiment, one of the most famous in composition studies history. Novel life-course and educational changes tend to erase earlier positions—a fact about human potentiality that makes it hard to document, as life-course and knowledge-transfer experts have often noted.

narratives for the official record, and subsequently wrote himself into a career with the Coast Guard.

Such accounts may disturb English teachers who want to believe that they have their students figured out by the end of the course, but teachers who trust in student potential may be cheered. Indeed it can be argued that unpredictability is an essential ingredient of potentiality. If an outcome is totally predictable, then it makes more sense to say that a person had the readiness for it than the potential. The trouble is that even more than potential learning, unpredictability badly fits the framework of college courses. Rather it is predictability that upholds institutional teaching. Students are admitted to college and sometimes placed into courses on the basis of scores on national examinations taken two years earlier, examinations validated by predictability formulas correlating high school test success with college academic success.[8] On the first day of class, required assignments, attendance rules, grading standards, and other fixed expectations are handed to the students, in state institutions sometimes done so by state law. During the course, any unpredicted jump in quality of work is regarded with suspicion—did the student cheat, plagiarize, receive help? English teachers usually declare that among their most important criteria for papers are originality of ideas, expression, and individual interpretation, yet analysis of their actual commentary on papers reveals the bulk of it is devoted to marking points where the student transgress from pre set standard usage or from pre-approved interpretations (usually the teacher's). Perhaps it is only fair that even teachers suffer from this outlawing of unpredictability. After the course, if the teachers' grade distributions deviate too much from the expected distribution, the burden of proof is laid on the teachers, often in the chair's office.

One would think that it would be English teachers who would fight most against the banning of unpredictability, since unpredictability lies at the root of their discipline. As cybernetics has long argued, unpredictability is essential to communication. If a message is totally predictable to the reader, it does not communicate anything. It may serve

---

8. Even though the statistical correlations are pitiful, around .3. Such a poor correlation coefficients mean that what the test scores really record in connection with later academic success is unpredictability. They leave about 90 percent of college performance unaccounted for. In terms of writing performance, the statistical calculations would be more honestly called "unpredictability formulas."

other purposes, epideictically authorizing an already agreed-upon action or celebrating an itch for war. But just as potentiality is a necessary function of the human capacity for language (Chapter 2), unpredictability is a necessary function of the human ability to pass on new information. The students who on a test only echo their teacher's reading of *Hamlet* have not really authored pieces of writing, only proved that they got it. What teacher would want just that? By extension, the students in an English course who do not gain any knowledge or any skill that may change their future life-course have not really learned, just demonstrated some short-term knowledge. And what teacher would want just that? Just as what teacher would want to teach students who have no genders or voices to express, what teacher would want to teach students who have no future lives of their own?

In all honesty, some teachers would. They are the kind of educators who stress the other cybernetic rule, that if a message is totally unpredictable it is unreadable. They argue the obvious, that you cannot teach what you do not know and by definition the unpredictable is unknown, that teachers do not know the future of their students and therefore cannot teach to it. We would argue, however, that, yes, teachers cannot know the future of any student, and that therefore they must teach to it and must do so because it is unpredictable. They can teach to the unpredictable by not doing two things—a pedagogical *not-doing* that might go a long way toward maintaining their own potentiality as teachers (see Chapter 2). They can stop teaching a particular way of writing as if it were the only future way available to students, when it is not. And they can stop teaching as if students don't have futures beyond the last day of class, which they do. Positively, they can start teaching unpredictability itself, how students must use it in communicating new information, how students can produce it as a feature of good writing, how students must accept it as a condition of future writing contexts. English teachers should teach students that in their life-courses nothing is more predictable than that they will encounter the unpredictable, and should teach them how to maintain the discursive potential to deal with that fact.

LIFE-COURSE, UNPREDICTABILITY, POTENTIALITY, SINGULARITY

The hard fact of human life-course unpredictability and its hard tie with human potentiality have hard connections with the next part of this book, the fact of singularity. So far we have stressed that English teachers can rouse up students' waiting powers of imagination, intellect, and rhetoric, can allow students room for full authorship and readership, and can concede their need to *not be* occupied by work that would threaten the continued viability of their ongoing potential to read and to author. To all of this, teachers must commit their own potentiality, as readers, evaluators, and diagnosticians. And that commitment is embedded in singularity.

For with each new course the teacher is faced with the unpredictably new or, in our word, with the singular. The teacher has no recourse but to engage with *this* student, explore *this* topic, take advantage of *this* context—particular ground no teacher or student, reader or writer, test maker or test taker has ever experienced before. In English studies, English pedagogy, and English testing, of course, the singular is a concept of even more disrepute than potentiality, voice, or unpredictability. In the scholarly literature, there are veritable taboos on words such as *individuality*, *originality*, and *unique self*. So among other pleasant tasks, the next six chapters of this book will need to remind many readers that human singularity is a fact as solid and inescapable as the floor on which they put their feet in the morning.

Here is the gist of the next six chapters. On the one hand, authors cannot be passive in their engagement with readers. They write to readers whom they know are each unique, each with singular lives, positions, understandings, and interests. On the other hand, readers never act passively either. As Peter Brooks (1984) describes it, readers set out on an "active quest" (19), as if each unique text were "the meaning of the cipher left by a life" (34), sifting through and sorting out particular messages, discriminating among particular viewpoints, inferring new text in relation to text previously read, shaping an answer to the singular text in the process of reading it. This kind of interpretive reading assumes a heraldic import similar to Cobbett's sand-hill *tableau vivant* and could still be called "Life-Course," but there is a difference. Perhaps it is closer to the scene George Yeats has set for us. Now the two people are a novice reader-writer and a mentor reader-writer. Between them stands a piece of text—unfinished draft or widely published masterpiece, it matters not. The text is now public, and has had or may have lasting importance to one or both of them. The two seem to be asking: What do we do with this piece next? The answer, if and only if it has potential, will be unpredictable. And if and only if it turns out singular will it be useful.

SINGULARITY AND ALICE SHELDON

I was always just being me.

Alice Sheldon

In the 1920s, as she is growing up, Alice Sheldon is known as a loner, one of a kind. She remains a oner all her life.

At six years of age, on an African trek with her parents, she walks or is ported some 1,000 miles in search of the mountain gorilla. At nine she becomes an avid reader of *Weird Tales* and other pulp science fiction. At sixteen, in the Corcoran Gallery in Washington, DC, she has her first art exhibit and sale—a nude for which she served as her own model. At nineteen she meets a man at a Christmas Eve party and four days later elopes to marry him. At twenty-six, divorced, she works as an art critic for the *Chicago Sun*. At thirty-one, in August 1942, she enlists in the WAAC, serves as a supply officer, gets transferred to the Pentagon to study photo intelligence, is assigned to the European theatre, meets and marries her second husband, Ting, a CIA man, seducing him by beating him in a game of blindfold chess. At thirty-two she and Ting buy and run a chicken hatchery in Toms River, New Jersey. At thirty-seven she moves with Ting to Washington, DC, and works for the CIA. At forty-one she enrolls at the American University, encouraged to pursue psychology by Rudolf Arnheim. At fifty-one, she earns a Ph.D. in perceptual psychology at George Washington University. At fifty-three, she places her first science fiction story with *Analog*. Even she could not have imagined such an unpredictable life-course.

She was a oner but also a loner, gregarious yet alienated, adventurous yet shy as a night animal (as we have noted, one of her *noms de plume* was Raccoona). She said she submitted her first science fiction stories anonymously because "The one thing in the world I wanted was something I'd done *solo*, all by myself, unhelped" (Brown 1985), yet she hated the attention that she received when her cover was blown: "All my wonderful anonymity is gone; the reader is tied to the specific person" (*Contemporary Authors* 1983, 445). At 65, still faithfully married to

Ting, she confided in a letter to Joanna Russ that at heart, though not in deed, she was a lesbian.[1] As we have noted, her last communication with the rest of the world was to announce her suicide yet plead to be left alone to accomplish it.

In her fiction and elsewhere, she wrote often about singular beings, human and nonhuman, alienated from others yet finally in tune with themselves. Responding to the news that she had been identified as James Tiptree Jr., she wrote to Jeffrey D. Smith, the editor who had helped spread the discovery, about her secret reading of science fiction as a child during summers in the Wisconsin woods: "I'll tell you one thing: You haven't read fantasy or SF unless you have retired, with a single candle, to your lonely little cabin in the woods, far from the gas-lights of the adult world and set your candle stub up in a brass basin and huddled under about sixteen quilts . . ." (Tiptree, 2000, 310). In a letter to the *Saturday Review*, responding to a man who had argued that men are naturally more creative than women, she wrote about men and women, "Rather than belaboring each other over the head to prove that we are the real lovers of humanity, let us just look at each other, plain and simply, as individuals" (Phillips 2006, 157). In "The Women Men Don't See," the short story of hers most people have read, and sadly sometimes the only work they have read, two women depart Earth with some extraterrestrials, choosing an unknown life as aliens with them rather than continue their life on Earth alienated by men and their "huge authoritarian organizations for doing unreal things." In "The Milk of Paradise," a more characteristic short story, Timor is the only human on a muddy alien world ironically named Paradise, where he is raised by ugly creatures called Crots; then he is returned to Earth, where he is repelled by everything human; finally he is taken back to Paradise, where he is received again by Crots, at first to his hor-ror and then to his love.

---

1. "I *like* some men a lot, but from the start, before I knew anything, it was always girls and women who lit me up" (Russ 1990). Among Sheldon's papers, her biographer Julie Phillips found a notebook dating from around 1935 with some drunken scrib-blings: "Oh god pity me I am born damned they say it is ego in me I know it is man all I want is man's life . . . wasteful god not to have made me a man" (Phillips 2006, 85). The man in her Yeats would have called her daimon; Alice called him "Alex." Nearly fifty years later she described her alias James Tiptree Jr. as the "man who for a decade had made himself part of me" (*Contemporary Authors* 1983, 445). Yet Alice Sheldon was a fierce feminist, and used her male pseudonym to help her skewer male chauvinism with a gusto and success that astonished and delighted science fiction readers. Such can be the complexities of anonymous authoring.

What would it be like to have Alice Sheldon as a student in an English class today? It's like imagining Timor on Earth. Think of the current push toward co-authoring, peer evaluation, oral presentations in front of class, monitor screens open to the gaze of others, computer networking totally accessible to the instructor, stress on conventional style and audience placation. Getting lost in the crowd, the anonymity of conformity, seems to be what late adolescent students want and what their English teachers want for them. Not Alice Sheldon. For her was the anonymity that protects the self. At Sarah Lawrence College, she would stay up all night to write her papers and then secretly leave them on the professor's desk in the morning, "like the elves" (*Contemporary Authors* 1983, 445). In officers' training school, required to deliver a two-minute lecture, she walked to the lectern, announced her topic, threw up, and then fainted. After her James Tiptree Jr. cover was outed, she wrote, "It was a lovely thing being nobody!" (445). A nobody is precisely the one thing that pedagogy, policy, and worship of the public image will not allow a student to be today in the English classroom. Yet Alice Sheldon survived the classroom and the lectern. She graduated magna cum laude from American University.

In so many ways, she was unlike the rest of us. Just like the rest of us.

8

SINGULARITY AND THE TEACHING OF ENGLISH

The single and peculiar life is bound,
With all the strength and armour of the mind,
To keep itself from noyance.

William Shakespeare, *Hamlet* III.3

The lenses are useless now, there cannot be two eyeballs again like
hers, a curious thought in so populous a world.

William Gibson, *A Mass for the Dead*

We have been exploring potentiality as a nurturable and sustainable capacity that feeds authoring in many ways, from motivation to creativity, from student five-finger exercises to widely read works of expert hands. For social philosopher Giorgio Agamben, potentiality is more than that. It is the very foundation of a free community and its evolving ethos. In *The Coming Community* (1993), he advocates a new social kinship of people, united in their willingness to make room for one another's potentialities—potentialities that, as a consequence of the nature of human potentiality itself, singly would be distinct one from another. It would be a community where individualism does not exist but where individuals do, a "community without presuppositions and without subjects" where each person would bear "a singularity without identity" (64). In some ways, the current book argues that it lies within the potential of the discipline of English to be and encourage such a community.

Human potentiality remains a psychosocial theory or metaphysical concept, but human singularity is a fact. Singularity is the ontological grist and phenomenological food of potentiality. For English studies, the relationship between the two bears an important difference. Potentiality in discourse is theorized by moving from what is imagined for the future to what is singularly realized. In contrast, singularity of discourse and discourse-making becomes evident by looking not ahead, but back—for writers and readers back to their prior experience, family make-up, habitual language style, or accomplished life work. For the English profession singularity means, among other things, that since the history of each and every student is unique, each and every text and interpretation a student produces is unique. This recognition lends dignity both to the writer engaged in the act of authoring and the reader engaged in the act of reading, as well as to the teaching professional who helps better those acts.

As we have seen (Chapter 1), singularity is a given and a motivation for working authors, but currently in the English profession the neglect of singularity runs deep. Sometimes it appears more like an aversion. That is the excuse for the polemical nature of this chapter's short introduction to the concept. Our chain of argument offers, we hope, a bit of a lifeline in some very turbulent waters. First, in the profession's thoughtful rejection of writing taken as isolated from society and culture, the profession has unthinkingly conflated the single author with the singular author, throwing out the baby with the bathwater. Second, human singularity needs to be re-authorized as a fact—a fact demonstrated in any number of ways and intuitively felt and known by all of us. Third, such knowledge and feelings are a necessary ground for authoring. Consequently and last, teachers who disregard singularity may be withholding from their students one of the primary motivations and privileges of writing.

THE MYTH OF THE SINGLE AUTHOR

Some words become so tarred with association that they may not be worth the effort to cleanse. We are willing to risk our professional reputations by sticking with "potential" and "voice," but "individual" we will regretfully leave on the cutting floor of the profession's history. In English studies "individual" is now linked with "individualism" and a host of fellow travelers: "originality," "unitary genius," "personal writing," "autonomous writer," "isolated author," and—the most familiar expression, and the one we will take as generic—"the single author." The trouble is that all of these terms have been implicated with behaviors and institutions well deserving of critique: oppressive patriarchy, relentless materialism, capitalistic ownership, agonistic argumentation, egocentric illusions about discourse production of many stripes. At the same time, the terms have been employed in ways that unfortunately sever the connection between authoring and singularity. It is assumed that a single author means a singular author, and if the first is a myth so is the second. This fallacy is so pervasive that it deserves some critique itself.

Individualism is the god-term under indictment. Generally, individualism stands indicted as an ideology that undercuts discursive group actions attempting to change established and oppressive policies and practices. For feminists the social and political individualism of the eighteenth and nineteenth centuries licensed the kind of cutthroat competition that kept women submissive and in the home and, among other inequities, kept male-driven forms of discourse established and female-preferred ones silenced or belittled. For neo-Marxists, economic individualism underwrites all forms of capitalistic exploitation (including copyright laws that control distribution of ideas) and, through a strategy of divide and conquer, undermines collectivist efforts at counterhegemony. In all this indictment, rarely is it noted that individualism theorizes humans down to a single unit but not necessarily to a unique unit.[1]

In the profession-wide attack upon the idea of the single author, with its collateral damage to the idea of the singular author, critics have adopted a strategy of divide and conquer themselves. The division is between the act of writing and the use of the product of that act—between what Roland Barthes (1953) calls *scription* and *texte*. Our concept of authoring moves toward a uniting of the two, and it does so in part by rewriting the notion of the single author instead of erasing it.

The most convenient eraser that profession has found is the second division, *texte*. The proof goes beyond arguments from the history of text production; for instance, that typewriters and digital printers no longer convey the distinct authorial signature of a handwritten document, or that print and digital reproduction no longer issue the unique texts of pre-print transcriptions. Under deconstruction, the human agent of text—herself, himself, or themselves—disappears as soon as the text is produced and can never be retrieved. Under radical social constructivism, any singularities of the author are, along with the rest

---

1. This is a point Raymond Williams makes in his entry on "Individual" in his 1976 *Keywords: A Vocabulary of Culture and Society* (136), but that is erased from Bennett, Grossberg, and Morris' 2005 revision (183-184). Philosopher and feminist Adriana Cavarero notes postmodernism's collapse of individualism and singularity: "Because of its stubborn affection for the fragmentation of the classical subject, the post-modern view finds suspicious—in principle—the *uniqueness* of the self, in so far as it is too perilously close to the idea of a unitary, substantial and self-referential subject" (2000, 69).

of the text, stamped or stereotyped into a uniform and reproducible unit, naturalized in conformity with current interpretive conventions. The William Shakespeare who wrote about the "single and peculiar life" is no longer a single and peculiar author, but rather a socially coined and exchanged "Shakespeare" that readers borrow from whatever sociocultural knowledge or ideology that happens to be current. Under poststructuralist language theory, the text itself cannot contain any unique signature of the author because language "always already" is composed of signs that must be familiar to be transacted. And most radically, under strong versions of literary cultural theory, the "individual author" is just an "intersection of cultural codes and sign systems: authors and their authority are mere language effects" (Couser 1989, vii). It seems to follow—incorrectly, as it turns out—that the idea of a unique author must be a delusion.

In short, the radical versions of *texte* do not support the idea of the single author because there is no author with presence in the written product. The counterargument is not often entertained, that if the authorless text cannot confirm the idea of a single author then neither can it disconfirm it, much less disconfirm the idea of a singular author. A second counterargument simply reasserts the continued presence of the author in the written product, a position of Giorgio Agamben's (2007) that we will take up in Chapter 14.

If some of this *texte* theory feels moribund, the attack in terms of *scription* is still very much alive in the profession. Beginning around the time of the first Reagan inauguration, on both the composition and literature sides, a number of professional trends have converged to discredit "the myth of the single author." New Historicism traces the nexus of political, scientific, religious, and cultural ideas that compose an intertextual literary "*scription*" without, it seems, the composing author needing to be aware of them. Cultural studies ferret out the unspoken multiple authorship of productions ranging from movie scripts and annual reports, to comic books and greeting cards. Critical discourse analysis uncovers the ideology that moves authors as if they were factory-produced puppets.

Technical-writing programs train students to write in teams because that is the way the workplace writes. Writing-across-the-curriculum and within-the-discipline pedagogies stress shared writing assignments because lab reports, social work case reports, and research reports are often multiply authored. And especially among the general writing faculty, increases in student population, the advent of the networked computer classroom, the appeal of the feminist promotion of caring or non-agonistic discourse, the theories of language socialization and discourse communities and cultural-historical activity, all have encouraged multiple-writer classroom practices such as collaborative writing assignments, peer evaluation, group presentations, and team portfolios. Emphasis at one point always urges censure at another, and this stress on multiple authorship seems to go hand-in-hand with denunciation of single or isolated authorship—although, as we way, logically the one does not necessarily refute the other.

In short, the postmodern debunking of the "myth of the single author" is extensive. It has generated books (e.g., Stillinger 1991). A critique of the debunking itself could be as long. We'll confine ourselves to three areas important to current English studies: interpretation, collaboration, and the personal.

In *Rescuing the Subject* (1989) writing studies theorist Susan Miller argues for a renewal of the interpretive act. She advances a "textual rhetoric" that would re-conceive composing as a socially constituted activity, and text as a material good distinguished by the absence of the author. She wants to "Investigate the human 'writer' without necessarily surrounding that person with the now easily deniable claptrap of inspired, unitary 'authorship' that contemporary theorists in other fields have so thoroughly deconstructed" (3). So far, fair enough. But in her rejection of the unitary in authorship she tends to neglect the unique in authoring. For example, she puts scare quotes around the name William Wordsworth to show how readers construct a "Wordsworth" without the evidence that some of his poetry may have been written by his sister, Dorothy. Miller's evidence comes from Dorothy's journal entries that contain verbatim lines, or wording close to verbatim, later appearing in William's published poetry. Miller's revision of the authoring of the poetry we call "Wordsworth" entails an authorship construction of its own: "Wordsworth [male] Hiding Dorothy [female]."

Our point is that *Rescuing the Subject* offers this construction without rendering the authoring of the poems, however it happened, as singular. Missing from her argument, for instance, is individuating biographical evidence that William's handwriting was execrable and Dorothy often wrote out fair copies of his poems and letters, or that since he habitually composed while walking and took frequent walks with his sister, so he might orally have given her lines she later recorded in her journal. Miller's "textual rhetoric" helps rescue the interpretation of writing from simplistic notions of authoring, but its focus on intertextuality and hidden multiple authorship seems to block appreciation of singularities of the author and the act of authoring that could assist in the rescue.[2]

Running parallel to unacknowledged co-authorship is acknowledged writing collaboration, another scholarly locus where "single" authorship is often dismantled and singularity of authors elided. The fact that two or more authors work together to compose a piece of discourse doesn't forbid any of them from being singular. Yet in "Collaboration and Concepts of Authorship" (2001), Lisa Ede and Andrea Lunsford's persuasive call for more privileging of collaborative scholarship in the humanities, the picture of authors as singular barely flickers behind a stark foreground where the notion of an author as a "single, isolated individual" is denounced as a "modern construct" with roots traced to capitalism's emphasis on intellectual property, Western culture's stress on rationalism, and patriarchy's obsession with lineage and "autonomous individualism" (354). Only twice does the sense of a writer as singular peep forth. Both times are qualified. Legal scholar Lani Guinier's position that authors can combine available voices and create a new voice that "is singular and plural at the same time" (a position we agree with and will return to) is introduced as "an ingenious argument" (362). The other time is the notice of interpersonal clashes that may make scholarly collaboration difficult, where Ede and Lunsford's only example is "personal preferences shaped by ideologies of the autonomous author" (363), thereby leaving unmentioned the possible existence of ideologies of the *collaborating* author that also might shape personal or individualizing preferences.[3]

---

2. Scare quotes are now part of the conventions of literature and composition scholarship. They signal that the concept so enclosed is socially or culturally constructed. A critic's choice of which items to scarify often reveals tacit constructions of the critic; the construction of others are marked, but not one's own. So Susan Miller renders Dorothy without scare quotes. Apparently journals of Dorothy are really hers but the poetry of "Wordsworth" not really his. In the above quotation from *Rescuing the Subject* (1989, 3), Miller puts scare quotes around "writer" and "authorship," but not around "claptrap."

3. The notion of originality of texts, which we will argue follows from the singularity of writers, is lumped by Ede and Lunsford in with the myth of the single author. They refer to "the impossibility of making a truly original contribution to knowledge" by a dissertation writer (358) and to "the old cloak of the originary author-genius" (359).

The reference to "personal preferences" casts us into the muddiest of discursive waters. Is "person" or the sense of being a person also constructed, and if so, is the traditional composition assignment of the "personal essay" invalid or dishonest? As philosopher and feminist Rebecca Kukla (1996) argues, ontologically the features of the self cannot be attributed to the single person, but rather are determined by the social context in which they occur, and epistemologically people do not have "privileged access" to their own nature or mental states. Indeed, it may be as self-contradictory to speak of the "personal self" as to speak of the "single author." Not surprisingly, students tend to be unaware of this, so proper to the classroom are exercises in "decentering," which will help extract them from their mistaken idea that they are the hub of their universe: work such as peer review, group projects, and writing collaboration. A personal essay assignment would not serve to decenter, and in fact could more firmly lodge young writers in their egocentric misapprehension of themselves and their relationship to the cultural surround.[4] An argument congruent with Kukla's is made by educators who believe that college students should immediately be trained in academic discourse and its impersonal or group voice. It takes a staunch college teacher to assign the personal experience essay anymore, or if they do (and no doubt sub rosa the pedagogical tradition carries on), they rarely defend the practice in print.

The few who do rarely point to the uniqueness of the writer, the writing, or the text. For instance, none more staunch than composition researcher Thomas Newkirk and no more passionate defense of the personal essay than his book *The Performance of Self in Student Writing* (1997). Newkirk pays the price, naturally. One reviewer called his defense atavistic, "jumping back over two generations of critical thought on the social situatedness of the self" (Kameen 1999, 103). But even Newkirk doesn't admit the singularity of the writer. He sees students as occupying "subject positions" and "trying on" or performing various literate subjectivities that chance their way. "The student who writes personally," he asserts, "is not revealing a unique self" (1997, 95-96).[5] In a sense, Newkirk's resistance to singularity completes a cir-

---

4. See Chapter 9 on *recentering* as a more reasonable term than "decentering" for college English teachers, and a way toward writing assignments less dubious than the "personal essay."

5. Newkirk argues that were a student to reveal a unique self in an essay, "then it would be pointless to generalize about it" (96). That sounds like a generalization to us. Besides, aren't generalizations constructed from singular particulars? We would also

cularity begun by Susan Miller. She quotes poetry by "Wordsworth" but resists a particular writer named William Wordsworth. Newkirk quotes a student's essay about her dying grandfather but says that the subject position is "not one she invented." Neither the writer nor the writing is singular.

The temptation is one more time to hoist these extreme constructivist constructions and performative performances by their own petard. When Clifford Geertz in his highly influential book *Local Knowledge* (1983) says that the ideology of individualism promotes a "bounded, unique, more or less integrated motivational cognitive universe . . . organized into a distinctive whole and set contrastively both against other such wholes and against its social and natural background" (229), why does the term "unique' and "distinctive" have to contrast with "background"? Singularity and environmental surround are not mutually exclusive. Nature and society could have constructed us as singular. When psychologist Polly Young-Eisendrath warns of the "ideologies of mental separatism" that advocate "the fallacy of individualism, the shared belief that separate physical bodies endow us with separately unique and creative minds" (1988, 154), on what logical grounds are "separately" and "unique" attached? Singularity and separateness are not mutually inclusive. Common causes can unite people each different from one another. When Lunsford and Ede charge that Peter Elbow's theory of composing "requires not social interaction but mining the depths of the self, searching inside the self for a unique voice" (1994, 427) why are "social" and "unique" set up as contraries? Singularity and sociality are not mutually exclusive. A oner need not be construed as a loner. Nor is the reverse true. A person, even an author, even a student author, may act in ways that are non-isolated, non-separate, non-individual, and that person can still be one of a kind.[6]

---

note Newkirk's unsurpassed case studies, where he individualizes participants to the point of singularity and where he does not hesitate to generalize about them. Even if *The Performance of Self in Student Writing* really does jump back over two generations of social constructivism, that wouldn't damage its keen analysis of the way cultural studies affirm moral positions as counterproductive as the ones they castigate, or its shrewd argument that the genres and styles advocated by cultural studies surreptitiously promote academic life (104-105).

6. Ede and Lunsford's "Peter Elbow," by the way, cannot be found in the writings of Peter Elbow. For instance, in his *Writing Without Teachers*, which they cite in support of their characterization, neither the phrase "unique voice" nor the notion of unique voice appears, and half of the book promotes classes in which students in writing groups learn by interacting with each other.

As much as the next person, we buy into critique of individualism, demystification of the isolated writer, Miller's textual rhetoric, Ede and Lunsford's defense of collaboration, Kukla's decentering, Newkirk's performativity, and much of the rest of the professional captivation with social situatedness. We just want to restore an absence or, better, to right a balance. All we are saying is that the English profession seems to have lost sight of singularity in its swing during the last two decades of the twentieth century toward the collective. In a letter (admittedly personal) to his brother, Friedrich Hölderlin (admittedly a Romantic) once wrote that "There is only one quarrel in the world: which is more important, the whole or the individual part" (1998, xvii). Historically, at least in higher education, the opposition between whole and part has proven less a quarrel than a pendulum. Three decades ago personal autonomy was valorized as a sign of adult maturity and a desired outcome of the undergraduate curriculum, love of uniqueness was recognized as a trait of the creative person, centering was promoted as a psychological exercise that will enhance writing, and individualized instruction was touted as an important goal of higher education. Then within a few years the autonomous, unique, centered, individualistic author is declared a myth and a threat. Rise and fall, but the same ocean. Part and whole, member and group, resistance and conformity, one doesn't refute the other.[7] And singularity, which is a physical fact along the same lines as gravity and heartbeat, has been there all along.

---

7. Our own sense of the false dichotomy of individual or society is expressed perfectly by the Jewish sociologist Norbert Elias, in sentences written in 1939 in exile from Nazi Germany: "Every human society consists of separate individuals, and every human individual only becomes human by learning to act, speak, and feel in the society of others. Society without individuals or the individual without society is an absurdity" (1991, 75). It is interesting that today the linguist of the American English department may be the most likely to hold a working theory of this interdependence of social-group language and the singular language user, between the sociolect and the idiolect, perhaps because linguistics applies a finely discriminating set of tools for language analysis. Charles J. Fillmore notes that the issue was explored by Ferdinand de Saussure, the linguistic forefather of deconstruction, and William Labov, the godfather of sociolinguistics, as a kind of paradox: "one studies the community-wide possessions by examining the speech of a single individual, and one studies the individual aspects of language by studying groups, and knowing where variation occurs" (1989, 33). Especially French stylistics has continued exploring this tension between the social and the singular, sometimes where it might be least expected. Bernard Gardin (2004) finds individuated language use in union worker texts, Frédéric François (2006) in children's texts. See also our discussion of American sociolinguist Barbara Johnstone in Chapters 9 and 10.

THE REALITY OF THE SINGULAR AUTHOR

The next seven paragraphs are an exercise in decentering, for readers who believe that basically everyone is alike.

Basically we are also all different.

This is most obvious on the physical level. In theory and measurement of material things, singularity reigns, from astrophysical calculations of the instant of origin, when the universe appeared from a single point of no size (an instant called "the singularity"), through chaos theory and its argument that every moment of particle-composed events such as our bodies is non-replicable, to the technology of social identification that everyone including the courts accepts and relies on: fingerprinting, pupil-scanning, DNA analysis, birth certificate, social security number, postal address, IP computer address, the optical prescription of the glasses William Gibson saw on his grandmother at her funeral. One of the few axioms shared by physics, philosophy, and common sense is an assertion about singularity, that only one object can occupy one space at one time.

As we have already seen in Chapter 1, the human brain does not escape singularity. Gerald M. Edelman argues that because the brain responds neurologically to experience, physically no two brains are alike. His reasoning involves a "simple calculation" showing that a human being's genome is inadequate to write his or her synaptic brain structure. Hence, the way that one's body modifies synapses and selects particular neuron clusters must be due in part to "individual experience in an open-ended world or environment" (1989, 31). Since environment necessarily varies (only one object can occupy one space at one time), each person's brain is therefore singular.

Edelman's findings suggest that the most salient singularizing force is life experience itself. With humans this force is naturally conveyed in language through life-histories. Early in her career as a novelist, Willa Cather said that "There are only two or three human stories and they go on repeating themselves as fiercely as if they had never happened before" (1913, 113). Yet for the person living and telling the stories they never *have* happened before. Who but Jan was born in Spokane, was educated in Seattle, now teaches in Corpus Christi, and travels to Seattle, Denver, Pueblo, and San Antonio to see her five children and seven grandchildren? Who but Rich celebrated his twelfth birthday by cutting his ankle on a beer bottle in the family trash heap on a farm in Missouri and was given a cocker spaniel puppy named Craig by his sister to make up for the seven stitches? With brain chemistry, offspring diaspora, stitched ankle, and the like, human singularity is a physical reality manifesting itself over time, ineluctable. More in the next chapters on the study of life-histories and the lifestories that recount them, but one of its most repeated conclusions bears anticipating here, that "each of us acquires a unique personal narrative that we share in parts with many, many people; brother, sister, friends, parents, but which in its entirety is ours alone" (Mason 1988, 25).[8]

Because a person's life-history is singular does not mean, of course, that it is isolated. There was a curious contradiction in heyday social constructivism. Its "social" message argued that people are partly shaped by their milieu. Its most radical "constructivism" message argued that preexisting codes stamp our sense of self into ready-made subjects or identities that can be circulated and accepted as legitimate by others. But milieu is always unique (only one object can occupy one space at one time), so how can subjects be ready-made? Old-fashioned sociology can resolve the contradiction, arguing as Elias did that in day-to-day behavior, society and the member of society co-exist as die and coin, one unable to function without the other (1991, 60). But so can current study of life-histories. Paul Smith, for instance, sees an inextricable merger of subject-position created by society and singular self created by the person. People may borrow narrative plots from their culture, but their unique situations create a "self-interest" that "is bound up with—indeed, in part built up by—a singular history" or "self-narrative" (1988, 158). This is not a radical stance. Everyone knows herself or himself as unique. Exceptions are amnesiacs, autistics, autocopic paranoiacs who are convinced that their exact double is pursuing them, and severe schizophrenics who may believe they have no self.

Dyed-in-the-wool constructivists would answer that self-belief itself is at epistemological stake. Self-belief is based on self-knowledge, and knowledge is socially constructed. Even the sense that one is

---

8. Strange that life-history is not a research focus much utilized in literature or composition. The closest is the case study, which became popular with composition researchers in the 1990's and often shows, usually tacitly, the singular development of academic and workplace writers. There are hundreds of such studies, written by teacher-scholars but rarely read by the English teaching profession as a whole, an abundance of buried evidence for singularity. They might help convince the profession that it is communities, groups, categories, and classifications that are humanly constructed, not individual human bodies in space and time.

unique—whether true or not is irrelevant—is historical and has been learned. There are plenty of counter-answers, but the one with the most appeal to us again comes from psychology. It argues that the radical constructivist argument indulges in the fallacy of division. Psychologist Ulric Neisser points to five kinds of self-knowledge.

Ecological: "'I' am the person here in this place, engaged in this particular activity."

Interpersonal: "I am the person who is engaged, here, in this particular human interchange."

Extended, based on personal memories [or lifestories]: "I am the person who had certain specific experiences."

Private: "I am, in principle, the only person who can feel this unique and particular pain [or emotion]."

Conceptual: a "network of assumptions and theories" like roles or marital status, internal entities or faculties (that is, intellectual), and social status (1988, 36).

Even the last, conceptual self-knowledge, entails singularity. Any one of the "assumptions or theories" may operate as a category in a non-singular way (for instance, "upholder of the First Amendment"), but, as Neisser observes, the "network" is composed of so many categories that combinations are unique for each person (52).[9] The parts may be collective, but it does not follow that the whole is collective (the fallacy of division). The whole, the individuating combination of the parts, will be singular. Of course it is possible that the self-believer's sense of uniqueness (perhaps a student's) is delusional, just as it is possible that the observer's sense of collectivity (perhaps a teacher's) is delusional. But those delusions themselves are also singular.

---

9. In his argument for the singularity of the constructed self, Neisser is obligated to a psychologist from a previous generation, Gordon Allport, who often argued similarly against nomothetic diagnosis that reduced patients to only a type of mental problem ("sociopath," for instance) rather than idiographic diagnoses that ended with patients seen as singular. Allport also applied the idiographic argument to the diagnosis of students by teachers: "Children, like adults, differ most of all in the complex pattern that results from the interweaving of their intelligence, temperament, security, interests, and motives. So infinite in number are the ingredients of personality that their permutations and combinations and final organization (influenced by an infinite diversity of genes and of environments) produce individuals who are unique." Allport says that "each personality is inevitably, ineffably, and ineluctably unique" (1960, 64).

Self and language—at least since Lacan—entail one another, and postmodern language philosophy joins hard science and psychology in defending singularity, though advocates of radical postmodern theory rarely note this. Just because modernist philosophers such as Hannah Arendt (1958) posited uniqueness of humans does not mean that postmodernist philosophers rejected it. It is true that since 1977, when Derrida published his watershed piece "Signature Event Context," academics have accepted the death of the author, the death of originality, the death of the shifting "I," and so on. But how far on? In reducing readers and writers to "subject positions" and texts to linguistic placeholders, the "deaths" might seem to include the singular language event. But Derrida never denied the unique event. In fact, for Derrida these "deaths" are based upon the fact that events *are* unique, noniterable, and have to step aside for language to function in its essential quality of iterability. The argument in "Signature Event Context" is that a signature asserts over and over that a unique event has occurred: "what must be retained is the absolute singularity of a signature-event and a signature-form" (1977, 180).

Finally, *texte* itself. Despite Chomsky, whose generative grammar requires the premise of novel utterances, and despite classic reader-response theory, which contends that every text is unique because every act of reading is different because every reading by a reader (even of the same piece) takes place at a different time and in a different context, one of the legacies of the radical postmodernist's debunking of origins is a common misunderstanding in the English profession about the possibility of unique text. It's as though there were no singular expressions left. This misunderstanding is also based upon the fallacy of division. What holds for a part (a word) does not necessarily hold for the whole (a combination of words, such as a sentence). The fact that novelty is the norm even at the sentence level can be easily shown with Internet search engines. At this writing, Google.com scans over three billion web pages. A Google search for the single word "chapter" comes up with about 266,000,000 hits, for "singularity" about 4,700,000, and for "authoring" about 1,710,000 hits. Little novelty in the use of these words—that is, in the isolated appearance of them in published text. However, the simple word string "authoring a chapter" has only 4,780 matches. And the string "chapter on singularity" has only 3 matches. "Authoring a chapter on singularity" has none. Even the two-word string of "potentiality, singularity" records no instances. In actuality, it is difficult to invent any full sentence of ordinary length for which Google can find a match (this one has zero matches). Even the most ordinary book or essay is almost entirely composed of sentences that have never seen print before. This includes student essays.[10] As Chapter 1 notes, human language processing is built to deal with "always new" as easily as with "always already." Just because a reader comprehends a sentence doesn't mean that the reader has met it before.[11]

SINGULARITY AND AUTHORING

The event in its context, the human life in its living, the text in its writing, and the text in its reading are all singular. Fact—but is it a fact a writer needs to know *to* write? Granted that every act of human authoring is a unique event, it still does not follow that the author is necessarily motivated by a sense of that uniqueness, even an unconscious or intuitive sense. So it is in practically uncharted territory that we stake our claim. Good writers and good readers must believe in the

---

10. Excepting cited or plagiarized sentences, of course. A teacher who charges anti-plagiarism services such as Turnitin or Cheatbusters with over-detection may forget that they also provide overwhelming evidence that the workaday student sentence is unique. The plagiarism search programs would not function otherwise. Examples easily show that, regarding expression at the sentence level, the default state is uniqueness. In 1973, in a chapter in an Edinburgh Press book on computer use in literary studies, Sidney Michaelson and Andrew Q. Morton wrote about the classical scholar William C. Wake: "Wake was soon able to show that what is most characteristic of an author is not his few personal idiosyncrasies but the rates at which he performs the operations which he shares with all his colleagues" (1973, 70). In 1980, Susan Hockey, in a Johns Hopkins University Press book on computer use in the humanities, wrote, "Wake was soon able to show that what is most characteristic of an author is not his personal idiosyncrasies but the rate at which he performs the operations shared with all his colleagues" (1980, 136). No one would buy the argument that the similarities between these two sentences is due to chance or cultural currents.

11. Need we add that resistance to singularity and reliance on totalizations is the bread and butter of political language and that totalitarian regimes are not the only illustration? In the past fifty years alone how many non-combatant Afghan citizens have been killed in combat, and of them how many have been singularized in the West? Any exception to the general practice is shocking. In 1988, a few days before the Soviet Union started withdrawing its troops from Afghanistan, the Central Committee of the Communist Party sent a letter to all Party members explaining its decision. The letter numbers the Soviet dead and wounded in Afghanistan and then, astonishingly, says, "There is a reason people say that each person is a unique world, and when a person dies that world disappears forever. The loss of every individual is very hard and irreparable" (*Harper's* 2009, 24). Reading such language in a public governmental document is like finding a live plant growing in the middle of an asphalt parking lot. Not that the Soviet communiqué mentions the number of dead and wounded Afghanistanis.

singularity of their acts; to do otherwise would be to undermine their potentiality as writers and readers. Singularity, as we have said, is the phenomenological food of potentiality.

We offer three pieces of support for this position. First, psychological studies have connected the personal sense of uniqueness with qualities associated with healthy discursive activity. Fredric A. Powell (1974) reviews studies in "perception of self-uniqueness"—a perception, it should be noted, which is not questioned by psychologists, though they tend to measure it along a continuum of weak to strong. According to Powell's summary, at the weak end of the scale, people who see themselves "the same as others" also tend to judge themselves negatively; at the strong end, people who see themselves as unique in some ways tend to have positive self-images. These appraisals of one's own likeness vis-à-vis others have real effects. In one eye-opening experiment, C. R. Snyder and Howard L. Fromkin (1980) randomly divided research participants and then told one group that psychological tests showed them unusually like other people and told the other group that the tests found them unusually different from others. Then the participants were given a "unique uses test" in which they had to list as many different uses as possible for an object (such as a shoe). Subjects who had been told they were very similar to other people devised more uses than subjects who had been told the opposite. The explanation is not that a sense of non-uniqueness fosters creativity; nearly the opposite. Participants who were told—at random, remember—they were non-unique resisted that qualification and tried to disprove it.[12]

Second, as Chapter 1 records, testimony of working authors finds them persistently claiming the singularity of and in their acts of authoring. Gish Jen says about a period of not writing, "Most of all, I missed the orientation that came with experiencing myself as distinctly—exhilaratingly, uncomfortably—singular. (How firmly this frames the real world.)" (Darnton 2001, 107). Rimbaud's famous line, *Je est un autre*,

---

12. Snyder and Fromkin conclude that "individuals *want to perceive* themselves as having some differences and are constantly struggling with cultural and social forces that inhibit the expression and self-perception of uniqueness" (1980, 198). The effect was especially strong for female participants. Note that for the participants it doesn't matter if the qualification is accurate or constructed—put into quotes, so to speak. Phenomenologically, actual singularity and perceived singularity are still singularity. "None of us lives," Paul Smith insists, "without reference to an imaginative singularity which we call our 'self'" (1988, 6). The word "imaginative" is superfluous even if, as we argue, the singularity is real.

as pure an expression of non-singularity as you will find ("I is someone else"), seems to express an anomaly. George Steiner notes this fact and quotes the line as expressing the essential deconstruction of the self and the erosion of the author, adding, "I have, before, cited some of those who know best: the poets, the artists. I have found no deconstructionist among them. I have found none who can, in conscience, accept the constraints on permissible discourse prescribed by logical atomism, logical positivism, scientific proof-values or, in a far more pervasive sense, by liberal skepticism" (1989, 227).

Third, a logical support. In the authoring of discourse, how can anyone personally *act* in a way that recognizes consequences without sensing herself or himself as singular? It seems hardly possible to imagine someone who wants to write and who at the same time wants to believe that the writing will emerge from a context that has happened before, will say nothing new about the situation, will do so in sentences that have been written before, and will be read by people who will get nothing new out of it. What use would such writing have? No matter where an act of writing is located on the individual-society continuum, its viability entails uniqueness.

SINGULARITY AND THE ENGLISH CLASSROOM

This chapter, finally, will wax polemical.

At the top, we opined that English studies could become a professional community where the singular potential of each of its members, including its students, would be allowed room and respect. Judging from trends in the scholarship and practice of the last three decades, it seems that the little action the profession has performed in regards to that future has been to avoid it. Generally it has moved further away from Agamben's "community without presuppositions and without subjects," where each person would bear "a singularity without identity" (1993, 64). Instead the swing has been toward discourse theory that believes language users can never escape presuppositions, social critique that insists even resistance to subjectivization must operate from subject positions, and classroom practice in which group identity stands as beginning and end. There have been plenty of countercurrents, and many if not most members of the profession are likely to deny it, but as a whole we have drifted with the nationwide fin-de-siècle tide that has moved toward conformism and collectivism in things cultural, economic, political, and educational.

How far have we drifted? Here are three vignettes.

In a LAN classroom, a teacher has students connect with a member of their collaboration group and share their ideas about that student's collaboration, with the other students and the instructor reflecting on these messages "sent through the free space of computer conferencing." As a result "the environment in the computer culture went far beyond the instructor's expectations in establishing a community of trusting, diverse individuals—a community required both in the composition room and in the larger society" (Fey 1992). Digital space is free just because it is digital? Having a one-on-one conversation heard by the teacher and the rest of the class will make a student more trusting? And such oversight is required in our society? This course was conceived in LAN days when the clunky Interchange function of Daedalus was considered cutting edge. Today, with standard course-management systems such as Blackboard, WebCT, or Moodle that connect through the Internet and consequently that make every digital act in the class technically accessible worldwide, a teacher can easily construct a classroom community that national security agencies would envy and dystopian science fiction might dream of, where everything private is made public, where everything divulged is weighed and judged, where "diversity" exists only within some group, and where the requirement for membership is eternal vigilance of one's neighbor.

A teacher requires her students to write a series of assignments exploring their different selves, the "familial self, the writing self, the political self, the public self," so students will understand that "the 'real me' operates within the boundaries of social context" and that "personal narrative should be perceived as a product of ideology" (Marinara 1995). Why not so students will understand that "the real society" is shaped by acts of singular selves, or that ideology is a product of personal narrative? Why is the predicate "operates within" instead of "resists"? Why is "real me" put in quotes and not "boundaries of social context"?

The English composition homepage of a large university enthrones "collaboration" in these words: "Contrary to the myth of the isolated author in the garret, successful writers do not work in isolation. Writers collaborate extensively. Writers develop their best ideas by discussing issues with colleagues, by researching others' ideas, and by exchanging comments about one another's documents" (University of South Florida 2008). *Myth* "of the isolated author," that anyone still believes or ever did believe? *All* writers "collaborate extensively"? *Best* ideas?

Are these vignettes extreme cases? Maybe. But the catchphrases are discipline-wide. Their contradictions sound like feedback from a cheap loudspeaker. Lip service is paid to students as "diverse individuals" with a "real me." But the true power is handed over to a heavy-handed gang of collectives: collaboration, colleagues, social context, product of ideology, computer culture, community. In this pedagogy where student response is "required" by an unanswerable agency called "larger society," the unspoken message is the closeting or erasure of singularities in student writing.[13]

Of all professions, English should hold itself accountable for the language it deploys. Yet one moment members will be convincing students in class that the "isolated author is a myth," that "authorship is constructed," and that "the individual is an intersection of group identities," and the next moment alone in their faculty office be penning a letter to the editor of a scholarly journal arguing that another scholar has misread their intentions in a piece of their own authorship. It's quite human, of course, to lump other people into groups but keep oneself separate, unconstructed, and singular. But with the issue of singularity the profession betrays contradictions that are hard to call anything but self-obfuscation. Teachers put manifestoes on their course websites declaring the isolated writer a myth and collaboration a must for the student's best writing, and then during examinations isolate students to make sure they will "do their own work." They publish articles that apply Deleuze and Guattari's "facialization machine," an unlocalizable social process that regularizes persons into recognizable social identities (1989), and in a crowded auditorium they each instantly pick out the face of their spouse thirty rows away. They apply historical analysis to show that the "unitary author" is effaced through

---

13. One of the reviewers of our original manuscript, encouraged by anonymity to speak directly, wrote, "I don't know what the authors mean by 'singularities in student writing.' I suspect one could find a social background for any 'singularity' they cite." But why must social background forbid the uniqueness of persons or their ability to convey that uniqueness in writing? Any number of English teachers can set on the table any number of singularities in student writing (for instance, Victoria's "Later, as I talked with Jan and Rich Haswell about their research project, I saw my essay in a much richer context"), but has anyone ever produced or ever will produce a social background?

social norming, and they distrust statistical analysis because they think it effaces the single student writer or reader with numerical norming.[14]

Self-obfuscation may be the wrong term. Slippage might be more accurate, such as the dissonance that Chapter 4 hears in the theory of multiple voices held by teachers, compared to the pedagogy with which they enforce a single, academic voice. There is certainly slippage, for instance, in the profession's conception of singularity and handling of computer technology. It uses computer file sharing such as Google Docs or EtherPad to foster group work in class, technology that permanently records every textual change, yet it thinks of over-the-air provisioning technology as a collaborator in hegemonic plots against their own individual freedom; for instance, when the U.S. government commandeers giant databases maintained by Internet providers to spy on users without court warrant, or when Kindle and Amazon.com, unannounced, erase the files of a digital book consumers have bought and stored in their own "personal" or "home" computers. On the one hand, scholars claim that computer-mediated synchronous discussion in the networked classroom reflects the fragmentation and dissolution of the "individual" subject. On the other hand (beginning early in the history of English departments and computers), they claim that computer analysis helps aid in authorship studies—that is, helps flush out an individual writer hiding in anonymity. And what English teacher has not used Internet search engines to flush out the student writer who may have had the temerity to collaborate without showing the teacher the citation conventions that will discursively isolate the student's own work from that of others'?[15]

---

14. Statistical method does nothing of the sort, of course, although the application of statistical results may. A statistical mean or correlation or trend line treats and uses each datum equally. Compared to a statistical point-distribution display, the run-of-the-mill English studies assertion ("other silenced groups such as racial minorities and those with working-class origins," etc.) looks like a hastily erased chalkboard. A statistical mean (for instance, "7.31") is a generalization composed of recorded unique events; an expression such as "racial minorities" is a generalization usually without them.

15. Use of computers for authorship detection has continued to this day. In 2002, the U.S. Information Awareness Office (whose motto is "Scientia Est Potentia", "knowledge is power") put out a call through their Defense Advanced Research Projects Agency (DARPA) for project proposals to aid in combating terrorism. One of the suggested areas was "Entity extraction from natural language text," that is, identification of individual terrorists from the text of anonymous public manifestoes (Defense 2002). Don Foster describes some of this activity—he was an academic trying to identify Shakespeare's unattributed publications through computer analysis

Much as the concepts of potentiality and unpredictability, singularity jibes ill with the regulated framework of English courses. To fit into the semester, class size, and academic credit system, everything needs to be squeezed into familiar classifications, from literary works to class activities to the students themselves. Auden's brilliant libretto to Stravinsky's operatic take on Hogarth's *The Rake's Progress* isn't taught, because it escapes conventional teaching categories (straight or satiric, poetry or prose, music or language, Enlightenment or Modernist?). Single student presentations are not assigned because there is not enough time in the semester for that many. Plus-or-minus grading is resisted because it might mean only one or two students could graduate with a perfect four point. Singularity upsets all the pedagogical rubricization that saves so much time in dealing with large numbers of students, such as the gender-tailored diagnosis, handy toolkits of rhetorical skills, predictability formulas, and response and rating rubrics discussed in Chapters 1-6.[16]

In part, English-teacher neglect of singularity may owe to ordinary human avoidance of the unpredictable (see the previous chapter). When teachers classify students—that is, grade them as "B," see them as "young male," label them as "non-English major"—they may feel they are banking upon known information. If they interact with a student as a singular person, however, teachers must admit that there is information they don't know. And what they don't know may be used to undermine or limit their power or authority as a teacher. It is illuminating to sit with a first-year student away from his or her peers and the classroom environment, where conformity and anonymity so easily cloak the student's uniqueness. It is refreshing to experience how, one-on-one, the singularities of student and teacher begin to emerge. But as

---

and was hired by the FBI to use his skills to identify the Unabomber. According to Foster, the basic assumption of "literary forensics" is "that no two individuals write exactly the same way, using the same words in the same combinations" (2000, 5). Although the CIA initiative failed, the Unabomber's sister succeeded, intuitively recognizing his style and leading to his arrest.

16. We take the term "rubricization" from Abraham Maslow (1962/1968). He is referring to the classification of patients by psychotherapists into types, instead of "using concrete, idiographic, patient-centered experience-language" to see a patient in "his individuality, his uniqueness, his differences from all others, his special identity" (126). The nomothetic procedure of rubricization abstracts a person into categories of age, occupation, nationality, gender, status, mental condition, etc. Maslow notes that patients hate such treatment. Rubricization is used most frequently when psychotherapists "are ill, tired, preoccupied, anxious, not interested, disrespectful of the patient, in a hurry" (129).

this happens, the safe structure of pre-set rubricization begins to totter. This student reports for a national animal shelter website? Maybe she doesn't really belong in the "B" cell. The more teachers get to know students individually, the less blanket diagnosis of group reading and writing "problems" seem to fit, and the more the student's needs begin to appear idiopathic (in medical parlance, a problem of unknown origin that seems to occur spontaneously for no known reasons), that is, idiographic. Doesn't the existence of human singularity mean that in every student there is something unknowable, therefore something unpredictable, ungradable, maybe even something unteachable? With the fact of singularity enters the inevitability of secret, the one Derridean notion most anathema to English teachers (see Chapter 14).

Teachers will face these questions about singularity and find ways to deal with them only by asking about the effect on the student. How can students not interpret the current emphasis on self-identity only within the community of others, on learning only as co-learning with each other, on collaborating in writing only as part of an embeddedness in the larger culture—interpret it all as anything but a promotion of groupthink? How can they not interpret the current lovefest of education with standardized, anonymous, high-stakes testing as an argument that singular behavior will be punished?[17] First-year students may be especially susceptible to nomothetic gestures of teachers. They have just left two intimate groups—family and school cliques—that were small enough to recognize and treat them as singular persons. Now they are in large lecture classes where the professor does not know their names, or in small classes (of which English departments are justly proud) where eccentric readings are pressured toward the center with group consensus, and the uniqueness of authoring formally declared a myth.

---

17. The complex incompatibility between mass testing and singularity is a topic large enough for another book. Studies have shown, for instance, that in independent scoring of student essays, as raters sense information that individuates the writer, their rating of the essay goes up and their agreement with each other's rating goes down (Barritt, Stock, and Clark 1986; R. H. Haswell 1998)—a tendency that seems reasonable until we consider it as a reason why testing companies cover up author names. The clash between standardized examinations and student singularity has been long noted, from Fred Newton Scott, who argued in 1909 that such testing opposes the ideal educational task of promoting the unique development of each student (12), to Sharon Crowley's testy comment in 1985 on the plight of female students when "in the discursive gangbangs that are holistic readings, even her name is expunged from her texts" (95). It's time for the issue to be revived.

PASSING THE SKEPTRON BACK TO SINGULARITY

Singularity is making a return in English scholarship. Compositionist Robert P. Yagelski (1999) argues that literacy makes sense only in local acts of "individual agency" and illustrates the point with case studies that render students as unique persons. Literary theorist Amihud Gilead (2003) explores the way novels convey human uniqueness, noting for instance that Proust not only insists on the singularity of human beings, but also exhibits what Gilead calls "panenmentalism," a denial that there is "intrinsic similarity" in people. In feminist studies, Mona Ozouf (1997) argues that French women have always assumed the status of *singularité*, not feeling the American need to band together to resist some patriarchal global war against women. In narrative studies, Samira Kawash (1997) wonders how political analysis changes if racial identities are seen in terms of singularity, which would be equivalent to dissolving social groups into "disorder, excess, non-identity," into a new community that would recognize the unrepeatability of singular selves and the "irreducible otherness of the other" (213-214).[18]

As we argue in Chapters 11 and 12, a return to singularity will not mean a wholesale repudiation of postmodernism, just a questioning of its more extreme pronouncements and an expansion of many of its central tenets into areas it has so far eschewed, including a new look at neglected scholars, at neglected positions of scholars well-known, and at fields of knowledge that have maintained a path through postmodernism quite unlike that traveled by the discipline of English. Because of this book's interest in the classroom, the next five chapters will delve into life-histories of students, teacher knowledge of those histories, personal topic assignments, and diagnostics of eccentric writers. But the chapters are also interested in theory and philosophy that support human singularity. We have found useful not only Agamben's vision of singularity without identity, but also Derrida's argument that naming underlies any resistance to the violence of totalization (1995), Barthe's evocation of the "impossible science of the unique being" as the only way to explain and defend singular interpretations (1981, 71), and Adriana Cavarero's synthesis of feminism, narrative, voice, and singu-

---

18. Gilead notes the passage in *Remembrance of Things Past* where Marcel's grandmother assures him that he will be all right staying in a room separate from hers in the Grand Hotel at Balbec, that she could not mistake his knock on the wall from anybody else's. And why not, asks Gilead, when "genuine love is the intimate, veridical acquaintance or familiarity with the singularity of the beloved person" (2003, 25)?

larity (2000; 2005). We will also use the contribution of human developmentalists and lifestory experts, who through the last half-century never lost their love of human singularities traversing time, and who therefore envision post-secondary educational goals sometimes at odds with those promoted by English studies: personal autonomy instead of group identity, self-authoring instead of group authority, recentering instead of decentering.

We are not the only ones who sense that it is time in English departments for the skeptron to be passed back around to singularity, to hear its distinctive and—dare we use the word?—*deconstructive* perspective once again.

9

SINGULARITY AND NARRATIVE:
CHARACTER, DIGNITY, RECENTERING

The people in whom the system personifies itself [celebrity spokespersons] are well known for not being what they are; they became great men by stooping below the reality of the smallest individual life, and everyone knows it.

Guy Debord, *Society of the Spectacle*

Whatever kind of poor job I was in my own eyes I was Hari Kumar—and the situation about Hari Kumar was that there was no one anywhere exactly like him.

Paul Scott, *The Towers of Silence*

In *Reading for the Plot* (1984) Peter Brooks reflects on a change in the world's inexhaustible appetite for stories, a shift not in the appetite but in the stories. In the past, we repeated master plots, overarching Narratives (with an uppercase N). Mythically, we told stories of origin; spiritually, we told stories of fall, redemption, reincarnation, salvation; teleologically, we told stories of purpose, of nature, of ultimate end. For the most part such Narratives disappeared after the Renaissance, Brooks observes. Since then, history has replaced theology as the authoritative narrative, and we now tend to speak of personal identity in terms of the remembered past, and of social purpose in terms of a projected earthly future. Paradoxically, since the demise of Narratives we use narratives (lowercase n) with a new urgency, "as the key discourse and central imagination" to order, organize, and explain a secular world (5-6).

Serious scholars have shown their own inexhaustible appetite for stories, especially in the last half-century. It seems the scholarship of every major professional field has taken a "narrative turn": anthropology, organizational studies, literary criticism, legal studies, cognitive science, discourse analysis, psychoanalysis, journalism, historiography itself—you name it. On the member/society and singular/collective scales, in many fields that turn has weighed ponderously on the social and collective end of the beam. Narrative is analyzed as a cognitive frame, discursive paradigm, or behavioral guideline assigned by society, culture, or ideology, and received by subjects in order to make sense of their lives. Fairy tales conform to thirty-one universal plot features, history follows narrative tropes as few as four in number, children shape their moral behavior to fit family tales, juries are unconsciously persuaded by cultural story lines hidden in attorney's questions and summaries, the most ordinary public acts such as walking into a restaurant enact pre-coded social scripts, discursive genres both fictional and non-fictional obey or deliberately transgress (and acknowledge by transgressing) traditional plot lines.

Supposedly, the influence of pre-written narrative enters deep into each of us. What we may believe is our own private story of our own life-course, not told fully to anyone else, still borrows its plots from elsewhere. Developmentalists Jan-Erik Ruth and Gary Kenyon summarize the theory: "Life stories reflect standard mythical scenarios in a culture drawn from literature, drama, and sacred heroes of the past, as well as present media heroes from TV and film" (1996, 5). Supposedly, even the "self" to which we feel our life-history is happening constructs itself from stories told by the world outside of us. According to James M. Day and Mark B. Tappan—pursuing their exploration of storytelling, human development, and moral action, the self is "an inhabited, decentered actor, in a theatrical world of possible stories where all action is rehearsed, justified, and reviewed according to the narrative possibilities inherent in the actual context(s) in which action occurs" (1996, 71).[1]

In this and following chapters we will tread a narrow line. On the one hand, we want to affirm the value of providential narratives; their virtue of explaining events, choices, desires, and lives over time; their distinct way of capturing subtlety, healing trauma, sharing wisdom, expressing social identity. On the other hand, we want to believe that in life or in writing the fact of human singularity alters the way people

---

1. The radical position on narrative and social construction can be uncompromising: "There is no selfhood apart from the collaborative practice of its figuration" (Battaglia 1995, 2); "The self is social in its entirety" (Burkitt 1992, 215). The next chapter, however, will present some current scholars of life-history, such as Mark Freeman and Paul John Eakin, both believing constructivists, who see an interaction between self and society, a society in which the singularity of lived experience is routinely expressed and communicated.

interpret narratives presented to them. In this chapter we will restrict our gaze to the reading of novels and autobiographies and further to three critical aspects of literary narratives, aspects often taught in English courses: character type, moral vision, and discovery (Aristotle's anagnorisis). Taking up two novels, one by Michael Ondaatje and the other by Paul Scott, and a non-fictional piece by Melanie Thernstrom, we hope to show that singularity is written into each of these works and keeps readers, including student readers, from otherwise cheapening the authors' representations of the complex worth of human beings. Recognition of singularity, we argue, is necessary to elevate type to *character*, moral to *dignity*, and discovery—usually taken as a moment when self-centered hubris is decentered—to *recentering*.

At the same time we will argue that while narratives may capture such qualities, they do not create, bestow, or endow them. Many champions of narrative insist otherwise. The danger is to assume that singularity and coherence of the person are the product of the *representation* of singularity and coherence in the narrative and do not exist apart from it. To say that identity is like a story is not the same thing as treating people as if they are characters shaped by story. This will be our concluding, cautionary point.

CHARACTER: "THAT SUBTLE ART"

Robert Coles remembers his father saying, "character is how you behave when no one is looking" (1989, 198). As an adult and a psychologist, Coles realized that even if the behavior is an act of self-scrutiny, someone is always looking. Character, perhaps first learned socially and conditioned by the reactions of others, is "how you behave in response to the company you keep, seen and unseen." In that response, however, character does not necessarily or totally turn on social or cultural affirmation to grow or maintain itself. Character is the site of personal agency that can, if it wants, turn on the social. It can be subversive, it can be resistant. In short, as Michael Ondaatje insists in *The English Patient*, character is a "subtle art" (1992, 70). Like potentiality, it is one of the quintessential acts of self-authoring and partakes of the singular. How you are different and think yourself different from others play a role in how you choose to behave when no one is looking.

The question is how this notion of character relates to character as it is authored in narrative, both in the sense of fictional characterization and of the human character they project. Any good novel would serve to study this question. Michael Ondaatje's *The English Patient*—a novel popular in college literature classes—provides an answer that is a little startling in its simplicity. Characters in a novel achieve character only when they achieve singularity.

There is any number of ways students can see this in *The English Patient*. One is through a complex motif that might be termed "art-into-self." Characters navigate an art-infused landscape where they encounter, among other texts, Herodotus' *Histories*, Kipling's *Kim*, Cooper's *The Last of the Mohicans*, and Stendahl's *The Charterhouse of Parma*. These texts do not serve merely as ambience or intertextuality, but are reshaped by the characters who read them. The copy of Herodotus had been made by the Patient into his commonplace book and stuffed with his own creations: corrections to Herodotus' "lies" and inaccuracies, sketches, maps, additional glosses, archaeological field notes. So on what turns out to be his suicide bed in the war-ravaged villa of San Girolamo, he listens not just to the *Histories* being read to him by the nurse Hana, but also to the history of his singular life.

The copy of Kipling's novel belongs to Hana and has her notes etched in the flyleaf. *Kim* and the *Histories* become part of her, adding to the sentences and moments of her life (12). Thus it does not surprise her, in looking up from the pages of *Kim*, to find Kip, the British sapper and bomb defuser, walking into the villa "as if out of fiction" (94). As for Kip, he is not bookish, but he is taken by paintings, or rather he takes them into himself. In those hellish days of the war, with all of Naples booby-trapped by the retreating German army, when the sappers expected to die at their job, Kip sleeps at the feet of a painting in the villa depicting the Annunciation: "If he is going to explode he would do so in the company of this woman and the angel" (280).[2]

The characters all translate art into themselves, converting a historical construction into something singularly theirs. The Patient's "Herodotus," Hana's "*Kim*," and Kip's "Annunciation" (in quotes like Susan Miller's "Wordsworth") are unlike anyone else's. In the process of individuating these works of art, the characters individuate themselves

---

2. The art-into-self motif appears also in the sequence of paintings that the characters encounter. The patient gazes at a garden painted on the walls of his bedroom. He associates David Caravaggio's name with the great painter, and even casts himself in the role of Caravaggio the elder and Kip in the role of Caravaggio the younger in "David and Goliath" (116). Occasionally, Kip feels as if he is in a painting (104); at other times he wants to comfort Hana by surrounding her with a painter's landscape (114).

and help create Ondaatji's fictional representation of their character. Kip, stunned by a painting of Isaiah in the Sistine Chapel, "the face like a spear, wise, unforgiving" (77), is especially drawn to the mouth because he thinks the mouth reveals character, "that subtle art" (70, 219). Humanly-designed artifacts whose originating creators are gone and whose interpretation is open to vicissitude are translated back into a living and unique art work.[3] Character is self-portraiture.

Of the many ways Ondaatji singularizes characters into character, the most revealing is with his central protagonist. The Patient is both eponymous and anonymous, the "English patient" of the title whom the military authorities are trying to identify. That is not easy, since Ondaatji's plot has stripped him of all *identity*. He is nameless, nationless, documentless, and raceless (his skin has been burned off). Literally faceless, he lacks those characteristics that, in Deleuze and Guattari's term, allow facialization. In the novel, the Patient's identity is altered, debated, bartered, hidden, and investigated like a piece of war matériel, and readers have to deal with the title of the novel as a truth or a lie (is the patient really "English"?). Normally identity is located in a name, a nationality, one's cultural heritage or biological lineage, the color of one's skin, the side one assumes in war, one's function in a family or a marriage. Identity establishes front lines and fault lines, between loving and owning, between being named and remaining anonymous, between belonging to the Axis or the Allies. Yet ultimately in the novel identity is not the prize. In the end, the English patient's identity is still not determined.

Instead it is his unique character that has been established. Outside chance that causes the extreme defacialization of the social and personal identity of the Patient cannot erase his unique character, which emerges through the particulars of his humor, his erudition, his knowledge of music, his guilt, his thwarted love for Katharine, his quirky and tragic life-history. In sum, the Patient is the fictional embodiment of Agamben's ideal community member, who has "singularity without identity" (1993, 64). This antimony between social markers and personal character is a major point of the novel, and one students should not miss.

In discourse, character in this sense is achieved when individuating information frees the figured persons from types, groups, movements,

---

3. The villa San Girolamo is appropriately named after Saint Jerome, who translated the Hebrew and Greek Bible into Latin.

and other frames that would otherwise lock them into easy categories. Individuation is the only way for the writer to generate character, for stock information (national citizenship, ethnic origin, etc.) would only generate identity. Singularity releases the stock character from the public stocks.[4]

While the central plot of Ondaatji's novel makes this point, with the Patient creating character as he lies bed-bound but freed of the nationalized war that created his tragic plight, so do the tales of other characters in the novel. Caravaggio, the professional thief turned spy who had known Hana in Canada, learns to love her when he stops trying to give her an identity and instead tries to read her character.

> He realized that during the last two months he had grown towards who she now was. He could hardly believe his pleasure at her translation . . . this wonderful stranger he could love more deeply because she was made up of nothing he had provided. (1992, 222)

In the same young-love storyline, Kip still loves Hana fourteen years later, after he realized that she was "someone who has made her face with her desire to be a certain kind of person" and that it "will always reflect a present stage of her character" (300). Character, like potentiality, is a capacity that can be nurtured, maintained, and lost. It resides, the narrator tells us, in "that pure zone between land and chart between distances and legend between nature and storyteller. . . . The place they had chosen to come to, to be their best selves" (246).

This sense of developed or developing character is opposed to the Theophrastian "character," the seventeenth-century literary genre that expounded on stock types such as "young raw preacher" or "the fair and happy milkmaid." It differs also from Aristotle's *ethos*, sometimes translated as "character," since ethos, or the persuasive force of the speaker's credibility, belongs to the audience, not to the speaker.[5] Our

---

4. The thoroughgoing social constructivist would argue that "individuation" is only a node of intersecting pre-written codes, an argument that, as regards literary characterization, goes back to the structuralists (e.g., Jonathan Culler 1975). Maybe so. But, as Gordon Allport and Abraham Maslow noted, outside of books the result is still singular (see Chapter 8). So why not inside books as well?

5. It also differs from E. M. Forster's idea of "round character" (1927/1954, 67-78). Forster says that flat characters are formulaic. Their character can be described in one sentence. Round characters are more complex, and surprise us when a new aspect of their character emerges during a new scene. None of this has anything necessarily to do with singularity, a notion Forster does not broach. Both flat and round characters can be singular or not. With her insistence that the uniqueness of persons be never

working concept for literature students is character as a lifelong work of art rooted in whom one chooses to be and wants to become, since that concept supports their own self-concept as singular and their own life-course potential. Since assigned narratives often explain the choices that shaped character, students can capture character and suspend it in time, like a photograph or a painting beneath which one sleeps. But narrative is not the basis of character—although it may be of identity. Rather, narrative is the most natural way of expressing the unique particulars that express character.

DIGNITY: "IN THE POWDER BARREL, HUMAN BEINGS"

The literary quality of character has no necessary connection with morality, if we take morality to be socially approved systems or rules of behavior. Corrupt character in narrative is just as legitimate and can be just as singularized as sterling character. Neither does what we will call discursive dignity have any connection with morality. But dignity is deeply ethical, in the sense that it functions as an ethical axiom: every person has dignity by virtue of being singular. Not everyone, of course, may display that dignity. Imagine a person who in no way acts differently from others. That person may have a purpose (as a link that holds a social chain together), a use (as achiever of a goal set by someone else), a value (as slave on whose head a dollar value is set). But if that person doesn't think his or her own thoughts, doesn't achieve a distinct place, can't be recognized as a particular person in a crowd, then that person lacks dignity. In the works of the real world and in works of fiction, that character will be treated without dignity, both by other people and by herself or himself.

Our talking point for discursive dignity is one literary character, Barbie Batchelor. In Paul Scott's *Raj Quartet*, his four-novel sequence on India's Partition, Barbie serves as a minor stock figure in *The Day of the Scorpion* (1968/1998) but becomes, it seems against the author's will, fully singularized and the fulcrum of the next novel, *The Towers of Silence* (1972/1998). We choose Barbie because archived materials of Scott offer a rare view into an author's arduous singularizing and

---

forgotten, Hannah Arendt comes close to our sense of character: "the moment we want to say *who* somebody is, our vocabulary leads us astray into saying *what* he is; we get entangled in a description of the qualities he necessarily shares with others like him; we begin to describe a type or a 'character' in the old meaning of the word, with the result that his specific uniqueness escapes us" (1958, 181).

dignifying of a particular character. The authoring of discursive dignity, at least in this case, took many months and exacted a heavy toll on the writer. We find in the authoring of Barbie a lesson for students in both literature and writing classes.

As we know from Paul Scott's own words, his exploration of the interior space of his characters partly serves a philosophical purpose: to challenge the divisions that work to sort persons into groups. Group alignment, role differentiation, labels of identity and value—for Scott these are the evils of his day. No wonder he was attracted to Raj experience as a fictional setting, and to British India's separation from its mother country and partition into India and Pakistan. Difference creates partition, and partition between races, classes, and genders, once entrenched, forces human beings into divisive oppositions. Scott agrees with Ondaatje that the value of the individual does not ultimately stem from the community in which he or she lives, nor from race or gender, nor from nationality. Value comes from the fact that each person has a chance to create and preserve "an inner dignity and sense of destiny" that cannot be compared to anyone else's (Scott 1963/1985, 183).[6]

The adulation of difference that saturates contemporary literary theory would not have rung true for Scott, who witnessed the dismantlement of the British Empire. "The world is full of conflicts—*and correspondences*," he wrote in 1975. "When I write about India these are always in my mind"(Tulsa 9:5; our emphasis). In an address to the Writers' Summer School in Swanwick ten years earlier, he articulated a claim that encapsulates the future purpose of the Quartet: "There have been enough distinctions, and it is time to recognize that there are only, in the same powder barrel, human beings: human beings in need perhaps of redefinition" (1986, 31). To explain what he means by

---

6. Scott's belief in a hard-earned and self-conferred uniqueness of every person was shaped before the Raj Quartet. In *The Birds of Paradise* (1962/1985), a novel written several years before the Raj Quartet, the protagonist, William Conway, has returned to India only to discover that he can't stay away and he can't fit in. In a first draft of the novel, Conway says, "To me, each new day is like an arrival in strange territory with invisible luggage. In my mind is the map of the journey that's gone and an illusory map of the one ahead. In my luggage there is what I remember of the past & hope for the future & they are tied together by that frayed but only serviceable rope: my personality, my experience of myself, my sense of my own continuity, what I am, what it feels like to be me, what it feels like to be me in relation to what it might feel like to be them" (Austin 4:3). Hereafter archived material will be identified in the text by box and folder number. "Austin" refers to the Paul Scott archives in the Harry Ransom Humanities Resource Center at the University of Texas at Austin. "Tulsa" refers to the Scott archives, Series I, in the McFarlin Library at the University of Tulsa.

"redefinition," Scott describes how the radical youth of England during the early 1960s were dressing and behaving differently from their elders, attempting to overthrow traditional gender roles and redefine their own identities. This is not the kind of redefinition he had in mind. He was tired of seeing his fellow citizens categorized and divided in groups pitted against each other, girls who should have long hair or boys who should not, allies of the West or of the Soviet Block, radical Tories or reactionary socialists. For Scott, the term "inner dignity" is ultimately unconnected with an individual's success in meeting superficial social standards about how to wear one's hair. Nor does dignity connect with liberal reform. "An Act to legalize abortion has nothing to do with a concept of the dignity of unmarried mothers." That "dignity should be a human dignity, and our notions of that have faded," he laments. "We're no longer certain what a human being is" (1986, 49). Later each volume of the Quartet will explore this uncertainty and try to draw the contours.

Scott's belief in individual uniqueness and "human dignity" sounds like the "individualism" or "humanism" that was decried by, among others, American neo-cons and English professionals in the 1980s and 1990s.[7] It seems also vulnerable to those kinds of postmodernists who want to "demystify" subjectivity into a non-cohesive, opaque, and fractured self. Scott's "redefinition" of what it means to be human, however, escapes these critiques. It escapes them because it begins with the fact of human singularity, which stands outside their parameters. In all of his novels, but most explicitly and tellingly in the Quartet, human beings are first and foremost singular individuals, admittedly grounded to the place they inhabit and shaped by ties to family, nation, race, and history; but not inalienably grounded or totally shaped, finally free to define themselves. They must be free agents at some level, or else they would not be singular. Scott says his novels as imaginative acts attempt "to create something so that it may exist in its own right, or to create something that may exist in order to demolish what exists and is undesirable" (1986, 147). In a word, his fiction challenges and attempts to transform the historical through the singular. Even within the regimented code of the Anglo-Indian community, for instance, there is, as Samira Kawash puts it, "the unique, the unrepeatable, the unknowable, the irreducible otherness of the other" (1997, 214).

---

7. Scott has not escaped such charges from postcolonial critics attacking his "universalistic, univocal, and monologic humanism" (JanMohamed and Lloyd 1997, 235).

No better illustration of Scott's endowment of a character with dignity through narrative singularization than Barbie Batchelor. The bare facts of her life paint her as common, in more senses than one. No different from most other missionaries in India before the Partition, she grew up poor, felt the true call of Faith, worked to save the pagans, and ended up at the bottom of the Raj's social scale. Open Barbie's steamer trunk, which accompanied her all through India, and we find, however, her life narrated in the form of unique objects: pictures colored by her Indian students, a personal facsimile of a picture of Queen Victoria entitled "A Jewel in Her Crown" (Barbie kept her smaller copy in her trunk while her companion missionary Edwina mounted her larger one on her wall), old exercise tablets in which Barbie used to write letters she never mailed. As Scott explains, Barbie is loyal to her trunk, "even more loyal to it than to her God," because it works as

> a symbol for the luggage I am conscious of carrying with me every day of my life—the luggage of my past, of my personal history and of the world's history—luggage crammed with relics of achievement, of failure, of continuing aspirations and optimistic expectations. (1986, 118-119)[8]

Barbie's trunk itself is not lacking in narrative adventures. Barbie secretly asks Sarah Layton to hide it in the mali's shed at Rose Cottage, where it is discovered by Sarah's irate mother and causes a native wallah disastrously to lose control of his tonga in an apocalyptic rainstorm.

The adventures interweave with Barbie's story, which has its own entanglement in the narratives of others. The pictures colored by her students trace a story, not simply about Barbie's students but about Barbie's relation with them. In one little girl's picture, the sky is not colored blue. Why? Because previously the girl had colored Jesus' face blue, like Krishna's, and Barbie had taken away all the blue crayons. Why is Barbie's picture of Queen Victoria smaller than Edwina's? Because Barbie had not left Muzzafirabad as a hero as had Edwina, who once heroically turned away rioters at the school door. What does Barbie most want to be in the future? To save her own Unknown Indian. Yet she gradually comes to understand that the Unknown Indian is exactly the person she had neglected in her years of service.

---

8. The trunk differs from the ceremonial silver in the regimental mess in Pankot because it is a living, valued receptacle. It expands and contracts and moves around like a living thing, with objects retrieved or dislodged at need. In contrast, the silver in the regimental mess had not changed in forty years.

Thus this self called "Barbie" comprises a life-history that tells what she has done, failed to do, should have done, is doing, wants to do now, and hopes to do in the future. As we will see in the next chapter as a characteristic of lifestories, hers is interwoven with the story lives of many others, but ends unique to her.

Thus Scott singularizes Barbie, but how does he dignify her? Just as at first she appears common (non-singular), she also appears common (low class). Scott can write scenes in which dignity is explicitly at issue. In one poignant and violent episode set in a hospital room, Raj-proud Millie Layton literally wrestles with the older Barbie for control of events, like a demon narrator intruding and trying to rewrite Barbie's life: "You were born with the soul of a parlour-maid and a parlour-maid is what you've remained," Millie sneers. Barbie tries to stop Millie from phoning to have her removed from the hospital room; Millie forces Barbie to her knees ("imprisoned by her own violence in this penitential position"), and in a culminating insult throws a carafe of cold water over her. Does such a confrontation destroy Barbie's own dignity? It could have, but it does not. Barbie

> held an edge of the table, getting purchase to rise which she did without dignity but perhaps honourably. Who could say? She did not know. Dignity and honour were not inseparable. At times, and this was one of them, they seemed far distant for both of them. Without another word she retrieved her handbag from the floor where it had fallen and left the room.

Barbie "recovers" herself and understands, better than Millie, that by trying to shame her, Millie has demeaned herself (1972/1998, 234-235).

But Scott does not need such scenes to establish Barbie's dignity. He has already given her that by endowing her narrative with singularity. In the narrative of Barbie's life, Millie is not superior to Barbie because of her social standing or her economic class. Neither is she equal to Barbie only because they are endowed with the same rights based on a shared abstraction called "humanity," as liberal humanism would have it. Rather, as Seyla Benhabib (1992) would say, Millie and Barbie share the same dignity because they are both unique human persons. Through singularizing scenes such as in the hospital room, Scott has endowed both Barbie and Millie with different *characters*. By many moral codes, Barbie's character is less despicable than Millie's.

But through the same scenes Scott has brought out the dignity that both have.

It might seem that privileging millions upon millions of singular individuals would only deepen the kind of divisions among people that Scott targets as one of the evils of colonialism. Scott's narrative argument concludes the opposite. In doing so, he uncovers a deep paradox. Since a character's sense of *identity* originates outside of the character in the larger group (whether that group be defined by religion, race, class, gender, or nationality), effort must then be devoted to keeping that group intact. Group survival then dictates that emphasis be placed on differences among groups. Group difference breeds division and hatred, which in turn make those people who identify themselves only through a group more intent on maintaining its coherence, its privilege, and its safety. Something sinister must happen, so the logic of group difference goes, when black and white races commingle and marry, or when Indians assume roles in the government that Britons now have.

This dynamic is at the core of power relations and explains why interlopers such as Barbie Batchelor must be kept in their place. The paradox is that the original need for self-affirming identity ends with an identity that disaffirms self. Scott believed that differences among persons holds precedence over differences among groups: "there are only, in the same powder barrel, human beings." Singularity, or a unique, person-based sense of self, breaks down divisions and barriers because the group becomes less important than the knowledge that another person—regardless of differences in race, nationality, religion, etc.—is also a unique and dignified individual.[9] Scott comes close to

---

9. This tenet of Scott's worldview is voiced not only by characters who serve as his moral guides, but also by characters who are not necessarily trustworthy yet who are still able to recognize this truth. There is the fact of uniqueness that racists like Merrick, nationalists like the Pandit, even adventurers like Jimmy Clark, all recognize with a forceful reminder: "'I'm not quite a girl. I'm this one,'" Sarah snaps at Merrick (1968/1998, 429). Even Hari Kumar, aka Harry Coomer, during the most cruel and dehumanizing night of his life, comes to this realization:

    I wasn't to be compared, I was myself, and no one had any rights in regard to me. I was the only one with rights. I wasn't to be classified, compared, directed, dealt with . . . . I wasn't to be categorized by type, colour, race, capacity, intellect, condition, beliefs, instincts, manner or behavior. Whatever kind of poor job I was in my own eyes I was Hari Kumar—and the situation about Hari Kumar was that there was no one anywhere exactly like him. So who had the right to destroy me. *Who had the right as well as the means?* The answer was nobody. (1968/1998, 302)

Levinas' insight that recognition of the uniqueness of others entails responsibility for them (1969). It is an insight that provides seed and cohesion for a different kind of group, one such as Agamben's future community, whose members have singularity without identity.

For students in English courses, whether in the interpretation of discourse or the authoring of it, the lessons from Scott's achievement in character dignity are obvious. But not obvious is the labor needed to achieve it. It is easy for a writer to imagine other humans (even oneself) through generalities. Authoring *identity* takes a few phrases already placed on the tips of our tongues by the culture (see Chapter 11). Authoring *singularity* is far more difficult, an act of love in more ways than one. Direct evidence for this fact lies in the Paul Scott archives, where notes, drafts, and letters trace his long travail in revealing Barbie's dignity. The paper trail is fortunate for us, since it documents a case of authoring as it really happens. It is not a narrative entirely pleasant to read, although that may turn out also fortunate, since the unpleasantries help dispel the common student hope that good writing can be accomplished in a relative trice, without the "preparedness" working authors feel (see Chapter 1).

Scott said that in the moral landscape of his novels he consciously tried to give voice "to people who would otherwise remain inarticulate" (Tulsa 10:24). Barbie Batchelor, aged and retired missionary, is one instance. But Barbie—who became the cornerstone of the third novel of the Raj Quartet, *The Towers of Silence*—turned out to have a character very difficult to voice. By June of 1968 Scott had decided to divide what he had thought would be the third and last novel of the Raj sequence into two novels. The new third novel, *The Towers of Silence*, would be the "slow movement" of the Quartet, to contrast with the fourth, *A Division of the Spoils*, "far more a book of action" (Tulsa 13:18). Critics have praised *Towers* for its economy, its meditative leanness, and its symbolic density. Yet of all the novels in the Quartet, it seems to have been the most difficult for Scott to get finally under way. The writing is "simpler, more direct," admits Scott, but he adds, "This wasn't consciously sought, but it is part of the explanation of the awful trouble I had with it, I think" (Tulsa 13:18).

He would find the key to the book in Barbie, but not easily or quickly. In June he made a sketch of the "main blocks of interest" for *Towers*, which had a rectangle for "Indian Nationalism & Unity" containing arrows for Muslim and Hindu separatism, and another rectangle for

"English Traditionalism" that includes the established military (the Layton family), the younger military generation (Jimmy Clark), the aristocracy (Lady Ethel Manners), and the diplomatic liaison with the Indian government (Nigel Rowan). At the bottom Scott places a third rectangle labeled "The Pressures of EVENTS: The moral drift, the momentum" (Austin 33:1). Apparently Barbie, who does not fit readily into any one of these three blocks, is not yet a main "interest."

Scott began drafting *Towers* in July of 1968, and four months followed of uncoordinated scenes that illustrated the dismantling of the Raj but, as Scott put it, seemed only to show that it was his imagined novel that was "breaking up." At the end of October, Scott was still trying "to crack the bloody nut" of *Towers* (Austin 33:1). In a section dated December 18, 1968, Scott lamented,

> I don't know how to write this. There's too much of it. I'm looking for the form that fits the content. I need an attitude. While I'm disturbed in my mind about this novel, I can't think myself into an attitude at all. I want something that conveys the deep love of the alien landscape, which somewhat corresponds to the devotion of Indians to their cause, the idea of the nation that is to be, but doesn't arrive (Austin 33:1).

For three more months, Scott wrestled with sections that try to convey "the deep love of the alien landscape," including multiple drafts of a scene when Susan Layton's dog Panther dies in her Aunt Mabel's rose garden: "the Laytons as a family had come to the end of themselves & were breaking up, floating away in different directions as though surrendering to strange & diverse currents" (Austin 33:1). The scene fit his purpose but lacked cohesive power.

Then with no warning, in a new scene dated April 3, 1969, Scott resurrected Barbie Batchelor, who had appeared in a minor role in *Day of the Scorpion*. Barbie had been befriended by Mabel Layton and given a room in Mabel's house, Rose Cottage, but Mabel has died and Barbie is being evicted by Mabel's daughter-in-law, Millie Layton. Scott commented that Barbie's two "besetting sins" are acting without intention and talking without cease. "Barbie never intellectualizes. That is her point. She is a victim," Scott noted in the margin. But at this point in the manuscript Scott did not (or could not) move forward in time. Maybe he was following an author's intuition that, as we have noted in Chapter 8, singularity is made evident in discourse by looking back, not ahead. He described Barbie's answering an ad in the paper, her meeting with Mabel, her attachment to her luggage, her previous acquaintance with Edwina Crane, but Barbie continued to puzzle and frustrate Scott. With every new entry, he moved farther and farther back in the past rather than following his plan to move ahead by three years. In a note dated 2:15 p.m., April 10, 1969, Scott wrote: "It's necessary to put at least one foot on the path she's gone by (leaving not exactly a trunk so much as a disruption: a ragged swath in her cornfield)" (Austin 33:1).

He retreats back, finally, all the way to 1942. It is a breakthrough. He quickly describes Barbie's encounter with the devil, who hungers for her soul—she feels an emanation, a nausea enter her room at Rose Cottage. He develops more fully her love-hate relationship with God, the hailstorm of her prayers, her devotion to Mabel, and her relationship with Edwina. In an entry dated August 15, 1969, Scott even attempts a chapter called "The Apotheosis of Barbara Batchelor" (Austin 33:1). *Towers* is on its way. At the end of March 1970, Scott has Barbie encounter Ralph Waldo Emerson and thus assume the important task of philosopher and seer for the book (Austin 33:3, notebook #2).

But Scott still was not content. "Rewrite from graveside scene," he noted in the margin. "Put backbone into Barbie. She has become a memsahib" (Austin 33:4, notebook #1). He meant that, for him, she is more than just another Raj woman imprisoned by culture and history. In a word, he could see her dignity and wanted to make sure the readers see it, too. A character who unexpectedly arose to jump-start a stalled narrative, a woman originally imagined as vacuously verbose with no political sense, a person who was thus no more than a victim, had taken command of the novel. In a letter to John Willey dated September 6, 1970—after more than a year struggling with the authoring of *Towers*—Scott heaved a sigh of relief: "The inner sense of excitement has come right. . . . So I feel pretty confident about the final sections of Barbara Batchelor" (Tulsa 13:17).

In addition to its meditative quality, *Towers* differs from the other three novels of the Quartet in its almost exclusive dependence upon a single perspective. "The Quartet has step by step narrowed itself down to the viewpoint of a single character," Scott observed (1986, 168).[10]

---

10. If an author does not make a character the center of consciousness, that does not mean the author is denying that character dignity. If there is a villain in The Raj Quarter, it is Ronald Merrick, the chauvinistic officer who tortures Hari Kumar to

Barbie became the still center of the entire Indian experience, the wait before the political storm (1945–47), neither exclusively British nor Indian, accomplishing Scott's need of "something that conveys the deep love of the alien landscape, which somewhat corresponds to the devotion of Indians to their cause, the idea of the nation that is to be, but doesn't arrive" (Austin 33:1).

In the narrative and particulars he invented for her, Scott found Barbie's singularity and dignity, but the finding required an act of authoring that was prolonged, agonizing, and stubbornly resistant to conventional narratives. He may have called Barbie's story an "apotheosis," but it is less meaningful to ask how that master Narrative shaped his novel than to ask how Barbie's *petit récit* changes the way apotheosis is conventionally conceived. Critics who argue that acts of authoring are not original need to sit face-to-face with Scott's creation of Barbie. The dignity he made manifest in her was forged out of a sense of singularity quite at odds with the *dignitas*, the public show and masculine clout, which Roman rhetoricians once praised.[11]

RECENTERING: "THE REAL THING, NOT A PHOTOGRAPH"

One of the master Narratives still trusted by many English teachers is decentering, discussed in the previous chapter. Here is the academic plot of decentering, *á la* Paul Bunyan and Vladimir Propp, the narratologist of the fairy tale. The student heroes, a sister and brother, intuiting some lack in their lives, leave home for college only to find that a giant named Ignorance is terrorizing everyone there. The heroes are eager to do battle with the giant, but unawares are kept weak and defenseless by an evil spell. We know the name of the spell, since on a shelf in the cottage of a wicked mage is a half-empty vial labeled

---

promote his own career. As Scott notes about Merrick in a 1975 letter to an admiring reader of the Quartet, "There is not a single paragraph in the entire million words written from his point of view. He is peripheral, marginal. But central." That is, he has dignity. Scott thanks the reader for noting that the last word in the Quartet referring to Merrick is "compassion" (Tulsa 9:24). Compassion is the emotional response by author and reader to a character's dignity.

11.   In Imperial Rome, *dignitas* meant rank, social esteem, honor, prestige, public distinction, entitlement to respect. In current English, "dignitary" still carries some of that meaning. In classical rhetoric, Quintilian named *dignitas* as one of the three elements of style (the other two are *elegantia* or taste and *compositio* or arrangement). Earlier, in *The Poetics*, Aristotle had defined *etikos* (traditionally translated as "dignity") merely as the quality of a style that distinguishes it from the ordinary—a sense still present in the English word "etiquette."

"Illusion of Egocentricity." Fortunately an aged and wise donor comes to the aid of the heroes—a teacher with a different magical potion called "Decentering." Decentering counteracts the spell Illusion of Egocentricity and allows the heroes to discover allies in a friendly pack of animals, to wit: a parrot named Convention, a swarm of microbes named Culture, a one-eyed owl named Literacy, a colony of prairie dogs named Others, and a voluminous flock of starlings named Academic Ways. Together, after four years of suspenseful battle, victory is finally achieved over the giant Ignorance. Modestly, the heroes select a single piece from the reward due them, the jewel known worldwide as Degree. They return home, only to discover that their parents are being held captive by another giant, a younger sibling of Ignorance named Insufficient Stuff, and—but that is another story.

Usually in a more serious tone, English teachers and scholars tell variants of the tale of decentering, in support of acculturation, enculturation, entrance into the academic community, acquaintance with the literary canon (old or new), acquisition of literacy, ESL education, service learning, career preparation, and no doubt other pedagogies named and unnamed. The ur-plot is maturation. Students enter college with an adolescent inability to see the world or use the language from any other perspective than their own narrow world or their own limited language. Maturation is a term not much favored in English departments anymore, but that was not true back around 1980, when "decentering" first appeared in the professional literature. Compositionists such as John Mellon (1979), Andrea Lunsford (1980), and Andrew Wilkinson (1980), for instance, took the notion of decentering from Jean Piaget and used it to explain maturational deficiencies in first-year college writing. They argued that egocentric students needed to shift from the developmental stage of concrete operations to formal operations, from dealing with physical problems through simple hands-on reasoning methods such as classifying into groups and arranging in a series, to dealing with logical problems through abstract reasoning. This was despite the fact that Piaget had identified decentering (*décentration*) and the discarding of egocentrism (*égocentrisme*) as achievements of the concrete stage, and had located the shift from concrete to formal operations at around age twelve.

One could debate whether the misapplication of Piaget is or is not due to a tendency of the English profession to see entering college students as less mature than they really are, but what is not debatable is the tendency of the profession to lag in its application of theories of human development. By 1980, experts in development had already radically modified Piaget in their efforts to describe "postformal" maturation during the college years. One of their consistent conclusions was that typically *de*centering had already happened by entrance to college, with a vengeance, and that what happens next, if it happens at all during the next four years, can best be thought of as *re*centering. It is late adolescents who fixate and alienate themselves in tidy, formal, abstract systems of thought and who gradually move from that untenable position. The move, for instance, toward an understanding that systems of thought are not fixed but dialectical (Klaus Riegel 1973), toward a growing experience of concrete, pragmatic contexts (Michael J. Chandler 1975), or toward a more autonomous bending of inflexible moral codes under personal, real-life situations (Gisela Labouvie-Vief, 1980). These and many other views that locate a shift to postformal recentering with college-age persons are not just epiphenomena of the liberal 1970s, but are conclusions based on empirical study of thousands of hours of interviews. They are conclusions still largely accepted by developmentalists today, most of whom would agree with Robert W. White's venerable insight from his pioneering 1952 study of life-histories that "the over-all trend, starting from childhood, might be described as a trend from absolute received values to a personally wrought value system" (397).[12] In the plot of recentering, the hero still does battle with Ignorance, but the evil spell is the Illusion of Received Certitudes, the counter-potion offered by the teacher donor is Recentering, and the allies are Personal Life Experience, Contextuality, Resistance, Hospitality, and—it follows as night the day—Singularity.

This clash between the two narratives of decentering and recentering begets countless flashpoints of conflict in the profession's efforts to gain insight into students during the college years. We will visit a few of those conflicts in following chapters. Here we continue our interest in the reading of discourse, where narratives of decentering and recentering may underpin quite different interpretations. In particular, we will focus on that moment in the traditional literary plotline called "recognition" or "discovery." Recognition is that moment when the protagonist learns something crucial, a piece of knowledge that leads, usually

---

12. For a contemporary psychological account of developmental recentering, see Jennifer Lynn Tanner (2006).

right away, to the dénouement of the action. King Oedipus learns that his wife Jocasta is his mother and forthwith blinds and exiles himself. The more meaningful term for recognition is Aristotle's original one, anagnorisis (or un-ignorance), because it marks a jolting shift "from ignorance to knowledge" (*Poetics*, Ch. XI). But ignorance of what to knowledge of what?

The narrative of decentering would argue that the ignorance is of others and other ways outside oneself, and the knowledge is of the need to see and follow their ways. The narrative of recentering would argue that the ignorance is of the false certitude of abstract constructs, social and political, in which one once believed, and the knowledge is of realities and contextualities in accord with which one can retune one's life. In, recentering, anagnorisis leads to "discovery" or the uncovering of truths, whereas in decentering, anagnorisis leads to "recognition" or the rethinking of one's position.

Application of either recentering or decentering may change the way one interprets a piece of discourse. Decentering sees Lear as discovering (too late, since the plot is tragic) that he is just another "bare forked creature" equal to other people and living in a universe larger and wiser than any one person. Recentering sees Lear as recognizing (again too late) that his mental and governing powers have not remained the same as they once were ("I am old now"). For the decentering plotline the central sin is pride (*hubris*), seeing oneself as more important than one really is. For recentering the central sin is sloth (*accedia*), wearily relying on old certitudes because they are easier. Recentering and decentering are both legitimate yardsticks by which to measure a piece of discourse, but one may turn out more insightful or more appropriate than the other.

Take Melanie Thernstrom's memoir, *The Dead Girl*, published in 1990. In part, the book is an elegy for Thernstrom's closest high school friend, Roberta Lee, who was murdered. A Berkeley student, Roberta went out jogging with her boyfriend, Bradley Page, and did not come back. Five weeks later her body was found buried in a makeshift grave. Melanie—attending Harvard at the time—was devastated, traumatized is not too strong a word. So the book is also a bibliotherapy, an attempt of the author to write herself out of grief. Consolation and cure are folded within each other, and in terms of narrative plot it would make sense to expect an anagnorisis leading to some kind of healing uplift.

Such a story line is readily provided by the narrative of decentering. The author will discover that her grief has been self-serving and introverted, and she finds her way out of it by recognizing the social structures already in place to deal with the death of a loved one. She will be brought back to normal life by ceremony, legal trial, daily routines, and religious verities ("It's God's will," "You have to keep on living"). The publisher's blurb promotes the tale of decentering. Melanie and Roberta both belong to a generation that is "adrift in a spiritual void," "alienated and often depressed," but Melanie manages to rescue herself and "move toward adulthood" by writing an account of "loss and redemption."

Recentering also fits some standard advice for dealing with trauma. An unforeseen and violent event destabilizes the victim of trauma. The person's secure worldview is suddenly broken and safe routines are no longer certain. The cure is to reestablish that worldview and those routines. According to Judith Herman, recovery from trauma involves "establishing safety, reconstructing the trauma story, and restoring the connection between survivors and their community" (1997, 3). Writing about the event aids this recentering, because the "trauma story" utilizes providential narrative lines that are familiar and socially accepted. A shattered world is gradually glued back together. A restorative way "emerges by reaching beyond whatever is piecemeal and fragmentary and finding a unitary and all-encompassing ground," says Arthur Egendorf, an expert on war trauma. "Concretely this means that healing unfolds through engaging our experience as a whole, rather than analyzing things in bits and pieces or specifying causes, effects, and categories" (1986, 10). Uncaring and crude as it sounds, decentering advises the grief-stricken person to stop feeling sorry for him or herself and join the rest of the world again.

The trouble with the tale of decentering is that it doesn't fit *The Dead Girl* very well. There is a sense at the end that the narrator has undergone some recognition and put her life back together, reestablishing, for instance, some old friendships. But there is little sense that she has "rejoined society." Nor is her cure brought about by tailoring Roberta's death into familiar stories. Melanie tries this method and explicitly argues throughout the book that it doesn't work. And instead of finding restoration or consolation by "engaging our experience as a whole, rather than analyzing things in bits and pieces," Melanie's central moment of anagnorisis, as we will see, involves the recognition of one singular bit of her life, unique to her and nobody else.

In the end, Melanie Thernstrom discovers that life-as-narrative is a metaphor, not a literal fact. In her grief she has attempted to fictionalize the traumatic events. She tells stories of Roberta's disappearance, the murder, the days of desperate search, the dramatic confession of guilt by Roberta's boyfriend Brad, and then his recantation. None of this really assuages her own guilt. Even the trial, with its hopeful, conventional narrative of crime, confession, and just punishment, offers her no healing story (Brad eventually is convicted of manslaughter but insists on his innocence, and afterward Thernstrom does not know whether he is speaking the truth or not). She tries to think of her friend as a particular kind of character: brilliant, sensitive, prone to depression, suited to play the role in such a tragedy—in fact, doomed to die (1990, 276).[13] But it is a "strange and unsatisfactory way to think about people," Thernstrom finally reflects, "as if they were like poetry, and could be interpreted thus" (92).

Thernstrom is not immune to the seduction of the illusion that lives are stories and therefore meaning can be, will be, interpreted. This is "a most serious human enterprise," she notes, "the sorting of interpretation into truth" (325). But in this recounting of events that the publisher labels "A True Story" on the cover, family and friends lose interest in views and interpretations. They do not want the contradictory stories Brad is telling; they want the truth. Thernstrom realizes that people who are alive are not characters, although "they are almost characters, and the decisions they make each day about who they are and what they ought to do are constantly forming a character, but it is not formed, or not quite formed, because they are still deciding, and because the story has not been written yet" (4). She realizes that Roberta needs to be dead for her story to be narrated. Then her story can be finalized by whomever is telling it and by whatever of the various epithets they call her, Rosamunde, Bibi, Bebe, B. B., Mei-hua, elaborate, formal, archetypal, literary, romantic, Chinese (5). For Melanie these narrational

---

13. Thernstrom explains, "In *Anna Karenina* you know that that initial scene is a foreshadowing from the moment you read it, if you read well. You don't have to wait six hundred pages to watch her actually jump in front of the train before you say: this is a tragedy. You know not because you know the story but because you know the genre. . . . We can be certain because in books events are meaningfully ordered, and people are suited to their fates" (112).

efforts at decentering provide no consolation. They only reinforce, because they depend on, Roberta's death.

In *The Dead Girl* recognition and consolation do come to Melanie Thernstrom. But the plot of the story she ends by telling about herself, in the last pages of the book, assumes the shape of recentering, not decentering. She rejects the certainties on which conventional narratives depend in order to rely on moments that happen to her, not in fiction but in reality, and not by a fore-constructed plot, but by chance. For instance, there is the moment she and a friend go to take their photographs in a street kiosk but find it broken, and her friend instead buys her some heart-shaped candies with messages written on them. There is the moment when another friend tells her, "Renegotiate . . . as time goes by you'll separate things out and rearrange them—once it is packaged differently, it won't feel so burdensome" (414). Or there is the moment she chances on a letter written by an old boyfriend, Adam, sent to her before their breakup after Roberta's death, in which he writes, "It isn't always a happy world, but we shall be happy in it— not by ignoring the sad, but by doing what we can" (414). There is her sudden memory of Roberta's mother handing her a flower during the reception after the funeral, part of the Chinese custom, Melanie says, of never returning a dish empty. Most saliently—if a particular point in the book serves as anagnorisis, this must be it—there is the moment late at night in a friend's bathroom when Melanie suddenly remembers Roberta's face. She had been unable to recall it earlier and thought she had forgotten her features, but now "I see her face. The real thing, not a photograph: her face."[14] She is sorting and rearranging all these bits and pieces from her past to make a new center for herself that will hold.

---

14. Yet Thernstrom prints a photograph of Roberta's face on the next page (which we will discuss in the next chapter). Roland Barthes provides an instructive parallel in *Camera Lucida: Reflections on Photography* (1981), a book he wrote in part as a reflection on his mother's recent death. He too had trouble recalling his mother's features, but then discovered a photograph of her as a child in a location he calls the "Winter Garden." The photograph consoles because it is both historical and present proof of his unique relationship with his mother. No one else can view the photograph the same way. For this reason he declines to reproduce the photograph, the only photograph in the book he discusses and does not print for readers: "I cannot reproduce the Winter Garden Photograph. It exists only for me" (73). The photograph of his mother helps Barthes recognize (it marks the anagnorisis of his book) the self-contradictory essence of photography as an art. The noeme or essential interpretation of a photograph, he says, is "that-has-been," which conveys both the "absolute particular, the sovereign Contingency, matte and somehow stupid" and a "protestation of singularity" or the unique reaction of the viewer (4). So as a

Recentering, the "renegotiation" or "repackaging" of one's world-view in the light of complex, singular, personal experience, is not only a plotline that may fit works of fiction and nonfiction. It is an explanation of what happens to people during their lives, not only occasionally in recovering from trauma but commonly—at least according to developmentalists—in sorting and resorting themselves in order to move into adulthood. It is a narrative that English teachers should apply more often to the undergraduates they face every day in class (Melanie Thernstrom was twenty when Roberta Lee was murdered). It is an alternate tale, and in some ways a more convincing one, to persuade students that the past writings of the world are an element not to be abandoned, but rather a part of their potential to be used in constructing their own changing lives. Its message is that the shared ideas of others are important, but so are personal, singular things. Memories are lost, writes Thernstrom toward the end of *The Dead Girl*, "but handed from the living to the living are things we have said, gestures, the breaking of a fruit in a certain season, a petal from someone else's bouquet, thoughts about language, the things that you wrote, gifts to give before you die" (421-422).

STORIES ALL THE WAY DOWN?

Toward the end of *The Dead Girl*, Thernstrom reflects, "I thought that fictionalizing was the way to make things more meaningful" (402). Of course, it can be. In her case, re-narration of her life-course turned out more meaningful than any fiction of it. But the recentering she factually experienced has also served authors as a fictional plot, an ur-plot if there ever is such a thing, from the *Odyssey* and the parable of the Prodigal Son to any number of novels, plays, short stories, and poems published last week. Certainly the ways that narration relies on singularity, what we have called character, dignity, and recentering, are

---

scholar of photographs he will have "to combine two voices: the voice of banality (to say what everyone sees and knows) and the voice of singularity (to replenish such banality with all the élan of an emotion which belonged only to myself" (76). We would say that the photograph of a dead person to someone who knew that person is a small narrative (about as *petit* of a *récit* as possible) of recentering. It dares to reaffirm the "originality of my suffering" (75; a quote from Proust's narrator recalling his feelings at the funeral of his grandmother). In essence, then, photography is three things: "contingency, singularity, risk" (20). Both Thernstrom and Barthes—one by denying a photograph to the reader, and the other by declaring her memory is not a photograph—narrate how they found consolation in the recentering of themselves in relation to a deceased person.

not the only means by which narration creates meaning. But does the melding of singularity and narrative technique issue any particular caution to English teachers caught up in our post-generation's insistence on regarding human life as narrative in constitution? In our substitution of small-n narratives for master Narratives, in our erecting of a narrative bastion against nihilism, have we again thrown the singular baby out with the bathwater?

The danger in reducing each singular human life down to nothing but narrative is that it partakes of the larger enterprise of reducing human beings to a subject position, or to a grammatical or linguistic reality. When Derrida's metaphysics of language has been embraced by English studies so literally and uncritically, then we do a disservice to both human beings and narrative itself.[15] In its complexity and patience, its slow unraveling through time, its imaginative richness that delights a contemplative reader, narrative can display personal singularity in its depth and mystery. If Scott is correct that "we're no longer certain what a human being is," narrative in its gravitation toward the singular can comfort us the way its shapely resonance echoes the meaningful and consolatory courses of our real lives.

In the ultimate dénouement, nevertheless, narrative does not substitute for the narrated. The "unique being," says Barthes in regards the interpretation of photographs, is an "impossible science" (1981, 71). The fact of singularity tells us that it is not stories, nor turtles, all the way down. Poststructuralism may disagree in its denying all origins, in its rendering down the self to a placeholder in language and life, or in its finding coherence only with socially constructed narrative. Yet how can a mere grammar-function be the teller of his or her own lifestory, for instance, and therefore the agent of his or her own life? As we will see in the next chapter, it cannot. As Aijaz Ahmad remarks, for English academics the temptation is to imagine that meaning and agency reside only with "the figure of the reader, the critic, the theorist,

---

15. Etienne Gilson (1965) would call this view "lingualism"—reducing all phenomenon to language and equating philosophy with linguistics. Clearly, according to Gilson, Derrida's claim is metaphysical in nature, since he places grammar as "the ultimate ground of all real and possible experience" (307). Gilson also suggests a parallel between Derrida and William of Ockham's "psychologism," which Gilson says conflates psychological analysis of human knowledge and philosophical analysis of reality (87). Agnes Heller insists that the paradigm of language is not the only paradigm of philosophy (1992, 274). Nor, we would add, is it the only paradigm of literary and composition theory.

as the guardian of the texts of this world" (1992, 36). That may be gospel truth for fringe postmodernists who deny original truths. But heed South African Antjie Krog's observation: "What you believe to be true depends on who you believe yourself to be" (1998, 125). And only the crazy believe themselves to be not singular.

10

SINGULAR AUTHORIAL OFFERINGS
Lifestories, Literacy Narratives, and the Shatterbelt

> *Great stories are the ones you've heard and want to hear again. You know how it ends but you want to know again.*
> Arundhati Roy, *The God of Small Things*

> *We know already! But that is a foolish thought. Anybody can know the story. To have been there is the thing.*
> Thomas Mann, *Joseph the Provider*

The dust cover for Melanie Thernstrom's *The Dead Girl* centers on a three-quarter view of the victim's face. Although the artist relied on a photograph of Roberta Lee, reproduced on page eight of the book, there is a striking difference between cover and photograph. Through cropping and especially through reshaping of the right eye, Lee's Asian features are effaced. This westernization of the author's Asian American friend may disturb readers for a number of reasons. Were the publicity experts at Simon and Schuster attentive to the history of United States' journalism, in which murders of young Anglo girls seem to prove more newsworthy than murders of young minority girls? Or were the publishers participating in the avoidance, common throughout the United States' marketplace, of race and racial conflict? (The erasing of race, of course, may be an act of racism itself.) There is a third reason to question the altering of the book's contents by the book's cover, one that most readers will not think of. That is the way the cover rejects an offering that the author is making to the memorial of her dead friend, and more fundamentally the way it strips the author of one of her own contributions to the story of Lee's death.

As the previous chapter notes, in the climactic scene of the book Melanie Thernstrom discovers that she has not forgotten Roberta's face. The "vision" comes back to her with the clarity and luminosity of real life: "I see her face. The real thing, not a photograph: her face" (1990, 428). This is a unique experience, happening once to her and her alone, by herself in the dead of the night. This particular "real thing" is her own memory and no one else's, a singular construction from the many years she and Roberta grew up together as close friends. Her narration of the late-night event in *The Dead Girl* serves as one of her personal offerings to the memory of Roberta. It is not different than the signed wreaths at the funeral or the single flower that Roberta's mother gives Thernstrom at the reception. Thernstrom's offering, however, is suppressed by the cover artist's doctored image of Roberta. It is not an inconsequential cover-up, since the counter-image on the cover will be the first impression readers have of the author's friend.

As a memoir, *The Dead Girl* is naturally packed full of such unique offerings by the author—personal memories, descriptions, stories, ideas, and stylistic turns that Thernstrom must have thought of as belonging only to her, now given to the reader. They are a fixture of the genre. But every other discourse genre also has room for textual constructions that authors can rightfully believe bear their own stamp. Such discursive space, such opportunity for the author to include in the text something uniquely of the author's own, is central and necessary for authoring itself. The space devolves from the ubiquitous fact of singularity. Yet it is another energy of authoring that English teachers can suppress in their students. And teachers are in a position to do a much more thorough job of suppression than that of Simon and Schuster's cover artist. Evident in nearly every piece of real-world text teachers lay their eyes on, and cited by many working authors as a part of their experience of authoring (see Chapter 1), the room for singular offerings may be shut off to students in the kind of writing genres teachers assign, in the ways the assignments are shaped, and in the way they are composed and evaluated. In this chapter we will consider the space for authorial offering in a genre that has been privileged for over a decade now in English classes, the literacy narrative, and contrast that space in a genre that has not been privileged but should be, the lifestory.

AUTHORING AND OFFERING

Except with the most subservient hash-slinging acts of writing, most writers are motivated by the thought that they are adding something of their own to the text. Possibly, the motivation is more unthought than thought, largely intuitive and therefore largely uninvestigated; another of those black boxes cluttering the workspace of English departments.

But the output can be seen easily enough. Although teachers may feel angry when they discover a plagiarized or bought paper because the student has attempted a scam at their expense, they also feel sad to think of students declining the chance to make the assigned writing "their own work." Although co-authors do not need to have their own words identified as such in the finished text, they do want something there that they can identify as their own. In acknowledgments and footnotes writers carefully record the distinctive contributions of others, in part to separate them from their own offerings. Scholars bristle when a piece of theirs is rejected because it does not "contribute to the field," and writers everywhere fight to save from the editor's knife certain passages that have personal meaning. As we have seen in Chapter 1, writers know they are unique and therefore have a unique contribution to make: "I am entitled to tell this particular story in a way no one else can," declares Amy Hempel (Wachtel 1993, 207). For their part, readers sign their name to a book they have bought and then mark passages as they are reading it, not so much as proof of ownership but as a way of marking the reading as theirs.

All this is deeply human. Even students in English courses show it. Anne Herrington (1992) once observed a college junior complying with a teacher's request to delete one of her ideas, but then sneaking the idea back in at another point in her paper. What is strange is the lack of a professional name for the phenomenon. We will call it authorial offering.

Authorial offering shares the same habitus of individual offerings familiar throughout our culture. They range from private to public, from surreptitious personalizing to showboat gifting. New college students start personalizing their dorm room the day they occupy it, with family photographs, favorite posters (signed if they are lucky), a dresser doily tatted by a weird uncle. About a half-century later some of these students will be publicly handed a gift, perhaps a Rolex watch with dates and their name engraved on the back, for contribution to a workplace. With reasonable longevity, a couple of decades later friends will send wreaths to their funeral, offerings that are singularized with a card bearing the names of the friends.

Our term "offering" suggests that the habitus always conveys public show. But the impulse to make an act or part of an act one's unique own can be completely private. Offerings appear anonymously at grave or memorial sites. In published pieces, serious writers hide messages that they assume no reader will ever discover.[1] In fact the dynamics of the habitus of individual offering always turns in some degree toward the private, as can be seen in the way expressions for it recall movement of the human body. A gift is a personal "gesture," a political aide has a "hand" in a politician's speech, an organizer of a formal dinner adds a personal "touch," a new novelist presents an original "voice," a performer has a "signature" piece, an article of furniture bears the distinct "stamp" of the designer, a young employee makes a "mark." In this figurative embodiment, authorial offerings suggest some atavistic connection with ceremonial sacrifices or sympathetic magic. For Agamben, "gesture" is the risk that any author makes in knowingly committing a piece of discourse to public interpretations, a bodily liability that remains with the discourse after it leaves the author's hands (2007, 61-72; see Chapter 14).

The space that discourse genres designate for authorial offering varies according to genre. The anonymous journalistic news item seems to allow none, and news that betrays the individual mark of the writer becomes another genre, news opinion, and carries a byline. Advertisements also look like they have no room for authorial offering. But brands sometimes are designed with a distinct flavor that suggests contribution from individual authors in the advertising agency or other times boasts specific authorship, as with photographer Steve Landis' ads for Calvin Klein jeans. At the other end of the generic spectrum, fictional works and political speeches, if serious and successful, almost demand the unique offerings of the authors. The undergraduate research paper is expected to contain some distinctive ideas of the student, not relay onward a mere patchwork of quotations or hash of restatements.

A mistake is to identify authorial offering with the "personal." Genres that insist on impersonalization can have room for the unique contributions of the writers, in fact may require it. Science reports and historical studies, for instance, usually bear an impersonal style, yet expect that the authors are advancing information that they can call their own because it has not been reported before. The personal essay, whatever that sobriquet means, expects authorial offerings but is defined not by them but by the topic, the experiences of the author. So a second

---

1. The most famous instance is John Peale Bishop's honeyed sonnet in which the first letter of lines reads F-U-C-K-Y-O-U-H-A-L-F-A-S-S. For this and other hidden acrostics in public discourse, see R. H. Haswell (2007).

mistake is to assume that authorial offerings are hard to achieve and not a technique for beginning writers. Yet no differently than concocting an original sentence, making a unique offering in discourse is easy as falling off the proverbial logos. The fact of singularity makes it so. Is the assignment literary criticism? A student who compares a recently published poem, say from the journal *Ploughshares*, with any other poem, even from the tiredest course anthology, cannot help but create unique commentary. Is the assignment a personal essay? All the student writer needs is a little honesty and precision about his or her own life.[2]

THE LIFESTORY AND THE LITERACY-NARRATIVE ASSIGNMENTS

Of course the teacher, like Simon and Schuster's unnamed cover artist, may have reasons to forestall authorial offerings of young writers. The teacher may require comparisons only of works assigned from the course anthology, or restrict "research" to material in a casebook, or forbid the "personal essay" in first-year English courses. Especially this last decision is worth exploring.

How much literature and writing teachers currently assign the personal essay in the actual classroom is not documented. Probably more than suggested by the kind of theorizing about the genre we note below. Yet even on theoretical grounds, there are good reasons to keep the assignment, at least certain forms of it. We would argue that in the grab bag notion of "personal essay" can be found a number of genres that in fact seem especially appropriate for college student writers. The convention of authorial offerings helps locate them. Which kinds of personal essays maximize the opportunities for students to express their own singular ideas, facts, and expressions? This is our ordering, from most to least opportunity:

---

2. At this point, radical social constructivists might object, arguing that verbal expression, concrete instantiation, and audience context may allow unique authorial offerings, but not ideas; there are no original ideas. The trouble with this argument is that it can't be proved. The educational system, however, regardless of social constructivism or rational argument, continues to find ways to punish authorial offerings of students. For instance, some of the latest computer programs for automatically grading student essays compare "maps" or clusters of words. The more digital matches with maps in model, highly rated essays, the higher the score of the student essay. The assumption is that word clusters correlate with ideas. As a result, students are not rewarded if they produce authorial offerings, that is, phrasing or ideas not found in the model texts. These computer programs with their conformist algorithms are widely used to grade college essay examinations in subject courses such as history or economics.

1. lifestory

2. personal experience

3. family story

4. literacy narrative

The ordering may come as a surprise. It would seem that the literacy narrative, an autobiographical account of the writer's growth in reading and writing, would allow much authorial offering, but as we will see, the way it is assigned and evaluated in English courses mitigates against it. By definition the family story is the creation of a number of family members over time and takes the shape of a personal offering only when one of them has modified it, usually unawares. The personal experience essay must be directed toward some "universal point," at least under traditional teacher guidance. That leaves the lifestory. Unfortunately, the genre is little discussed and apparently little used by English teachers and therefore needs to account for itself.

A lifestory is the narrative we create and tell, to ourselves and to others, of our individual trek across the small stretch of years so far allotted to us, from recollected past to anticipated future. It accounts for who we are and what we hope to become in terms of what we have done so far in our life. Lifestory researcher Charlotte Linde renders the genre down to one subject: "what you must know about me to know me" (1993, 20). It can be as extensive as a full-blown autobiography or as short as a joking aside ("I grew up in Forest Park in St. Louis, you know, so my sole ambition is to have a high-definition flat-screen TV bigger than yours"). It differs from the personal anecdote that relates what once happened to us, or from the personal chronicle that relates a series of events that happened to us, neither necessarily suggesting a shape to our life that explains who we are. The "whoness of the self," Seyla Benhabib says, "is constituted by the story of a life—a coherent narrative . . . through which actions are individuated and the identity of the self constituted" (1992, 127).[3]

----

3. Adriana Cavarero also argues (following Hannah Arendt) that lifestories, and more generally "the art of biography," allow description of *who* someone uniquely is rather than *what* someone is: politician, housewife, honors student, etc. (2000, 58). Literary scholar Susan Stanford Friedman believes that "individuals develop a sense of self through acts of memory, reflexivity, and engagement with others, all of which require forms of storytelling to come into being...the ongoing production of individual and communal identities constitutes a story itself" (1998, 153). Psychology philosopher Owen Flanagan argues that one authors oneself, transforms oneself, by being psy-

Across cultures no small-n narrative is entertained more widely than lifestories. Informal, intimate, and sometimes only intuited, they have been widely studied by sociologists, psychologists, philosophers, and historians, also by scholars such as Kenneth and Mary Gergen, James M. Day, Alasdair MacIntyre, Mark Freeman, Rom Harré, Don P. McAdams, Paul John Eakin, and many others. Lifestory, it has been argued, may be the ur-narrative that founds all others, from the seventh-century BCE *Gilgamesh* to tomorrow's assignment to write an essay on *Gilgamesh*. So far, however, English professionals have shown little interest in the lifestory genre, although it shows multiple connections with literary genres studied and written by English students everywhere.

However that may be, lifestory serves as the most natural and most capacious narrative vehicle for authorial offering. This can be shown through a list of the active traits that scholarly investigation has found in everyday lifestories.

Unique and cultural. Lifestory is one of the primary means by which people convey their sense of the singularity or "whoness" of themselves in transit through life. As Adriana Cavarero notes, the question "who am I?" "is a question that only a unique being can sensibly pronounce" (2000, 2). "Every human being is unique, an unrepeatable existence," says Cavarero, "which—however much they run disoriented in the dark, mixing accidents with intentions—neither follows in the footsteps of another life, nor repeats the very same course, nor leaves behind the same story. This is why lifestories are told and listened to with interest" (4). The plots of lifestories—the early but lasting influence, the struggle to the top, the irretrievable wrong turn, the return to the fold, etc.—may be influenced by culture, reading, popular media, and family talk, but the details are individuating and historical, "a sequence of unique, unrepeatable events," as sociopsychologist Mark Freeman puts it (2001, 284). Because lifestories are experienced and told as singular, they provide prima facie argument that people construct as well as reflect culture. Lifestories are "as much constitutive of culture as they are emergent from it" (1997, 171).[4] There is an element of de Certeau's "poaching" in every lifestory told (see Chapter 1).

---

chologically unified through narrative connectedness, which self-represents to self-understand and to self-actualize. To the extent that I can tell a coherent story about my life, Flanagan concludes, I am an "I" (1996, 65-69).

4. Currently, many lifestory experts posit a melding. Dan P. McAdams' position is close to ours: "The life story is a joint product of person and environment. In a sense, the two write the story together" (1988, 18).

Ongoing and periodically revised. If the sense of one's self and the story of one's life are inseparable, both are unstable since the second is still happening. Periodically humans rewrite their life histories, omitting previous key events and adding new ones, or giving old ones a new slant to fit a new plot. "We are in the middle of our stories and cannot be sure how they will end," explains historiographer Donald Polkinghorne, "we are constantly having to revise the plot as new events are added to our lives" (1988, 150). As we would put it, lifestories are the narrative expression of potentiality and its in-transit fusion of currency, continuity, and singularity.

Picaresque to purposeful. As humans normally mature, a major reorganization of lifestory often occurs in the late teen years, when a linear, picaresque plot ("Then we moved to Philadelphia, then my young brother was born, then . . .") is replaced with a purposeful, unifying one ("I think my interest in child psychology began when we moved to Philadelphia, where our block was full of young families with lots of little kids, and after my brother was born . . ."). One famous study finds students around seventeen years of age interpreting characters in a short story in terms of "plight," bound by their past to some unidirectional course leading to an undefined future; and people about ten years older seeing the same characters in terms of "dramatism," an arena of tension and conflict with an outcome shaped by social balances and imbalances (Feldman, et al. 1993). In terms of lifestory re-formation, many students entering college may be on a cusp. They would recognize themselves in the college senior's memory of himself as the high school junior applying to college who was put off by the "bizarre nature" of the application essay prompt that asked "Who Are You?": at that age "I have no idea who I am. Well, I have an idea, but I'm going to college to find out" (Karp, Holmstrong and Gray 1998). Entering students have the quiescent potential to fashion the "whoness" that adult lifestories demand.

Episodic and configurational. This does not mean that with age the singularity of picaresque episodes are lost in the larger pattern of some unifying life trajectory. Life-histories remain at once episodic and configurational. Particular events are remembered as particular, instantiations of the larger pattern, local stories that remain local. In one of the best essay summaries of the research, William L. Randall says that lifestories are never told as a "seamless whole, rather as a series of anecdotes of specific events, still lifes of particular moments, outpourings of pain, and bits of impressions from all across the years" (1996, 239).[5] People recount lifestories under the assumption that they are offering unique experiences to the audience, no matter what point they might imagine the narrative is making.

Moral and situational. Lifestories don't lack points. Behaviorally, they function as self-authored self-help manuals. Psychologists have proven them therapeutic. They allow people at emotional loose ends to bind themselves back together, sometimes to recognize that their old lifestory is self-destructive but can be rewritten. More commonly, lifestories operate as a moral lens through which one's actions can be understood, justified, and guided (for instance, "By being around children early I learned to respect them"). They are ethical arguments, but not necessarily arguments supporting a preset moral, as in a children's fable. Individual, experiential, and malleable, the narratives help a person adjust to new and unique ethical situations. Researchers often observe the social telling of a lifestory functioning as an unconventional contribution to muddy the ethical waters, a way for the narrator to complicate someone else's voicing of moral commonplaces.[6]

Fictive and nonfictive. In lifestories the boundary between fictive and nonfictive is constantly crossed in both directions. People recount their life as they remember it, but, as lifestory investigation has shown over and over, memory omits some parts and exaggerates, rationalizes, and invents others. The fictiveness of lifestories can be seen in the way they change over time. "Today's horror on the highway becomes tomorrow's tragedy, next week's exciting adventure, next month's amusing anecdote, and old age's illustration of the irony of life," explains Randall (235). Main characters, "imagoes," are reinvented to justify changes in moral beliefs and agendas. [7] With their lifestory, every person is a

---

5. Researchers who study the way people categorize have long known that the memory of singular, complex events ("exemplars") often functions as a sorting mechanism, as when one generalizes about Muslims based on a memory of 9/11 (e.g., Tversky and Kahneman 1974).

6. In their authoritative account of narrative and moral development, James M. Day and Mark B. Tappan say that with lifestories "Self's morality emerges from the conflicts and struggles that obtain from being an embodied site of contesting claims (rather than an idealized transcendental subject)" (1996, 73). For an example, see Ingrid E. Josephs' story below.

7. For imagoes, central protagonists and antagonists of lifestories such as the loyal friend or the family clown, see Dan P. McAdams (1996). He says that a fully formed lifestory will usually contain between two to five imagoes, and that as an adolescent matures into an adult, creating and refashioning them becomes the "central task of identity formation" (141).

novelist. There the space for the fictive means all the more room for authorial offerings. This last trait of fictiveness provides the most obvious contrast of lifestories with literacy narratives. In that academic assignment students are asked to remember and analyze significant moments in the history of their learning to read and write. Popular for more than a decade in first-year writing courses, the assigned mode is assumed to be nonfiction. Certainly opportunities for authorial offering await as much in the literacy narrative as in the lifestory. The focus is on the particular student's past, with all kinds of room to give the reader individuating facts. But as the literacy narrative is commonly assigned by teachers, that room is made difficult to enter. The reason is that many teachers subsume that narrative of one person's emergence and growth under the overshadowing presence of a community or cultural literacy that is already in place. The directions can be quite explicit. Students are almost forced to construct a plot that records the illusion of uniqueness deflated by the reality of commonality. Authorial offerings are effaced again.

This plot control is readily illustrated from the abundance of literacy narrative assignments that teachers have put online. For example:

- Tell a good story about how you have been shaped as a communicator.

- Who was most influential in your development as a literate person? Why was it this specific person/group of people?

- As this is an English course, you should strongly consider writing about how your literacy (in the traditional sense of the word) has been shaped, was affected, etc., by a specific event.

Textbooks often enforce the same assumption that preexisting culture or community trumps emergent language users and their singular offerings. Sara Garnes and her co-authors of *Writing Lives: Exploring Literacy and Community* (1996) create a characteristic assignment: "To focus on one or several literacy experiences you've had within a particular community and to describe the significance of those experiences in making you a literate person." Here are some of their prewriting exercises:

- List and describe those people and/or communities that have influenced your sense of literacy.

- Explain how your sense of who you are has shaped your experiences of listening, speaking, reading, or otherwise behaving according to the expectations of the community about which you're writing.

- Explain why you wanted to belong to a certain community (133).[8]

All too often the hero of the literacy narrative is just what the term implies, Literacy (or Culture, Community, Identity), an abstraction, not a singular person.[9]

It's worth returning to linguist Barbara Johnstone (1996) and her distinction between individuals constructing culture and culture constructing individuals. The danger with these literacy narrative assignments is when they promote the second exclusively, perhaps ending by squelching the motives of the more basic discourse genre, the lifestory, to which they belong. Johnstone's research argues that language is a tool for relatedness, true, but also for self-expression. "Self-expression," of course, is a term radical constructivist English teachers would like to believe is outdated, even delusional, and would like to toss out of the professional lexicon along with "voice," "individuality," and "single author." Yet Johnstone documents that "Speakers express their individuality not only when one would most expect them to but also when one would least expect them to, and their talk would not succeed if they did not" (x). Even in boilerplate situations such as thank-you notes, book reviews, or sales pitches, speech is less formulaic or conventional than we assume. No two people talk alike—a fact that cannot be explained merely by the infinite number of sentences that are possible in a given language. In sum, from her numerous studies of language use, Johnstone argues against assumptions "that we are linguistic crea-

8. The other assignments were found online in April 2008. Developmentalists might argue that when the literacy narrative assignment ends with abstract systems such as "culture" and "community," it is promoting an adolescent genre. In their lifestories, adults tend "to create a personal myth . . . to fashion a history of the self," whereas adolescents tend to create an "ideology" or formal system (McAdams 1993, 75-90, 102).

9. In a essay revealing contemporary pressures to erase singularity from the authoring of academic texts, Garnes and her co-authors (1999) tell how manuscript reviewers and an editor at St. Martin's Press made them rewrite their introductory essay, originally composed "in unique, personal styles" (257), to reflect "a unified voice" and a more "authoritative tone" (258). As we will also see in the case of Linda Brodkey (1996), Garnes, et al. advocate the literacy narrative as a way to critique and thereby resist culture and community. Through a kind of Freirean consciousness-raising, student writers are expected to deconstruct the early influences on their literacy. How literacy can rescue itself from its own formation remains a major conundrum.

tures of our social environments, not the agents of our speech at all but rather 'spoken by' our positions in society" (179).

One of the most distinctive uses of language by individual authors can be found in narrative where the singular self defines and articulates itself. Narrative genres and plotlines are readily accessible, picked up early, and "can be adopted or resisted, used predictably or creatively" (155). In short, teachers should expect that student authors will adopt, resist, and create with each narrative writing exercise given them—or any other genre of exercise. This is what everyone out of class does with the literacy assignments that life hands them. "The ways people talk about themselves," says Johnstone, and she means in both conversation and writing, "have to do with the particular selves they are creating and expressing in narrative" (ix). It is perfectly natural for them to turn assignments into signatures. As Johnstone observes, "expressing selfhood is both an important function of talk and a prerequisite for successful talk" (128). What our profession has neglected to theorize adequately are the motives and desires of authors who express their singular self as they speak and write.

LIFESTORY, LITERACY NARRATIVE, AND THE SHATTERBELT

Nothing wrong with asking students to write about literacy and introspect the way sedimentations of social, cultural, and community literacy *have* influenced their lives. But with particular students embedded in particular times and places, teachers should not assign the literacy narrative without some introspection of their own. What follows is a cautionary narrative about literacy narratives.

The two of us teach in a part of Texas that social geographers call the shatterbelt. It is a tipped diamond-shaped area whose points are Austin, Dallas, San Antonio, and, the furthest south, Corpus Christi, where we live. In the Texas shatterbelt, class, ethnicity, religion, and economic status are so mixed that one does not find the usual community or cultural formation where a single group dominates (as Anglo Protestant Great Plains farm culture does in Amarillo) or even where two groups have achieved a standoff (as Anglo and Hispanic perhaps have done in San Angelo). Historically, the Texas shatterbelt developed with a cotton economy in which the conflict between farmers (large and small) and processors (large and small) was further fragmented by infighting among tenants, sharecroppers, farm workers, and plant and shipping laborers—of Mexicans, Mexican Americans,

African Americans, African Mexican Americans, Amerindians, Asians, Germans, Irish, and people of other ethnic and national origins. Sociologists are interested in shatterbelts or shatterzones because they may be an index of the way our world is moving, with its increasingly mobile and mingling populations.[10]

We can attest that students growing up in a shatterbelt do not always experience the traditional class, racial, ethnic, and religious groupings and identifications as teachers might expect. In a recent semester, one of our students, Sara, provided the background to a poem she had written about growing up. On one side she had a grandmother from Culiacan, Mexico, who kept telling her that she must learn to cook Mexican, and on the other side a grandfather—a noble six-foot-six figure who went to a Baptist church three times on Sunday in a spotless white shirt, and who told her that she should never forget that her grandfather, his father, had been born a black slave in South Carolina and had married a Choctaw from Georgia. Sara ended by shaking her head and saying, as if in afterthought though not in carelessness, "I don't know who I am." In the same class, Josh said that it bothers Anglos because he speaks Spanish without an accent, and it bothers Latinos because he speaks English without an accent: "I can't win."

Our experience is that the customary literacy-narrative assignment does not always work well for students who have grown up in shatterzones. Students sense that the task does not fit them, because it presumes that they have been shaped by their culture or their community, a notion that they—along with their acquaintances—have a hard time getting a handle on. If community is the shaper of individuals within it, and if the students' community is so complex and shattered they can hardly describe it, then how are they to construct a meaningful or satisfying narrative of their growth toward literacy? How can one be shaped

---

10. Originally the terms shatterzone and shatterbelt were geological. They describe an area, usually along a major fault line, where over time opposing geothermal forces have smashed any sedimented or otherwise stratified formation. The terms have been picked up by anthropologists, sociologists, and political scientists (who have a history of stealing terms from geology, including "sedimented" and "stratified"). Shatterzone has been applied to areas such as the Balkans, the former Soviet Republics, the Middle East, the Mississippi valley during European settlement, and the southern Great Plains when warring Amerindian tribes, slave-trading Spanish, and various Northern European factions (ranchers, farmers, hunters) clashed. The classic human shatterzone situation is where neither of two super powers can gain superiority and local groups create continuous conflict. For our Texas shatterbelt, see Jordan, Bean, and Holmes (1984) and Foley (1997, 1-13).

by an abstraction that materializes in ways so splintered, crisscrossed, or polymath? For these students, the lifestory works better because it does not presume that individuals are necessarily formed under the sway of one or two predominant communities, religions, ethnicities, or any other social presences. For English professionals teaching in a shatterbelt, the replacement of the personal-experience anecdote by the literacy narrative has been perhaps premature.

The problems of both genres may be finessed by lifestory assignments, at least with shatterbelt students. For prompts, teachers can borrow one from the researchers (for instance, "What's happened in your life that has made you who you are?"), or can adapt one from the lifestories of authors, such as the two Muriel Rukeyser offers: "How has your life kept opening?" and "What shape has your life taken?" (Sternberg 1980, 217, 224). A prompt we have found productive is for students to tell a family story and then discuss how the story functions as a part of who they now are. This results in essays that on the one hand do not end with pointless anecdotes, and on the other hand do not dissolve the singular student into some goofy abstraction such as culture, society, or community.

Here is Adana's family story.

> When I was 12, my mother told me a story that her grandmother had told her. Mamaw, as my mother called her, was three-quarter Indian, and she told my mother a story about a young Indian princess who was given a beautiful doll on her 7th birthday. The princess was told that the doll was so rare and precious that it should never be given away. One evening, in the coldest part of winter, when there was no more firewood and the tribe was freezing, the princess offered her doll as a way to keep the fire burning. She watched the fire all through the night, crying softly until she saw the last ember turn gray, and she fell into a peaceful sleep. The next morning she woke to find the ground covered in beautiful bluebonnets as far as her eye could see. The mother of the princess said that it was a reward for her beautiful sacrifice for her tribe, and that the loss of one beauty requires the replacement with another.

Under the guiding hand of the literacy narrative, Adana could have taken her mother's story and proceeded toward the cultural. The prospects are enticing. There is plenty of grist for the literacy mill. It seems the mother had been influenced by European literary traditions, converting the Indian girl into a "princess" and ending with an Aesopian moral, "the loss of one beauty requires the replacement with another." Further, Mamaw's story rewrites an "old Indian legend" well known in Texas. There are interesting departures from the usual plot. For instance, in the early Comanche version the tribe is suffering from drought, the girl throws her doll into a ceremonial fire, and she disperses the ashes to the Winds, ashes that turn into rain (or in later versions of the legend that germinate into bluebonnets, the Texas state flower). Even further afield culturally, the child sacrificed to save the tribe can be attached to a universal plotline, with a number assigned it in the Aarne-Thompson Tale Type Index. In another direction, the mother can be analyzed as participating in the extensive commodification of the legend, from the roadside beautification projects of Jack Gubbels and Lady Bird Johnson to a children's opera, several best-selling fictional elaborations for young adults (for example, *Bluebonnet Girl*, or *The Legend of the Bluebonnet: An Old Tale of Texas*), and a video for teachers to increase "young children's cultural awareness with American Indian literature." All told, Adana could carry on with an essay that no doubt would please the judges for our department's annual student writing awards, perhaps entitled "My Mother's Middle-class Subject Position as Revealed through a Debased Comanche Legend."

Adana did nothing of the sort, since her assignment asked her to explain how her mother's story connected with the person she now is. The next step in her essay simply is to describe the circumstances of the telling. It would startle awake any English teacher reading adrowse through a pile of student essays. Adana writes, "This story was told to me by my mother while I was lying in bed crying because they gave my part in a play to another person." And that leads to her analysis of a battle for independence she is still fighting on at least six fronts, with her too-protective family, her father who wants her to live with him in Mexico, her religiously zealous aunt, her possessive friends, her irresponsible boyfriend, and her demanding supervisor at a local Whataburger who pressures her to work overtime with only an hour's notice. "They all want a piece of me, and nothing back," she says. She concludes that "All my life I've been asked to sacrifice what I hold dear, a bit here and a bit there, and to be honest I'm not seeing the bluebonnets yet and I don't think I ever will."

We doubt that a literacy narrative requiring Adana to describe how her ethnicity has influenced her reading and writing would have brought her to this bitter point of resistance. (The effacement of race may be an act of racism, but so may the enforcement of it.)[11] Instead of stamping her into some "literacy practice," the lifestory assignment allowed her to put her singular stamp on literacy. Her authorial offering takes the complex shape of lifestories in general. Hers is both unique and cultural, revised and on the verge of revision, directional in terms of her particular life rather than in terms of some discursive genre, episodic yet still generative, moral yet bound by her peculiar life situation.

In one of the most thoughtful defenses of the literacy-narrative assignment, Linda Brodkey argues that autoethnographic essays, which require "writers to cast their personal experience in a cultural frame," bring out "the presence" of writers better than do essays such as college admissions autobiographies "in which writers deliberately set out to distinguish themselves as unique individuals" (1996, 209-210). According to Brodkey, the reason is that the autoethnographic assignment forces students to see themselves *as* narrators and hence to present themselves more as they really are, since "all subjects are the joint creations of language and discourse" (89). We are not going to enter into the escapeless discursive debate over whether adult humans can ever escape discourse, but it seems to us perfectly arguable that humans live as well as narrate, and that there is an authorial presence that comes from writers seeing themselves as *living* and hence to present themselves thus, as they really are. Both kinds of assignments, the autoethnography and the lifestory, allow students to participate in "negative critique," which Brodkey defines as "any systematic, verbal protest against cultural hegemony" (106) and which we fully endorse. Our suspicion is, however, that as assigned by teachers often not as aware of the wiles of hegemony as is Brodkey, the literacy narrative can squelch critique by presuming the hegemony that it would negate. [12] And in areas where "culture" is badly fragmented,

---

11. A case in point. Ai, the poet who writes about the Southwest border shatterbelt, is one-half Japanese, one-eighth Choctaw, one-fourth African American, and one-sixteenth Irish (*Contemporary Authors*, ed. Frances Carol Locher [Detroit, MI: Gale Research, 1980], s.v. "Ai [Florence Anthony]"). She writes that "The insistence that one must align oneself with this or that race is basically racist. And the notion that without a racial identity a person can't have any identity perpetuates racism" (277). Her pen name, Ai, now the only name she goes by, is *alas* in Greek, *love* in Japanese, a cry of pain in Spanish, and a homophone of *I* in English—an apt synonym for our concept of authorial offering.

12. Brodkey's literacy assignments are as good as they get, respecting the person as

the lifestory offers a more natural narrative path to resistance against hegemonies of all kinds.

The lifestory simply helps students offer their unique "who-ness of the self," which is perhaps a different kind of presence than Brodkey is talking about. To Josh—who feels he can't win because he speaks two languages without an accent—it says, don't forget, it is you who have won, and it is the rest of us with our community expectations who have failed in becoming perfectly bilingual. To Sara—who "doesn't know" who she is—it says, think again of your grandmother from Culiacan, and your great-grandfather from South Carolina born a slave, and your six-foot-six grandfather going to church for the third time on Sunday, and remember that no one else in the world has such a grandmother and great-grandfather and grandfather, and tell yourself, well, then that must be "who I am." To Adana—whose mother alone of all mothers in the world once placated her daughter's social distress with a story distinctly hers, different from any other story ever told—it says, that's who you were and who you have the potential to stop being.

THE POTENTIALITY OF AUTHORIAL OFFERINGS

Rhetorically, lifestories can be very powerful, but in a way that current English studies theory usually does not intend. It can be argued that their rhetorical power emerges from a social situation minimally consisting of an author of one and an audience of one. So maybe the author's final motive for telling a lifestory is always persuasive, channeled toward a reader or listener. But the primal motive of the author to retell—and the crux is in the iteration—is always a need, however faint and liminal, of the author to change his or her life. Adana retells the story of her mother's story because it helps Adana change the story

---

well as the culture. Yet even they effect, it seems to us, a sly deterioration of authorial offerings. By sharing their literacy memories, students learn that their past experiences aren't unique (reading under the covers with a flashlight like Alice Sheldon, hating to draw letters with fat crayons, etc.). As she says, sometimes the first-draft anecdotes do not make it into their final ethnographic essays (209). In part, Brodkey's success with her autoethnography assignment may have to do with the age, experience, and motivation of her students, who were English graduate students and perhaps more of a mind "to cast their personal experience in a cultural frame." Our first-year university shatterbelt students sometimes say they are sick of writing about cultural and ethnic identity, which over and over teachers have made them do throughout school.

of her life, which will help her change her life, including possibly her relationship with her mother.

To a certain extent, the same is true of all authorial offerings. Uniquely ours, they are handed over to readers as a piece of ourselves, and in the transaction happens a loss and with the loss a change in ourselves. It must be a change we somehow want. Writing, says Rukeyser— and she is meaning every word precisely—is "the forces in our wish to share something of our experience by turning it into something and giving it to somebody" (Sternberg 1980, 228).[13] That is why the denial of authorial offerings is worse than mere censorship, which keeps the possible forces of language and ideas from readers. The denial of offerings negates forces in the writer as well. It negates the potentiality of people to rewrite their lives. Some very old and very deep sacrilege takes place when authorial offerings are curbed. The renewal will not come if the Indian princess is kept from giving over her doll. The way through mourning will not be found if Antigone is kept from burying her brother.

We have returned to Simon and Schuster's affront to Melanie Thernstrom's effort to transcend her loss, and we are touching on the problematics of bibliotherapy, or the use of writing to rescue oneself from personal trauma, which we take up in the next chapter. In this chapter we end by advancing a final and admittedly risky point about authorial offerings. Aren't they acts of resistance? At some level, aren't they gestures of Brodkey's negative critique, defying some hegemony, however tenuous or however benign? It seems to us they must be, by virtue of the stamp they always bear of the singularity of the author. This is mine and mine alone, they say, and to that extent I am not owned by whatever totalizing powers might control my life, be those powers armed with language usage, social tradition, family custom, group conformity, genre convention, institutional practice, fashionable habit, or cultural system. Here are three lifestories that take this hypothesis from under the shelf.

Consider the first as a minimal case. It is a favorite story of compositionist Cynthia Selfe. It happened many years ago. A student calls her on the telephone and asks why she had given him an F for a course.

---

13. Rukeyser explains that authorial giving is part of an "exchange of energy": "It's difficult to make the equivalent of an experience, to make a poem that is so full of the resources of music and of meaning, and that allows you to give it to me, me to give it to you" (Sternberg 1980, 229).

She explains that he never came to class or turned in any writing. The student then says, "'Dr. Selfe, that's exactly what I wanted to talk to you about. How could you even think of flunking me without ever reading a single piece of my writing?'" The story could end there as a kind of academic joke. But Selfe adds a final line: "Damned good question." And the story could end there as a kind of academic fable. But Selfe adds an autobiographical comment on the telling of the story, giving it a new footing and converting it into a lifestory. "I tell this almost everywhere: it seems to strike at the heart of the silliness with which the educational system sometimes presents us" (Haswell and Lu 2000, 172-173). So the story of her repeated telling of this tale of one singular moment in her academic life offers up a resistance to the ideology of course credit, tosses a particular bit of indigestible grit into a conformist educational system that pretends grades are earned solely by learning.

When lifestories contain stories told by other people (and many, such as Adana's, do), the resistances can be complex. Sometimes they resist one another. This literacy story is one of the saddest we know, another story of race effacement. It is told by Lex Runciman, remembering a moment as director of the writing center at Oregon State University. A concerned writing assistant comes in to tell him how a Vietnamese woman, in her thirties, had been working with him to gain the skills she needed to pass the two timed-writing essays on the Oregon teacher certification examination. Seven failures in a row. Then she came into the writing center to tell him that she had finally passed. How had she done it? Not with a tactic he had taught her. She had pretended she was a nineteen-year-old American girl. "She invented a past for herself—an American past—and wrote a fictional answer to the essay questions." She said her pretense was based on TV reruns and that she wrote the essay as she thought the American girl would have written it. All this "disturbed" the writing assistant, says Runciman. He adds that he now tells the story to novice teaching assistants "because it suggests to me the routine privilege of many, many American lives, because it calls into significant question the effort to use thirty-minute essays as genuine indicators, and because it emphasizes the fact that behind any prose (or poetry, for that matter) written by an individual there resides just that—a human individual working to make sense of what may well be a difficult subject" (Haswell and Lu 2000, 48-50).

The resistance is at once to others and to self. In the narrating of her experience to her writing center tutor, the Vietnamese woman is resisting the way the examination process effaces race, yet perhaps also her trust in her own ethnicity. In the narrating of her story to his supervisor, the tutor is resisting the writing center belief that native speakers can help nonnative speakers, yet perhaps also his professional ethic that all writing should proceed from sincerity. In the narrating of the tutor's story to novice tutors, the writing center director is resisting their cultural silencing of class privilege, yet perhaps also his own career tendency to forget how complicated and difficult any academic writing task really is.

In their singularity, then, authorial offerings serve the author by resisting the self-stagnation that comes with living. They resist the tendency to slide back into easy generalizations, to average uneven achievements, to routinize novel situations, to smooth the rough edges of life, to forget the uniqueness of the past. In a word, singular offerings help writers resist the loss of potentiality. Here is one of the most uplifting literacy stories that we know. It is a voice from another shatterbelt, another story of mourning and survival. It is the transcription by lifestory psychologist Ingrid E. Josephs of an Israeli woman who is explaining why she goes to her husband's grave and "talks" to him.

> Well, I do not get answers, but the memory of similar situations, that is the answer. That I spontaneously remember how he reacted when the chaos happened with the car. That somebody had crashed right into my car which I had parked in front of the house. And it was a day we came from the celebration of the final school exams of my daughter. And then the smashed car in front of the house. That he said: "We wanted to drink coffee now, and so we will do it." And we did exactly that. This calmness, this only comes when I am in panic, when I am standing on the cemetery and say, "Well, I have lived through something very bad," and then I hear that. And then I get also quieter. (Josephs 1997, 365)

Revisiting the grave, remembering the singular event, retelling the event, all help maintain this woman's potential to cope with life.

Authorial offerings—the husband's novel response to the accident, the woman's nonpareil response to the researcher—get passed along, each time different; lifestories offering a new little resistance to the adversities life keeps handing us, singular stories restorative in their singularities.

11

SINGULARITY, FEMINISM, AND THE POLITICS OF DIFFERENCE AND IDENTITY

Sex isn't a separate thing functioning away all by itself. It's usually found attached to a person of some sort.

Dorothy Sayers, *Gaudy Night*

The moral issue also involves a confusion about the importance of power in human communities [and] the false deification of power as the sole deciding factor in events . . . Wherever power does not limit itself, there exists violence and terror, and in the end the destruction of life and soul.

Karl Jaspers, *The Question of German Guilt*

In Chapters 3 to 6 we argue that when student writers are invited to exercise gendership as a rhetorical instrument and a means of expression and self-creation, they may discover, enact, and deepen their potentiality. True also of their singularity. For English professionals, to regard each student as singular is a moral necessity, since singular persons are what they actually face in the classroom and singular texts are what they and their students actually read and write. In this chapter we will measure our understanding of singularity and potentiality against the history of feminist discourse on gender during the last four decades.

In those years the values embraced by feminist theory—difference, positionality, political empowerment—are rooted in a complex and, to a large degree, coherent debate marked by critical reflection and honest examination. At first glance, it would seem that the emergent values run contrary to those that affirm the individual writer and so advance acts of authoring. A wide variety of feminists debating the central issues of gender identity and difference seem to have journeyed away from personal singularity toward political collectivity, or away from innate potentiality toward scripted performance.

But that would be to cut the historical journey short. While the dominant discourse of feminisms may still privilege difference and identity politics, there are subversive voices in the ranks advancing the cause of singularity: Samira Kawash, Seyla Benhabib, Gayatri Spivak, Adriana Cavarero, and others. As the following synoptic history makes clear, singularity may now offer a way out of a box that feminist theories have written themselves into. The feminisms of difference and identity politics seemed to solve the primary ill of early feminisms—binary essentialism—but brought with them losses that singularity may be able to recoup. Instead of an adversary, feminist theory is proving to be a tentative ally in our approach to authoring.

THE JOURNEY OF THE FEMINISTS

For American scholars, feminist theory since the 1990s marks a radical break from feminist discourse of the 1970s and 1980s.[1] As if to herald the new decade, Linda Alcoff described in 1988 what she saw as the "identity crisis" in feminist theory and offered a solution to that crisis (432). From Alcoff's perspective, female academics in the 1970s (following on the heels of the social upheaval of the 1960s) sought to articulate the principles of women's liberation and the gender revolution. These early years enjoyed a sense of unity in terms of purpose: to resist male oppression endemic in a patriarchal society. Such a purpose assumed an oppositional dichotomy between male and female, men and women—a division that saturated all conceivable contours of culture and society. But it was far easier to identify what feminists were resisting than whom and what each woman wanted to be.

With the influence of French feminists, American scholars turned the same critical lens focused on injustice and misogyny upon their own assumptions and distinctions. Should we speak of "females" or of "women" in our advocacy for equality? Is there a difference between sex and gender? Are women born determined by their biology, or must that biology be presented, understood, and played out socially and culturally as gender? Advocates of gynesis argued that the female, sexed

---

1. Our interest here is not to reconstruct the history of feminism, nor to trace the origins of certain views and lines of reasoning. Rather, we are interested in these two elements of contemporary feminism—difference and identity politics—and the discourse surrounding them (including exploration, dialogue, and debate).

body is foundational in terms of female psychology, chemistry, and means of expression and therefore shapes written and oral language. The gynocritics saw gender as the foundation of feminist practice, with gender transcending a biological imprint by including cultural, economic and social factors as forces that shape women's identity.

The sex/gender debate spawned a labyrinth of questions. If woman is equal to man because she is "as good" as he, are we not still accepting "male" as "norm"? If woman is "equal" to man but different, what unique insights do her experiences, perspectives, language, and writing offer? And what has made her different? If her environment shaped her and that environment is patriarchal, then either good comes out of oppression or the term "woman" should not be valorized at all. If a woman exists in her own right, if her innate femaleness (made manifest by body or text, or both) marks a distinct nature and distinct attributes, then haven't we essentialized femaleness just as the patriarchy has? And how do so-called third-world women fit into this essentialized, Western middle-class view of femaleness? Finally, if the term "woman" isn't grounded in reality, it is only a word—a construct—and why should we acknowledge or valorize it at all? For Linda Alcoff, such questions posed a serious dilemma: should we valorize gender and live with an oppositional dichotomy that essentializes "woman," or degender the subject and labor in a genderless, male world?

What is the escape hatch to the essentialism trap? The key, Alcoff believed, is found in the writings of Teresa De Lauretis, who introduced the notion of "positionality." The term "woman" does not designate a set of attributes that are objectively identifiable or universally applicable, but it is not therefore empty of meaning. Rather, "woman" is a position assumed by an individual based on specific social, cultural, and historical experiences, a position from which she can act politically. It is a term of potential. That is, a woman can elect to make gender an important platform or standpoint from which to take political action. Joined with other like-minded women, a group can advocate for equal rights or wider influence. That transition, from an individual's position to a group of individuals who share the same position, gives birth to "identity politics": the right and the ability "to construct, and take responsibility for, our gendered identity, our politics, and our choices" (Alcoff 1988, 432).

By the mid-1990s, critics like Liz Bondi were characterizing first generation feminists as women who valorized unity to the point of

suppressing difference. Bondi associates herself with second-genera-
tion feminists who understand that women's experiences are multiple
to the point of being fractured. Unity is impossible, and thus identity
based on essentialist assumptions must be deconstructed then recon-
structed on the basis of difference to sustain a system of power relations. Those relations, in turn, attract a critical mass that empowers
feminists, as a group, to achieve their political ends (1993, 96).[2]

Thus difference provides markers to designate various groups; those
groups mobilize politically and define themselves (their rights, their
goals, and their loyalties). For its part, identity politics sustains and
nurtures the differences that delineate groups, which vie to enhance
their own power.[3] To varying degrees, these concepts—difference and
identity politics—have pervaded feminist thought to the present day.[4]
Positionality, the foundational assumption (or mandala) that makes
them possible, has developed into two further articulations: "performance" and "strategic essentialism."

Building on the nearly unchallenged emphases on location, local-
ization, and subjectivity, positionality allows scholars like Judith Butler
(1990) to recuperate the term "woman," yet reject "sex" and "gender"
as ideologies that serve two patriarchal institutions: phallogocentrism
and compulsory heterosexuality. What we have become accustomed
to identifying as gender is really "an identity tenuously constituted in
time, instituted in an exterior space through a *stylized repetition of acts*"

2. For examples of scholars who early on embraced and advanced the view of male and
   female as oppositional dualities, see Nancy Chodorow (1978) and Annis Pratt (1981).
   Oppositional dualism can still be found in current discussions about how men and
   women read and write differently. Feminists discussing the benefits of binary thinking, especially the political advantages for women, of course can be perfectly aware
   of the polarities (e.g., Toril Moi 1985). And many feminist critics have analyzed the
   problems of research methodology based on assumed gender binaries or the negative consequences of selling gender polarity, among them Sandra Lipsitz Bem (1993),
   Deborah Cameron and Jennifer Coates (1988), Laurie A. Finke (1992), and Joyce
   McCarl Nielsen (1990). See especially Ivan Illich (1982)—not exactly popular among
   feminists—who argues that genders operate not as a particular kind of difference
   or binary opposition, but rather as ambiguous complements; to efface their distinct
   properties is the destructive need of an industrialized, desexed economy.
3. Deborah Cameron believes that "the gradual ascendancy of difference was
   almost inevitable given the ideology of twentieth-century linguistics" and the importance that difference plays in feminist theory (1996, 40).
4. Identity politics is also commonplace in at least two other discourses: ethnic/
   multicultural literary studies and postcolonial theory. See Richard Sennett's illuminating discussion of James Baldwin (1990), and Abdul JanMohamed and David Lloyd
   (1997).

(40). If true, gender is neither a set of attributes (whether tied to genitalia or society, or both) nor a state of being. It is a way of doing things, a way of living. Gender is performative. If we want to assume a particular identity, we must repeat certain acts that thereby over time appear as substantive.

While Butler uses performativity to call for the deconstruction of gender altogether, Diana Fuss (1989) argues for another kind of performativity—strategic essentialism—wherein women theorize and speak from a space recognized as female, and men theorize and speak from a space recognized as male. The act of writing "like a man" or speaking "like a woman" can advance a political agenda. Indeed, in recent years politics has proven to be the one unifying element for feminists. I am not a woman because I was born as one, act like one, assume the role of one, or stand where other women stand. Rather, I am a woman by choice and that choice is a political one. "Politics is precisely the self-evident category in feminist discourse," says Fuss, "that which is most irreducible and most indispensable" (36).

By defining gender politically rather than biologically or even culturally, this strand of feminism breaks with poststructuralism, an ideology notoriously apolitical. Butler, Alcoff, and Fuss see politics as embedded in all human interactions. Power is what has been denied to women; power is what all women desire (*pacem*, the Wife of Bath). It is "the force that emanates from action, and it comes from the mutual action of a group of human beings; once in action, one can make things happen, thus becoming a source of 'force'" (Benhabib 1990b, 194). But as Mary Poovey (1988) notes, power relations and the distribution of power depend upon the location and organization of *situational* difference. Therefore, feminists must recognize and acknowledge that all ideological formulations prove unstable unless they are grounded in politics.

It should be obvious that what we have described as the singularity of each person is a value that is unsustainable and unworkable according to identity politics, which holds that the group defines the attributes of individuals who are not unique but rather common in their shared identity. Potentiality, at first glance, could have emerged as a feature of positionality in its rejection of essentialism. But since positionality evolved into performity as scripted practice—visible, determined, recognizable, non-ambiguous—there is no room for potentiality, which would only subvert the iterability that defines performance.

As with all the paths that feminists have charted, there are those who focus on what is gained by an innovation and those who are concerned about what is lost. It is inevitable, therefore, that the triune propositions of positionality, difference, and politics would be challenged. No better place to analyze that challenge than in the debate over performativity between Judith Butler and Seyla Benhabib. We will review this debate in some detail, because it makes clear that while politics solves the essentialism impasse of the 1960s and 1970s, it subjects feminists to a new problem, the abandonment of the singular person of potential.

THE PERFORMITY DEBATE

For Judith Butler, performative action brings into being or enacts "that which it names, and so marks the constitutive or productive power of discourse." The subject position of "woman," identified and described through the language of a given society, may be imitated or carried out by an actant. Both the behavior imitated and the performing subject are political realities, shaped by the engagement of the actant with an external political field (1995b, 134).

Three tenets are embedded in this view. First, there is no stable subject for Butler, no "I" that exists apart from discourse and performity. The term "I," when used by or applied to herself, refers to the replay and resignification of positions that constitute "Judith Butler"—no differently than the discourse about William Wordsworth now constitutes "William Wordsworth." Such positions are not choices, but "fully embedded organizing principles of material practices and institutional arrangements" (1995a, 42). If such a view conflicts with previous descriptions of the human subject that incorporated stable identity markers, then we are witnessing the "death of the subject" or the "deed without the doer" (49). For Butler, this is a liberatory end that opens up the word "subject" to new uses. The individual can rightfully be called a "doer" if we understand that term to mean the "uncertain working of discursive possibilities by which it itself is worked" (1995b, 135).

Grounded in this view of the subject is the second tenet of performity: the embedded or "constituted" subject. Given that the actant can imitate, can he/she also initiate acts? While it might seem so, Butler insists that the subject is a product of prior signifying processes. Even when it "institutes" actions, such actions are the effects of prior actions. Still, Butler can speak of agency as "the capacity for reflexive mediation, that remains intact regardless of its cultural embedded-ness." The "culturally enmired" subject can negotiate its construction insofar as it is able to vary and thereby subvert the "regulated process of repetition" that substantializes the subject (2001, 110-113). This agency, however, is not in any way a free or autonomous capacity of the subject.

That is because the third tenet of performity claims the politiciza-tion of all aspects of human interaction, including actions instituted by the subject. "Agency is always and only a political prerogative" (1995a, 46-47), Butler insists. Therefore, through the political, and only the political, identity is articulated. Nothing escapes power, even the subject position of the critic, since power is the sum total of actions shaped by previous actions that are embedded in "material practices and institu-tional arrangements" (42). Those actions are effects of previous actions, on back *ad infinitum*. The individual, situated in this endless chain of performative/constituted actions, is therefore determined in one sense and instrumental in another. The "subjecthood" of the actant is con-stituted through confrontation with the external political field that can exclude the subject, erase the subject from view, render the subject a figure of abjection, or otherwise deauthorize the subject. Within this adversarial condition, however, "woman" becomes "an undesignatable field of differences. . . a site of permanent openness and resignifiabil-ity" (50), so that future, multiple significations are possible.

At the risk of resurrecting what Butler labels "unproblematized metaphysical notions," Seyla Benhabib objects to this understanding of performity on the basis that the substantive "I" is too great a loss for feminism to suffer. Benhabib's argument is fundamentally ethical rather than political in nature, or rather it is both. Instead of denying the importance of the political, she observes that there is a "moral tex-ture" behind any "political" situation (1990a, 357). This moral compo-nent is too often neglected or denied in feminist discourse, a failure that also marks the limits of performity.

Fundamental to Benhabib's argument is her rejection of an "I" that is only an extension of its own past, of material conditions, or of anoth-er's actions. Neither is the "I" wholly constituted by discourse, for to be constituted for Benhabib means to be determined (1992, 218; see also 1995, 110). If the "I" is more than a subject position created by discourse, more than an imitative act performed according to political/material scripts, what is the self's ethical and political responsibilities to the other, given that both are "I"s existing independently of the discourse surrounding them?

Benhabib's answer comes from a position she calls soft or interactive universalizability. Taking difference as a starting point for reflection and action, Benhabib agrees that the "I" is not autonomous, but indeed shaped by a network of dependencies. Such dependencies do not suggest that the "I" lacks agency, however. Operating *in* the political realm, but *beneath* it as well—in a web of moral relations—each person must negotiate how he/she interacts with others. Underpinning such negotiation is "interactive rationality," not to be confused with the "timeless standpoint of legislative reason" advanced by the Enlightenment, but rather understood as a critical and intellectual process by which various principles (like performity) can be interrogated *by all concerned* (1990a, 356, 362). To negotiate anything from power relations into notions of "the good" requires a willingness to reason from another's point of view. This involves exercising what Benhabib calls the moral imagination, animated by "enlarged thinking" wherein "I" comes out of my domain to converse with other "I"s until an agreement is reached (1992, 6-9).

For Benhabib, Butler's notion of performity not only cashiers the "I" by reducing it to determinative mimicry, but also conceives of human relations as antagonistic and adversarial. If, as Butler asserts, the subject is constituted through exclusion, erasure, and rejection, then the only subjects I can affirm are those who share my position or group identity. Difference acts as a political wedge that widens the gap between "us" and "them." While Benhabib believes it crucial, as does Butler, to deconstruct rigid genderized thinking, the prospect of accepting the otherness *only* of fellow members of *my* group, *my* subject position, *my* performance identity, is the most abject form of ethnocentric thinking, threatening any possibility of ethical social relations (Benhabib 1999, 710; 1995, 117).

If group identity offers stability, it does so only through oppression, and thus spawns rigidity rather than generates safety. As Teresa Brennan observes, fixity not only emerges from essentialism but also from identification with groups and ideas (1996, 94). This single-dimensional, narrowed life is evident in both social space and interior space, so that "the repression of differences" occurs not only between oneself and dominant and subordinate groups, but "even within oneself" (Chaudhuri 1997, 268). The "I" gives way to a "we" that does not reveal who the singular selves are. This is the *we* of propaganda, which can create any subject and demand that the person addressed identify with it, which says "you ought to be one of us," and which is used by the missionary, the humanist, and the salesman. Even when group identity is conceived as performative rather than essential, it is always isolated and bounded, since it is based on the axiom of difference and the need to compete with other groups for political voice, privilege, and power. In the history of imperialism and prejudice, such an emphasis rarely works unto good. Group difference tends toward division and hatred, which in turn make those persons who identify themselves only through a group more intent on maintaining its coherence, its privilege, and its safety.[5]

In sum, feminism has reached what Mary Louise Fellows and Sherene Razack have referred to as the "difference impasse" (1994, 1,048). For political power women need to establish differences, differences create groups, groups exercise unacceptable political power. As Susan Stanford Friedman argues, discourse then cannot move beyond "the ignorance, anger, guilt, and silences about race and racism that are the products of power relations in the larger society" (1995, 5). The same impasse is reached with identity politics, which also corners persons into groups, committing the ultimate violation and victimization of persons, who should be "constituted through many group identities and cannot be reduced to any one collectivity" (18).[6]

---

5   An axiom of Paul Scott's, as we have noted. As Deborah Cameron rightly observes, difference is often thought of as a "given" of the natural order, and therefore intolerance of difference results in injustice and inequality. But Cameron says that in fact the reverse is true. Difference arises in a context of inequality—either through deliberate marginalization by those individuals or groups that don't want to share privilege, or by social/cultural/gendered practices imposed upon individuals or groups (1996, 40-44).

6. One inevitable consequence of identity politics is what Deborah Cameron calls "verbal hygiene" (1995). To be identified as belonging to a group, one must not only have the appropriate skin color, political-group allegiance, nationality, body parts, etc., but use language according to the norms and practices of that group. Language, above all action, is performative. To ensure that members talk the talk or master the discourse, groups must police their own members, reverting to stereotypes to self-define and to identify other groups—otherwise the subtleties and nuances of living could not be formulated into a recognizable and enforceable performance. And here the contradictions of identity politics are most obvious. Initially embraced as a way of rejecting the fixity of essentialisms, identity politics, in Teresa Brennan's words, "produce fixed points which, while they serve as reference points for identity, also restrict movement" (1996, 94-95). The restriction is precisely the degree to which one identifies with another person, idea, group, institution, language, dialect, or linguistic register. Reduced to prescriptive performance, identity is, in the end, only mimicry. And mimicry is the enemy of potentiality.

THE POLITICAL PARADIGM

As the last few paragraphs make clear, difference and identity politics bring with them grave ramifications. But they are only symptoms of a more destructive direction: making political power the ultimate value and attribute of feminisms. To define gender theory as political in scope, motivation, and purpose is, whether or not the consequences are intended, to expand the sovereignty of the state, which thereafter has an interest in what a woman wears, what she bears in her womb, whom she sleeps with, what she does in her bed, where she works, what she writes, and how she thinks. Michel Foucault's term "biopolitics" captures such a condition. Biopolitics (or biopower) begins with biological properties of populations (birth rate, for instance) and then, through regulatory mechanisms, furthers the goals and powers of the sovereign state. In the name of biopolitics, the singular self disappears.

Not many English scholars have dared take on the rhetoric of power and the paradigm of politics that dominate contemporary gender theory. From the policies on "political correctness" voiced by the National Council of Teachers of English to the identity politics of feminist, neomarxist, and postcolonial theory, artists, critics, and scholars are judged according to their political views and the extent to which those views dominate their work. While Diana Fuss heralds politics as "the self-evident category in feminist discourse" (1989, 36), the rise of politics and the focus on power relations are part of a cultural catastrophe. At least so argues Giorgio Agamben, who makes a strong and haunting case against the politicization of life.

In *Homo Sacer: Sovereign Power and Bare Life* (1995a), Agamben enlarges on Foucault's notion of biopolitics. To do so, he examines three different definitions of the term "life." He first turns to the ancient Greek distinction between *zoë* (life of all living creatures, or simple life) and *bios* (the form of living proper to an individual within a group, or social life). For the Greek philosophers, the life of the king, the artist, the doctor, the scholar, or the philosopher was distinct from the mere fact of physical existence or simple life. While human beings are, first, existing creatures (*zoë*), they have the additional capacity for political existence (*bios*). But in Greek thought, politics has no more jurisdiction over an individual's physical life than does art, scholarship, or science.

Next Agamben considers the ancient Roman form of simple existence or *zoë* that is not *bios* but *homo sacer,* or sacred life. Agamben is careful to note that "sacred" does not refer to what is holy or divine, but rather to what is obscure and impenetrable, or what Freud called taboo, the banned and dangerous. The sacred—whether materialized as altar, tabernacle, human, or goat—cannot be touched without contamination. The Romans regarded an individual designated *homo sacer* as one who cannot be sacrificed in ritual practices, but can be killed by anyone without that killing being considered homicide. Sacred life is an individual "whom anyone could kill with impunity" (72).

The fourth term Agamben examines is the Roman word *vita*, again "life" but again of a particular standing. According to Roman law, a father could take the life (*vita*) of his son, since the son was a member of the father's house. In the same way, the emperor could take the "bare" life (*zoë*) of any male citizen, since the citizen was a member of the body politic. Bare life, then, is the "originary political element" (90).

In what Agamben calls the most radical transformation of the modern world, the Western world dissolved the Greek distinction between *zoë* and *bios;* more specifically, governments merged bare life with the political realm, creating what Foucault called biopolitics. With that expansion of the political, the state or sovereign has jurisdiction over what was once exempt from political dominion—simple or bare life. In addition, other groups or professions such as science, medicine, and academics, once regarded as separate from politics, now are the handmaidens of the state. This sets the stage for a second transformation, of bare life (*zoë*) or social life (*bios*) into sacred life (*homo sacer*).

Who initiates this second shift? Agamben points to the sovereign, or "he who decides on the state of exception" (11). In recent decades, various emergencies have given governments the opportunity to declare states of exception, giving them extraordinary power beyond the limits of the law. As the sovereign's will takes the place of law, the rights of citizens are suspended (think of the Nazis' rise to power in 1933 and the U.S. treatment of "enemy combatants" post-9/11). As it extends over time, a state of exception becomes more "natural" and law more violent and all-encompassing. Once established to protect the rights and dignity of human beings, the law has become no more than the pure will of the sovereign, rendering law empty of principle and content. This is the ultimate nihilism of the biopolitics in which we currently live (51, 52).

In this state of politics, bare life (which for the Greeks stood outside of politics) now falls within the jurisdiction of sovereign power. Just as the Roman emperor could control the *vita* of his citizens, so the sovereign dominates the bare life of individuals within the political body, rendering bare life *sacred*, "as if supreme power were . . . nothing other than *the capacity to constitute oneself and others as life that may be killed but not sacrificed*" (101). Ironically, violent revolutions hailed as "democratic" have played into the biopower and biopolitics of the sovereign state. The French and American Revolutions made clear that political rights are not natural. They do not fall to human beings by virtue of their innate dignity or simple existence. Rather, rights are political and granted to citizens of states. The term "nation," Agamben notes, comes from the Latin *nascere*, to be born. The citizen is not a free and conscious subject, but instead a sovereign state's subject, a life of political value (128, 132).[7]

This condition marks what Foucault called "the politicization of life" or biopolitics. As defined by Agamben, modern man is an animal "whose politics call his existence as a living being into question" (119). In this sense, we have all been abandoned, not by falling outside the law, but by being abandoned by the law. At the same time jurists, doctors, scientists, legislators, and other regulators are caught up in the sovereign's process of deciding what kind of life is expendable. To the sovereign, all men are potentially *homines sacri*. Sovereign power is shared, of course, with doctors, scientists, politicians, and others who make use of lives (*zoë*) when they cease to be socially or politically relevant (*bios*). For example, military personnel, criminals, Black airmen, Native American women of childbearing age, residents living downwind from nuclear reactors, groups of citizens for experimentation selected by our own government without prior knowledge or consent, persons whose bare life can be threatened, altered, or even ended without reprisal.

What will happen to societies wherein bare life is politicized? For Agamben, this question does not require a look into a crystal ball. The specter is not futuristic, but rather graphically recorded in our recent

---

7. This merging of bare life and political life is true for both twentieth-century democracies and totalitarian regimes. Because biological life has become the "politically decisive fact," we can understand how parliamentary democracies in Russia, Italy, and Germany turned so easily into totalitarian states and why those states turned quickly back into parliamentary democracies (122).

past. The concentration camp is the "absolute space of exception" (20). Beginning as a space wherein the rule of law was temporarily suspended "on the basis of a factual state of danger," it was later given a "permanent spatial arrangement," becoming a "pure, absolute, and impassable biopolitical space" (169, 123). Various groups, including Jews, Sinti-Roma, and Jehovah's Witnesses, cripples, and political enemies, were all selected as sacred life, distinguished for their capacity to be killed with impunity (114).

What is Agamben's solution to the immorality or amorality of the biopolitical state? Until we can disrupt the tension between People (the whole political body) and people (marginal groups or a subset of People), there will always be "people" who are *homo sacer*. He calls for a clear awareness that "we no longer know anything of the classical distinction between *zoë* and *bios*, between private life and political existence, between man as a simple living being at home in the house and man's political existence in the city" (187).[8] In effect, he calls us to dismantle the political paradigm that contemporary feminists have fought to establish.

FEMINISM AND SINGULARITY

If it is true that the feminist agenda, separated from the political, will lack the muscle to instigate positive social change for women, it is equally true that the grim pragmatics of politics will co-opt the idealism and goals of that same agenda. Positionality, a term of power for Alcoff, and performity, Butler's proposed opportunity for resignifying the subject, in fact constrain the potentiality and singularity of the individual, and therefore sacrifice her or him to biopolitics. A particular person might select a group identity by choice, as Fuss envisions, but in fact existing groups, either empowered or seeking empowerment, will do the choosing based on preconditions of identity. It is that old maxim of the imperialist universe that Joseph Conrad described so well. You must be "one of us" to count.

In a sentence, biopoliticization erases the singularity of bare lives, both female and male, in order to use them for its own purposes. The

---

8. Agamben does not see gender or race, but rather class as the working demarcation of sacred life in contemporary culture. "In a different yet analogous way, today's democratic-capitalist project of eliminating the poor classes through development not only reproduces within itself the people that is excluded but also transforms the entire population of the third world into bare life" (180).

fact raises a crucial question for this book. Can the fact of human singularity serve as a means for English professionals to resist and even change the biopolitical conditions of modern life? The next two chapters address this question and answer it, at least tentatively, in the affirmative. For this chapter the question may be pointed more sharply. Is singularity a concept that has offered, or can offer a way out of the current feminist paradigm and its dilemmas with the political? The answer will also have to be tentative, but it seems that feminist theorists have begun to pursue this line of thought.

Samira Kawash (1997) agrees that the power of identity politics is the power of subjectification, or the power "to transform singularity into identity and to assign, regulate, distribute, and control identities." To the stable racial, political, or social collective, singularity is a threat; it marks "disorder, excess, non-identity, inassimilable difference" (213). Taken positively, singularity is a relational kind of power that corrects identity politics by exposing its boundaries and methods of exclusion based on control of representations. Because the politics of singularity involves "the unique, the unrepeatable, the unknowable, the irreducible otherness of the other" (214), it may bring with it a more accountable sense of justice, responsibility, and freedom—all renewed through the "together-touching" of singularities. It will also, paradoxically, bring what Kawash calls "perplexity," which requires feminist activists to suspend their own "stands of right and authority by which any particular interest or position becomes unassailable, self-evident, or commonsensical" (218).[9]

The distinction drawn by Seyla Benhabib (1992) between "generalized other" and "concrete other" also warns of the dangers of politicized or collectivized action and encourages feminism to embrace the singular. The moral posture of the generalized other endows other people, female or male, with the same moral rights as ourselves. This seems a positive act. People are treated according to norms of action based on *"formal equality and reciprocity"* (159), and constructed as reasoning and acting beings, capable of a sense of justice, able to formulate a vision of the good, and engaging in activity to pursue that good.

9. Kawash uses Agamben to argue that singularity and individualism are opposites, since the individual is conceived as autonomous and independent, while the singular is connected by location and by mutual uniqueness, unrepeatability, and irreducibility (214). In the same vein, singularity is not equitable with multiplicity (and its corollary, fragmentation) since "singularity is always plural, emerging within the mutually constituting relation of togetherness" (216).

The danger in thus generalizing the other, however, is foisting off on them an ethical posture they may not hold, and in thereby regulating them, becoming complicit in an act of politicization of which the activist may not be aware. In counterpoint to the generalized other, Benhabib's "concrete other" is embodied—a unique individual with a distinct life-history. Relations between concrete others is shaped by the "norms of equity and complementary reciprocity," rather than equality and normative reciprocity (159). The generalized other requires a commitment to an abstract Kantian principle, that every human individual is a being worthy of universal moral respect; the relationship with the concrete other means "that we as concrete individuals know what is expected of us in virtue of the kind of social bonds which tie us to the other" (10). One can value the singular, Benhabib argues, without discarding the social and cultural bonds among concrete others.

Gayatri Spivak (1995) also argues that Kantian or Enlightenment ethical arguments, which may promote benevolence or charity, violate the uniqueness of the Other. She distrusts essentialisms of all kinds. While recognizing their power in motivating and maintaining political action in periods of crisis, she argues that they can be addictive to the user and destructive to others, leaving little discursive room for the Other to answer. Her particular concern is with the relationship between subalterns and intellectual leaders, in which good intentions of activists may take on the reality of political coercion. So she advances, whenever possible, a one-on one engagement of activist and subaltern, which she calls "ethical singularity." The encounter is intimate, loving, and normal (not pressured by the sense of crisis). Exchange of information is as open as possible, although both participants will end up concealing much, not intentionally but as an unavoidable fact of their singularities. Indeed, Spivak admits that ethical singularity is experienced by participants as "impossible." For instance, "it is impossible for all leaders (subaltern or otherwise) to engage every subaltern in this way, especially across the gender divide" (201). Ethical singularity is an imperfect "supplement," but a necessary corrective to collective activity in resisting and bettering systems of law, production, health care, and education.[10]

---

10. Similarly, we will argue that there are limits to what a teacher can know of a student's authoring, and those limits are the unknowable in any act of authoring — unknowable even to the author—or what Derrida calls "the secret" (see Chapter 14).

Finally, for Adriana Cavarero (2000) people as "unique existents" is an ontological given (ix). Any denial of that given leaves people vulnerable to oppressive universalistic representations. Obviously, women have been totalized by a "patriarchal symbolic order" that defines them by *what* not *who* they are: "mothers, wives, care-givers, bodies to be enjoyed . . ." (53). They have also been universalized as belonging to the category of *impoliticità*, a class of people defined by lack-of-politics, with no bent or access to political action. The solution for women, however, is not to take up the male politics of symbolic order or universalistic representations of the subject, which would deny themselves and others as "unique existents." The solution is to exercise a political space described and promoted by Hannah Arendt (1958), an "interactive scene" where the activist reveals her uniqueness to others: "Actively revealing oneself to others, with words and not in deeds, grants a plural space and therefore a political space to identity" (22). Cavarero says that the public telling of a lifestory, with its self-representation of a particular identity—even if only to one other person—is a political act, one with political consequences. It should be stressed that Cavarero is offering a distinct notion of "identity"—not a cultural construct or the product of a social or political process of identification, but rather (although it must be interwoven with typological identities) a self-designed and "uncategorizable uniqueness," "a unique, unrepeatable, personal identity whose story a biographical text narrates" (73-74).[11]

It is significant that all four of these feminists imagine the singular engaging in the political via moments of one-on-one exchange. Kawash's "together-touching," Benhabib's "social bonds which tie us to the other," Spivak's "intimate" encounter with the subaltern, and Cavarero's "interactive scene" allow the fact of the singular both to resist and redirect the fiat of the collective. Instead of the singular being erased by the political, the political can be appropriated by the singular to further its own unique agendas. In many ways, of course, feminist theory and praxis can re-vision and revise the English profession, in classroom and in scholarship. But no way more immediate and lasting than with one-on-one encounters, one teacher (perhaps female)

---

11. Cavarero warns feminists of the universalizing yearnings of philosophy, which undermine the predilection that women seem to have for the unique: "Because this, from Plato onwards, has been precisely the mission that philosophy, seduced by the universal, originally decided to take upon itself: to redeem, to save, to rescue the particular from its finitude, and uniqueness from its scandal" (53).

conferencing with one student (perhaps male), one reader (perhaps male) engaging with one author (perhaps female). Some of the hazards and benefits of face-to-face singular exchanges both in and out of the English classroom will be explored in the next two chapters. For the moment, our caution is that any embracing of the political paradigm as the single heart and soul of feminism can only end with abandoning the singular self, and that cannot be a price feminists should be willing to pay.

12

SINGULARITY, SELF-LOSS, AND RADICAL POSTMODERNISM

*Listen to these words of Roustavelli, Shota: "Everything that you
take and keep is lost forever; everything that you give away is forever
yours."*

Prince Nicholas Tchkotoua, *Timeless*

*We sacrifice the potential life of the solitary self by enlisting ourselves
in the collective.*

Sven Birkerts, *The Glutenberg Elegies*

Loss of the sense of the singular self is threatened not only in established feminist theory but everywhere, including today's English classroom. The fact is an excuse, perhaps, for the odd mélange of topics
this chapter holds: the death-camp Muselmänner, the postmodernist
concept of subject position, the language strategy of the demeaning
epithet, post-traumatic stress disorder, a novel by William Faulkner, a
short story by Eudora Welty, and a student taking a capstone English
course whose brother had been killed in Vietnam thirty-four years earlier. From the mélange emerges, however, two contradictory images of
the human self: as a guarded coin useful for its exchange value, or as
a hoarded potential that must be used to stay alive. The chapter then
holds its own contradiction. Do not guarding and hoarding represent
the same human activity?

MUSELMÄNNER

In *Remnants of Auschwitz* Giorgio Agamben argues that the war crime
trials of post-World War II Europe contributed to the false notion that
the issue of the death camps had been resolved. What the world hoped
for in the war trials was justice in the legal sense. But law, as Agamben
observes, is directed only toward judgment, which is independent of
truth and justice (1999c, 18). In his own search for the meaning of the
death camps, Agamben discounts the "new theodicy" that asks how

it was possible for God to tolerate Auschwitz. Instead, he begins with a different premise, that human beings, not God, were responsible. Furthermore, he rejects the thesis that the experience of Auschwitz is un-sayable, as if the human extermination of millions of humans were some kind of mystical experience that defies language (32). As our previous chapter notes, in *Homo Sacer* Agamben views the camp experience as the most succinct expression, the logical end point, of a society in which the biocultural life (*bios*) of a person can be politicized into a biopolitical or "sacred life" (*homo sacer*), "a life that may be killed without the commission of homicide" (1995a, 159), a life controlled and destroyed at the will of the state. It is in the politicizing of life that Agamben locates the precise nature of evil revealed by the camps.[1]

Agamben consults the memoirs of survivors to excavate the camp experience and determine the voices of true witnesses. But he points out that survivors do not know the full force or full meaning of Auschwitz. The true witnesses of Hitler's killing machine are those who were killed and cannot speak of the experience. There was an exceptional population, however, whose condition perhaps can signify the meaning of the camps. Described by Bruno Bettelheim, Primo Levi, Jean Améry and other survivors, they were the Muselmänner, prisoners beat down by trauma, malnutrition, and forced labor to a state of utter apathy. The name means "Muslims," referring to the similarity between the characteristic body posture of these victims and a person in the Islamic position of prayer. Améry defines the Musselmann as someone who had totally given up, a "staggering corpse" with physical functions not yet ceased. Unconscious of their surroundings, focused only on food, indifferent to survival or escape, oblivious of others, these "walking corpses" or "living dead" were avoided by both inmates and guards alike. They were the "not seen" (41-43).[2]

For Bettelheim, the Musselmann is not only a clinical category but also a moral and political one. The condition marked an extreme situ-

---

1. In Holocaust studies, the term "Auschwitz" can refer either to the specific camp in Poland or to the camp experience in a broader sense. Agamben employs this second meaning throughout *Remnants of Auschwitz* because he finds the term "holocaust" misleading, an attempt to sanctify or justify those millions of deaths that are *sine causa*—"to give meaning back to what seemed incomprehensible" (1999c, 28).

2. Agamben notes the terms used for the same phenomenon in other camps. Muselmänner were called "donkeys" in Majdanek, "cretins" in Dachau, "cripples" in Stutthof, "swimmers" in Mauthausen, "camels" in Neuengamme, "tired sheikhs" in Buchenwald (1999c, 44).

ation wherein "man passed into non-man" under the control of an absolute power. Taking his cue from Bettelheim, Agamben argues that the Musselmann is "the site of an experiment in which morality and humanity themselves are called into question" (63). Stripped of all human rights and choices, the Musselmann "is the guard on the threshold of a new ethics, an ethics of a form of life that begins where dignity ends" (69). With the Muselmänner, "subjectification and desubjectification" have converged (106). They have been subjectified into *homo saceris*, killable people, by having been desubjectified out of community life (*bios*) through a gradual removal of "norms and models" (69): from citizen to non-Aryan, from non-Aryan to Jew, from Jew to deportee, from deportee to prisoner, and lastly from prisoner to Musselmann, "the final biopolitical substance to be isolated in the biological continuum" (85). The Nazis could therefore speak of the production or fabrication of corpses, rather than the death of persons.

It is this degradation of death that for Agamben constitutes the ethical problem of Auschwitz. He notes that Foucault speaks of sovereign power as the formula "to make die and to let live" (82), yet Auschwitz is the place "in which no one can truly die or survive in his own place" and where the self is witness to its own oblivion as a subject. This "self-loss" (107) is most obvious in the inmate's inability to control or find dignity in his or her own death: able to craft nothing of it—the time, the place, the method, the reason.

Although Agamben does not draw attention to the fact, the Nazi process of self-loss or turning persons into non-persons was also a process of de-singularization. As in many other camp-like situations before and after World War II, prisoners were subdued in part by rendering them faceless, depriving them of their sense of personal distinctness. They were assigned numbers, and guards were forbidden to call them by their personal names. In other ways language, that ever-renewable resource for singularization, was taken from them. They could not converse while working or marching, they could not talk to guards, they were not given mail from family; often, they were not allowed to write. They were guarded and treated like coin, one identical to the other in terms of a particular denomination, kept only for their exchange value (work for bread and cabbage soup). By the time malnutrition had rendered them valueless and finally dead, the prisoners had been constructed into total homogeneity. Their bodies were called *Figuren* (puppets or dolls) or *Schmattes* (rags). The near-dead, the Musselmann, had not only lost all potentiality, as Agamben argues, but all singularity as well.[3] As we have seen in Chapter 9, Paul Scott preserves the dignity of Barbie Batchelor, that prisoner in a lent room, by singularizing her. By contrast, the death-camp prisoner's final descent into the anonymous near-death state of Musselmann was marked, as Agamben says, by the total loss of human dignity.[4]

SUBJECT POSITIONS

In a coda to his uncompromising chapter on the Muselmänner in *Remnants of Auschwitz*, Agamben draws attention to a secret meeting of Nazi party leaders in 1937, wherein Hitler claimed to need a *volkloser Raum*, a peopleless space. He was not referring to any sort of depopulated landscape, but rather to central-western Europe—in fact, a densely populated region—where Himmler would construct a network of concentration camps. Hitler's *volkloser Raum* became the camps, eventually filled with hundreds of thousands of human beings that a state apparatus had declared usable, and if not usable then killable; turning them into numbers, and the numbers into Muselmänner wherein death was only an epiphenomenon.

Isn't the postmodern tenet of "subject position" a kind of *volkloser Raum*? Isn't the radical postmodern subject also a personless space, a vacant slot inhabited over time by others or by machinery deliberately or inadvertently developed by others, interchangeable as coin, denominated, distinguished, and guarded only in terms of their exchange value? In Agamben's terms, the subject has become "a

---

3. In *Discipline and Punish* (1975/1979, 192-194), Foucault argues that under the nineteenth- and twentieth-century regime of biopolitics, as power becomes more anonymous or de-individualized (*désindividualisé*), the people upon whom that power is exercised become more individualized. This political individuation, however, is a mechanism (or *dispositif*—see Chapter 13). A person's social security number individuates, allowing the state and legal apparatuses to apply their long arm and to exercise their will, but it does not singularize. Individual Jews bound for the death camps had been detected through unusually thorough German census records; once there, they lost their names and acquired numbers.

4. In *Remnants of Auschwitz*, Agamben argues that when the death-camp prisoners were made to bear all that a human could bear, then they had reached the end of their potentiality; their only choice left is to commit suicide, to enter the non-human. He also argues that the shame that survivors feel, otherwise inexplicable, derives from the fact that the camps forced them to recognize a truth about themselves—that they could be stripped of all "models and norms," that there was a life without dignity and they had lived it. Isn't the totally politicized life the perfectly non-singular life, the point at which members of the species are indistinguishable one from another?

substratum, deposit, or sediment left behind as a kind of background or foundation by historical processes of subjectification and desubjectification" (1999c, 158). Postmodern theory itself has suffered self-loss. Insofar as it frames the human person as a subject position, purely a construct of discourse, historical/economic forces, or other subjects' perceptions, the theory has surrendered to dehumanizing forces and assumed a despairing posture, a Musselmann-like acquiescence to the biopolitical.

With the postmodern privileging of the paradigm of language over the paradigm of presence, human agency no longer turns on the epistemic subject but, in Seyla Benhabib's words, "on the public, signifying activities of a collection of subjects" (1992, 208). In this framework, Benhabib continues, the human being is "merely another position in language" (214), which closes the book on the possibility of intention, accountability, self-reflexivity, and autonomy. With loss of presence—including that of the theorists, it must be presumed—comes loss of self.

We understand the offensive impact such a claim might have. In no way are we equating the experience of the death camps with the experience of the theory camps. Still, we argue that there is a disturbing parallel. Just as the Musselmann is "the site of an experiment in which morality and humanity themselves are called into question," certain aspects of postmodernism, especially its extreme rendering of singular human beings into non-singular subject positions, is the site of a theory that posits "a form of life that begins where dignity.ends." What the Nazis attempted in a bloody European carnage, recognized and resisted by people of conscience worldwide, in some ways has been repeated bloodlessly and with little apology in the Western academic world of English departments.

NAMINGS

Initially, there seemed to be gains in this absorption of the human self into language. For one gain, according to Kenneth Gergen, people, instead of feeling constrained into a single self, are saturated with a plurality of voices and can enjoy a "vertigo of unlimited multiplicity" (1991, 47). Isolated and self-engendered selves have been replaced with subjects who are happy to be freed of their own opaque coherence. "In this respect," Benhabib notes, "postmodernism presupposes a super-liberalism, more pluralistic, more tolerant, more open to the right of difference and otherness" (1992, 16).[5] Simultaneously, there has been an emphasis across the English profession on politically correct language, on sensitivity about racist or sexist words that can demean and hurt, or about pronouns and affixes, marked and unmarked, that signal to young women that they can be nurses but not doctors. This is the power of naming, of verbal representation. An English teacher does not condone such deployment of language because, if subject and language are collapsed, then I am less if your name for me is less.

In the radical constructivist framework, though, the name "subject position" is taken as more. It is understood that people are shaped and dominated by certain collective, economic, and historical forces. My identity can be named insofar as I am related or adapted to those forces. It seems obvious that "car mechanic" or "Broadway actor" carries more clout than any unrecognized personal name (of course, recognition would add clout—the quotes around "Wordsworth"). It does no good to resist this naming as dehumanizing, because resistance to naming is co-opted by the theory of it. The ability to resist depends on the sociolinguistic construction of the self, and "resister" has only so much clout as society and language allow. As Owen Flanagan puts it, "I am merely a location at which and though which, like all other locations, certain things happen" (1996, 6).[6] I am a subject position, imprisoned, with no escape possible. The only action left me is to inquire how "certain things happen."

So how do we name things? As it turns out, the inquiry keeps sneaking back to singularity.

Sometimes we are not comfortable with the praxis of naming among students. Two young women call each other "girl" or "bitch," seemingly without offense, despite the fact that others use "girl" or "bitch" to demean women. A woman called "bitch" is a woman who doesn't know her place, is uppity, or won't sleep around ("You're a whore if you do, a bitch if you don't"). If a male calls a female a "bitch," it sometimes has a different meaning or purpose than if a female uses the term. Linguists have thoroughly explored these contextual semantics of namings, of

---

5. Gergen calls this saturation the "populating of the self, the acquisition of multiple and disparate potentials for being" (1991, 69). He says this "multiphrenic condition" is not an illness but a normal state full of adventure and a sense of expansiveness.

6. In academic circles, Owen Flanagan owns a name with major clout: "James B. Duke Professor of Philosophy and Neurobiology at Duke University."

course. Notice, however, that in all cases the epithet is just that, a term that classifies a person rather than singularizes them. Categorically different from all these expressions would be the person's personal name (for example, "Sara" instead of "girl").

Or take some non-derogatory terms: "Mexican American," "Hispanic," "Chicano," "Latino." In the southern half of Texas, about half the population can be described by one of these terms. But those so named may not like the one chosen. Latino has connotations of region that don't apply to the United States. Chicano has political associations that are not always welcome. Mexican American may not apply to families who have lived in Texas as far back as the family can be traced, sometimes further back than "Texas" itself. In much of south Texas, Hispanic is sometimes embraced as a term that transcends these differences, yet many dislike it because it suggests a heritage that erases New World roots such as the Amerindian culture making up much of what we mean by Mexican. Consequently, the way these terms may be taken is idiosyncratic and unpredictable, and Anglos never use them in direct address. But there is another reason why, face-to-face, the ethnic categories are not used to qualify a person. The names are plural, and the person is singular.

Another set of namings, referring to another ethnic group, range from accepted to derogatory: "African American," "Black," "Negro," "nigger," "slave," "Sambo," and "Nat." African American is the term of choice now, but thirty years ago it was Black (Black Power, Black is beautiful), and in the 1950s Martin Luther King could use Negro as a term of respect. The word nigger is denigrating, except perhaps on the inner-city basketball court, where you might hear African American athletes call each other "nigger" without giving or taking offense. Slave is a word that doesn't necessarily connote race, since technically it refers to one bound in servitude, including one who chooses to sell himself or herself into servitude (historically, people from Africa have been a minority among slaves). According to legalist William Fisher III (1993), the term Sambo comes from the antebellum South and refers to the "childlike and undependable but loyal and unthreatening" slave, a kind of domesticated clown. The opposite of Sambo was Nat, a slave "fierce, rapacious, cunning, rebellious, and vindictive," someone who "defied all the rules of plantation society" (1,057-1,058). Is the term Black or Nat less dehumanizing than Sambo or nigger? However, all are far removed from the singular person who is perhaps constructed against his or her will by a group that will subjectify, define, dominate, and control.

Finally, consider this set of namings: "parasites," "vermin," *"figuren"* and *"schmattes."* These were deployed against the Jews by the Nazis. Joseph Goebbels wrote, "One might well ask why are there any Jews in the world order? That would be exactly like asking why are there potato bugs? Nature is dominated by the law of struggle. There will always be parasites who will spur this struggle on" (1998).[7] Individually naming Jews as vermin in the 1930s made it possible for certain collective actions to be taken later on. An insidious progression of official naming took place gradually over a decade. First Jews were named citizens of Germany, then subjects—a subtle change in language but not subtle in reality, for "citizens" enjoyed full civil rights (use of public libraries, for instance) and "subjects" did not. Ultimately, slave laborers forced to dig up mass graves and burn the bodies were forbidden by the Germans to use the words "corpse" or "victim." Rather, as we have noted, they referred to the bodies as *Figuren* (puppets or dolls) or as *Schmattes* (rags). These namings insult and violate the individuals who perished in a particular way, serving at once to subjectify and desubjectify human beings down to the non-singular, purely political state of *homo sacer*.

If we embrace what radical postmodern theory tells us, that the self is merely another position shaped by language, then how we are named determines our dignity and value. So in one sense, calling me "Sambo" or "nigger," "rag" or "vermin," "slave," or "subject position" is equally insidious and destructive, for in all these acts of naming I have been construed as a non-individual, without a sense of self or "whoness." Linguistically, the contrastive act of naming is the proper name. In her study of hate language, *Excitable Speech: A Politics of the Performative*, Judith Butler makes this point. The proper name "is understood to exercise the power of conferring singularity," whereas the denigrating epithet ("you, boy") "invokes a ritualized context" which confers qualities on the person that are iterated any number of times in any number of situations (1997, 29).[8] So the racist or sexist epithet is a denial of potentiality as well as singularity.

---

7. See Lanzmann (1995) for "Figurene," "Schmattes," and other characteristic naming in the death camps.

8. We depart from Butler where she states that it is the proper name that confers singularity upon a person. The singularity of a person and their actions is a physical fact not dependent upon language, and the proper name is a strategy by language to reflect that fact.

THOMAS SUTPEN

What postmodernism—or at least the most extreme reach of it— has done can be likened to the scene in William Faulkner's 1936 novel *Absalom, Absalom!* where Thomas Sutpen undergoes the watershed event in his life. In 1820, when he is twelve or thirteen, he is sent by his father to deliver a message to the owner of a Tidewater plantation named Pettibone. Child of a white family who had recently migrated from the Virginia mountains and who were so poor their house was worse than the slave quarters on the plantation, Thomas approaches the big house as an innocent: "he didn't even know there was a country all divided and fixed and neat with a people living on it all divided and fixed and neat because of what color their skins happened to be and what they happened to own" (Faulkner 1936/1986, 179).[9] Thomas walks up to the front door, which is opened by a black slave. Even before the boy has a chance to state his message, the slave tells him to go around to the back of the house.

The event shatters young Thomas. "He never even give me a chance to say it. Not even to tell it, say it" (192), he remembers years later. And during the hours after this humiliation, as he sorts out how to live with himself, he concludes with a strange but human twist of logic that whether he had delivered the message or not would have done the plantation owner neither good nor harm, and that therefore "to combat them you have got to have what they have" (192). The first step he takes toward that goal—Faulkner is explicit about this—is in having said "them" instead of "he" or "him." It is an issue of power for Thomas, and the first step is to switch from singular naming to generic naming, from this one owner named Pettibone to all owners. The only way he can see to beat the owners is to coin himself with the same die. Faulkner sees this solution as the root of Sutpen's moral demise and invites us to choose a different alternative, to break down divisions of inside versus outside, owners versus slaves, namings versus namings.

Radical postmodernists think like Thomas Sutpen. For instance, they encounter a man in a big house, whom they name the White Male of Enlightened Reason, and they resent and covet his privileged position. So they "demystify" the term by appropriating the house and enjoying the privilege of critical awareness, supposedly without being

---

9. And a country where, the passage continues in a succinct version of Agamben's *homo sacer*, a certain few men "had the power of life and death and barter and sale over others."

dominated by cultural forces, unexamined assumptions, hegemonic ideology, or manipulative naming the way the rest of us are. They guard the front door and send us around to the back, where all subject positions belong. The purpose of English studies is to make students aware that they are victims of impersonal forces, assuming that (somehow) awareness is resistance.

Unfortunately, awareness by itself is not liberatory and a "subject position" can be the posture of a slave. If an essentialized, monologic self (the White Male of Enlightened Reason) is the slave owner in our lives, why is it necessary to give him a different name—the Heterogeneous, Incoherent Self—at the cost of self-loss, at the cost of stripping the rich, dignified, singular self down to *homo sacer*, that is, down to a shamed self that is exchangeable and disposable?

THE TRAUMATIZED SUBJECT

Thomas Sutpen's lament lies at the heart of the contemporary understanding of trauma: "He never even give me a chance to say it. Not even to tell it, say it." Implied is the main cause of trauma, an unforeseen and incomprehensible rejection of the victim from the "norms and models" of life (Agamben 1999c, 69). Implied is also a method of healing, sometimes called bibliotherapy, the telling of the trauma by the trauma victim to others in a receptive, re-accepting social setting (see Chapter 10). One way to understanding the connections among self-loss, English teaching, postmodernism, and biopolitical culture is to realize the similarities between the postmodernist radicalized "subject" and the trauma victim.

Trauma is not confined to the postmodern experience, as we know. During the Civil War, traumatic reaction was named "railroad shock" or "railroad spine"; during the Indian and Spanish-American wars, "nostalgia" or "irritable heart"; during World War I, "shell shock"; during World War II, "combat fatigue" (Dean 1997, 26-27).[10] The current

---

10. In his study of the connection between war and the psychological, Dean notes that in 1916, during World War II, 40 percent of casualties were shell-shocked men. During the war, 200,000 were discharged as incapable. Of those diagnosed with shell shock, some were shot as deserters, some given the "rest cure" or treated with electric shock. After the war a "front-line" method of treatment was developed based on "proximity, immediacy, and expectancy" (31). Men were not removed from the front, in part to help them recover, in part because once removed it was most difficult to get them back to the front. Inpatient care at insane asylums shifted to outpatient care; physical causes gave way to psychogenic causes. During World War II, many potentially "defective enlistees" were screened out (the rejection rate

term, Post-Traumatic Stress Disorder (PTSD), emerged during the war in Vietnam and is a name finally legitimized in the third edition of the *Diagnostic and Statistical Manual of Mental Disorders* (DSM-III), published by the American Psychiatric Association in 1980. The arena for trauma reaches well beyond the theater of war. PTSD victims come from other violent experiences such as rape, incest, abuse, illness, industrial accidents, car accidents, natural disasters, political terrorism, and violent crime. The English classroom is not a sanctuary from trauma, as anyone teaching in September of 2001 learned. In our culture of violence, trauma is everywhere. "Nowhere are people exempt from feeling assaulted by forces that seem out of control" (Lifton 1993, 215).

The 1980 third edition of the *Diagnostic and Statistical Manual of Mental Disorders* defined "trauma" as "an event that is outside the range of usual human experience and that would be markedly distressing to almost anyone." In the 1994 fourth edition, "trauma" is defined as both an event and a state of being: "an event that involved actual or perceived threat to life or physical integrity," and "the person's emotional response to this event included horror, helplessness, or intense fear." Within these definitions fall not only victims but also witnesses to experiences that include threat to life or physical integrity, harm to family members, destruction of home or community, and violent accidents. As Judith Lewis Herman emphasizes in *Trauma and Recovery*, trauma is unspeakable—a violation of the social compact too terrible to utter aloud (1997, 1). As a result, trauma marks, in Jonathan Shay's words, "the undoing of character" and the destruction of the belief that "one

---

was 7.6 times that rate in World War I). Still, 438,000 men were discharged for psychiatric reasons during the war, and in 1943 the rate of discharge exceeded the number of enlistees. In 1943 the Army adopted front-line treatment. The age group that experienced the fewest problems was 18-25 at 6 percent, compared to 36-37 year-olds at 45 percent (37). After the war, methods of outpatient treatment spilled over into civilian psychiatry and "delayed stress" became an issue. Compare numbers in 1921, when 7,499 soldiers were treated for neuropsychiatric disorders, to 1944, with 67,000 (or half the Veterans Administration beds). During Vietnam steps were taken to minimize adverse reaction to combat, like the 365-day tour of duty. Only 12 percent of troops in Vietnam were diagnosed as psychiatric casualties, as opposed to 37 percent in the Korean War. In March 2008, the VA reported that of the 300,000 veterans of the wars in Afghanistan and Iraq, 68,000 or 23 percent were diagnosed with Post-Traumatic Stress Disorder (more than half had "serious mental problems"). The next month, Congressional hearings disclosed that while publicly the VA had reported 790 suicides among veterans in 2007, internally they had cited a figure of around 12,000 suicides.

can be oneself in relation to others" (1995, 53). Trauma can be a major contributor to self-loss.

Violence thus turns a person into a self-object of contempt and degradation. At the moment of attack, as Aphrodite Matsakis says of traumatized soldiers in Vietnam,

> one does not feel like a human being with the right to safety, happiness, and health. At that moment, one almost becomes a thing, a vulnerable object subject to the will of a power or force greater than one's self (1996, 23).

One Vietnam veteran explained why he does not feel he sacrificed to the war effort: "I don't have an identity. . . . I never gave myself because I didn't have a self to give. I don't have a person to give them. What they have is a shell of a person" (23).[11]

How can that person's sense of self-loss be restored? As we have noted, usually in trauma therapy healing is figured as a reinserting of the shattered victim back into preexisting social wholes. Hence the value of the victim's retelling of the trauma event, because narrative plotlines offer familiar constructs that will fit the pieces back into a unitary shape. Not all narratives, perhaps. In Arthur W. Frank's study of the stories told by people who have been traumatized by illness or chronic pain, he describes "chaos narratives" in which the victim can only produce a plot of "and then and then and then" (like adolescent life-chronicles). But he says chaos narratives are basically "anti-narrative," and the common trauma plots for example, friends discovered still true, or peace found again in the natural world—do help glue the shattered pieces back together (1995, 97-114).

Note that just as important as speaking or writing is the response of the audience. The witness to trauma must have a trustworthy community of listeners who are strong enough to receive the story and experience some of the terror, grief, and rage without suffering injury themselves, and who do not deny the reality of the witness' experience nor blame the victim. Telling narratives to others can transform involuntary re-experiencing into memories that can be controlled. Telling and retelling the moment of violence allows the victim to exercise control over the event—rearrange, reemphasize, reshape, re-cohere—and through willing listeners to reconstitute ties to the community, thereby allowing him or her to feel safe once again. Self-loss turns into self-return.

---

11. See also Shay (1993, 31-33) and Hallock (1998, 108-109).

The danger in this notion of trauma therapy is evident. What keeps the trauma victim from returning to the same conditions that allowed the original loss? If a traumatic event destroys someone's dependency upon social wholes, doesn't trauma therapy, even bibliotherapy, simply restore that dependency and therefore reestablish the vulnerability to another traumatic crash? Desubjectification and subjectification stand as concomitant. The return from self-loss must include a *terium quid*, an unnamed third term which effects a return with a difference—a catalyst that turns raw matter (the previous condition that allows traumatic experience, or the diminution of the self) into gold, a state of adamant value. As we have argued in Chapter 7, part of that difference may lie in a sense of the singular self and the trust in self-agency that comes with it.[12]

Postmodernism has had a major problem in dealing with traumatization, and for these very reasons. It not only posits as inexpressible the ontological conditions under which trauma occurs, it also cannot provide a *tertium quid* through which and only through which trauma can be permanently healed. Begin again with the postmodern notion of "subject," as in "subject position." Outside of contemporary literary discourse, the word "subject" may imply a condition of importance. The subject could be a focus of study, the basis for action, the end or purpose of another's love or devotion. Philosophically, the term can point to the essential nature or substance of a thing as distinguished from its attributes. Grammatically, the subject of a sentence written in active voice denotes the doer of the action. But the uncompromised postmodern subject, though formally/grammatically capable of playing an active role in a sentence, is conceived and constructed as passive, being only the *receiver* of action (there are only deeds without doers, we are told). Like the subject of a sentence, the "I" acts as a convergence of foci, but is rendered passive and receptive. I am perceived. I am what my race, gender, class, age, and profession make of me. I am how political, social, and economic forces shape me, without intention, accountability, self-reflexivity, and autonomy.[13] I am, as the

---

12. Building on the research of contributors to the collection of essays entitled *Writing and Healing*, editors Charles M. Anderson and Marian M. MacCurdy note that "As we manipulate the words on the page, as we articulate to ourselves and to others the emotional truth of our pasts, we become agents for our own healing" (2000, 7). The operative word is *agents*. Agency is the only counter to the passivity that underlies the sense of victimization entailed in the trauma history.

13. See Benhabib (1992, 214). The previous positive meanings of the word "subject"

denotative meaning makes clear, under the rule of another; under the rule of the Other.

Hence the postmodernist's universal condition of subjectivity pre-conditions the individual to victimization and, in a rewriting of the existentialist's angst, condemns all of us to a permanent state of no-resistance to traumatization. The description of the moment of trauma by Matsakis, quoted above, sounds ominously identical to a radical postmodernist description of the human condition: "one almost becomes a thing, a vulnerable object subject to the will of a power or force greater than one's self." If we believe Kenneth Gergen and we experience a constant "vertigo of unlimited multiplicity," our permanent state is traumatization itself. We have already lost the whole self that gets shattered at the moment of trauma.

Such subjectivity may work well for the rhetoric of certain political or social agendas. In the world of identity politics, being recognized as a victim of oppression, racism, imperialism, misogynism, etc., can be parlayed into an asset. Victimization can galvanize the sense of identity and unity within a group, as well as give members a moral high ground from which to resist injustice and demand their share of power. The trouble with the postmodern theory of victimization is the same as with the contemporary theory of traumatization: namely, how to deal with it. As trauma therapists are caught in a dichotomous closed circle of order-disorder-order, postmodernists (famously) are caught in dichotomous closed circles of their own: significer-signified-signifier, culture-individual-culture, constructed-construct-constructed, subject-subjectifier-subject, Other-self-Other. They too lack the *tertium quid*, the third term that would allow escape.

The problem is clearly shown in the postmodernist struggle with the issues of agency and resistance. How can a person take action in the radicalized postmodernist world? Judith Butler, for a typical instance, argues that the agency of subjects is constituted through subjectivization itself. "The constituted character of the subject is the very precondition of its agency" (1995a, 46). "Agency is always and only a political prerogative" (51). In other words, taking action in resistance to a politicized situation (and all situations are politicized) is determined by the situation. Not much freedom for the subject here. It's as if the therapist told the trauma victim that healing is preconditioned by the traumatic

---

may in fact work as a narcotic to make the notion of "subject position" more palatable to postmodern readers.

event. That may be true, but it doesn't help one get started on the path
back to psychological health, or avoid future traumatization.

It is not surprising that efforts to escape from postmodernism
often take the route of proposing a *tertium quid*, and that the source
of the third term comes from within the human. Paul Smith argues
in *Discerning the Subject* (1988) that a Lacanian theory of the unconscious serves as a mediating function to explain and allow resistance.
Wolfgang Iser (1993) offers the fictive as the bridge between reality
and the imaginary. Seyla Benhabib (1992) posits a "moral imagination"
that mediates between self and Other. In her last book, *The Mysterious
Barricades* (1999), Ann Berthoff explores the interpretive act as a third
term that resolves the impasse of dyadic theories of language and
action. And of course there is the uncompromising opposition to postmodernism in religious studies that so often stands on the continued
belief in a soul or inner light remaining in some essential way independent of subjectification and desubjectification.

A sense of the singularity of the self, we feel, may also act as a third
term. It is not from any social construction or politicized force that
one owes the understanding of one's singularity in the world. That the
construction or force is trying to erase such singularity gives it a reason and a way to resist the erasure. The multiple ways to further self-
loss by dehumanizing the singular individual—to generate a rhetoric
that enthrones subjectivity, to maintain an ideology that denies agency
of speech, or to apply a theory that curtails the full rights of authoring and self-authoring—map the very paths that individuals can take
in order to understand and deconstruct (the last has been the primary
route of this book).[14] This is why politicians and states hate and fear
the singular.

In sum, trauma through violent experience, and violation of the singular individual through discourse and ideology are near of kin, and
radical constructivists who would hand sole authority to the community or group and to the political, rhetorical, or symbolic order have
created a landscape wherein the subject may be totally constituted
and defined.[15] This is what self-loss truly entails. It is no accident that
whatever significant aspect of human experience we believe important,

---

14. See Caminero-Santangelo (1996, 76-78).
15. Noted by philosophers Martin E. Gloege (1992) and Louis A. Sass (1992). It is Sass
    who envisions celebrators of the death of the self "dancing round its burning image"
    (17).

from the traumatic to the restorative, we ultimately must look to the singular person—that mysterious black box—to understand and apply its import. The previous chapter ends with mention of several current feminists who theorize the need for women to accept themselves as singular beings in order to protect themselves from their own politicization and the politicization of others. We end this chapter with a study of two singular selves, both women, one fictional and one not.

RUBY FISHER

In some ways, a short story that appeared seven years after *Absalom! Absalom!* presents a reaction to traumatic self-loss opposite to young Sutpen's. In Eudora Welty's "A Piece of News," the second story of her 1941 collection *A Curtain of Green*, the hero receives a similar blow to her sense of self. Ruby Fisher is also Appalachian, young, dirt-poor, uneducated, and naive. One day, alone in the one-room cabin she shares with her husband, Clyde, she chances upon a sentence in a newspaper: "Mrs. Ruby Fisher had the misfortune to be shot in the leg by her husband this week." She has never been shot by her husband, yet her first words are "That's me." She begins to imagine what it would be like to be shot by Clyde, then falls asleep. She is waked up by his return to the cabin and she shows him the paper. "It's a lie," Clyde says. He adds, as if by way of proof, "Well, I'd just like to see the place I shot you!" Then, as he is burning the newspaper, he notices that it is from out of state. He says, as if in vindication, "That wasn't none of you it wrote about." No reader would predict Ruby's response, for which no literary convention serves as explanatory frame. "It was Ruby Fisher! My name is Ruby Fisher!"

The words are unpredictable, yet fit her character. The blow to Ruby's self does not come with her initial reading of the newspaper item. She assumes a mistake has been made and then uses it as a spur for some fantasies. What if Clyde did get angry enough to shoot her? The blow comes when he says that the name in print refers to another woman also named "Ruby Fisher." The newspaper item presents her with a dichotomous choice. Either language is arbitrary and has misrepresented her (subjectification), or is polysemic and therefore problematic (desubjectification). Instead, Ruby chooses a third way (*tertium quid*) that begins not with language but with the intuitive assumption of her singularity. Her possession of an absolute right to self-identity trumps any logical analysis of language.

It's easy to read the event as a humorous account of naive or even primitive identification of name with self. That would be to misread Ruby's essential vitality. Self-preservation is perhaps the more accurate word, or what in Chapter 2 we call phenomenological potentiality. "When she was still, there was a passivity about her," says Welty, "or a deception of passivity that was not really passive at all. There was something in her that never stopped." What never stopped was her guarding of her belief in her self as unique and independent.

Indirectly, we find out that sometimes Ruby exchanges sex for goods, stopping traveling salesmen as they are driving along her remote mountain road (the newspaper has come wrapped around a sack of coffee marked "Sample"). But she won't coin her name or her self. Young Sutpen encounters language that represents himself as a non-unique self, without privileges, and he responds by accepting that constructed self. Ruby responds by rejecting the language and its representation of her as non-unique: "It was Ruby Fisher. My name is Ruby Fisher." Hers is the voice of Victoria, our hero of Chapter 5, who reread her first-year essay—a piece that, sentence by sentence, most English teachers would categorize as typical first-year college writing—and declared that it says everything she stands for: "It's me, it's me!"

NORA

Nora belongs to no piece of fiction, and we have not given her a fictional name. When she faced her self-loss in 2001, she was forty-nine years old and taking Jan's English capstone class. The topic was the Vietnam War. At the beginning of the class she had told Jan that she wanted to do her class presentation on her brother, who had been killed in Vietnam in 1967. She faithfully read Tim O'Brien's *The Things They Carried* and the historical background material. Then a veteran of the war came to class with his medals, which he said did not represent the realities of the war. Later Nora, very angry, said she nearly walked out in the middle of his talk.

Along with shame (see Footnote 4, this chapter), anger is a common symptom of unresolved trauma. In a journal entry written just after the speaker's presentation, Nora described the day her family was notified of her brother's death as "the worst day of my life." She tells how her cousin who accompanied the body home, "angry and distraught," returned to service in Vietnam, was wounded several times, now walks with a brace, and "carries so much mental baggage." Nora ends the entry with a disturbing line: "I write this before confronting my own emotional baggage." On one of her PowerPoint slides she explains that to this day her brother's death remains a "guarded topic within my family." They had sealed his Purple Heart and Bronze Star and other effects in a trunk and kept it in the attic, unopened since 1967. In the trunk was also a photograph of the family receiving the medals, a photograph which Nora removed for her presentation and which the veteran who visited the class, a member of the psychology department, later said clearly showed four people in traumatic shock— mother, father, brother, and sixteen-year-old Nora. Nora finished her presentation for class, but she never gave it. She said she was afraid she would break down in front of the class. Jan showed the slides with Nora absent.

The healing disclosure of real-life trauma is not as simple as teachers might imagine—particularly a trauma guarded as long as Nora's had been. Nor is the restoration of self-loss simple.

Pierre Bourdieu (1977) notes two things about the social practice of gift exchanges. The material meaning (quid pro quo) is deliberately ignored, and the tempo of exchange is carefully calculated. Too quick of a return and too long of a return are both insulting (4-7). The same is true of all value exchanges built into cultures. Nora's cousin could return to Vietnam and retaliate in due time, but Nora had no way to get back for her brother's death. Her exchange was delayed for thirty-four years, building contradictory emotions the whole time—pride, shame, anger. At the end of the course, Nora wrote that she was not so angry now. Later she wrote Jan that she thought the family would be honored that her brother's story had been told. But she also said that she wished Vietnam had not been a part of the course.

From the trunk Nora also took two Vietnamese coins that her brother had sent home. She now keeps them in her purse, knowing that her brother had carried them in his pocket. For her, the coins have a meaning beyond their street-value meaning, a meaning that is perfectly singular. For her, no two coins on Earth could replace them.[16] Postmodernists have a name for her action: "excess," any semiotic act of humans that transgresses the boundaries set by conventional linguistic code, normal social praxis, practical material need, or healthy

---

16. Just as Roland Barthes refuses to show readers the photograph of his mother, since "It exists only for me" (1981, 73: see Footnote 14, Chapter 9). For more of Nora's story, and a reproduction of Nora's photograph, see Janis Haswell (2005).

bodily requirement. Another name for it might be "deficit," namely, a lack in radical postmodernist understanding of human trauma.

Either way, Nora's action helps distinguish between the two overlapping concepts of guarding and hoarding. The distinction is not between inner and outer control, where guarding might be something done to you by others, hoarding something you do to yourself. The distinction has to do with potentiality. Some things, such as Muselmänner, are guarded/hoarded for future use until they are used up, like a box of matches or a stock of canned goods. Other things, such as a sense of a unique personal self, are guarded/hoarded so they can be used continually, like embers kept covered overnight, or like Bobbie Ann Mason's starter dough rescued from today's bread and saved for tomorrow's. This is the difference between Nora's family guarding/hoarding the coins in the trunk and Nora's guarding/hoarding the coins in her purse. In some circles, not certain postmodern ones, the name for the second action is neither excess nor deficit, but sustainability. In this book's circle, it is potentiality.

13

SINGULARITY AND DIAGNOSTICS
Disposements, Interpretations, and Lames

It was when the trees were leafless first in November
And their blackness became apparent, that one first
Knew the eccentric to be the base of design.
　　　Wallace Stevens, "Like Decorations in a Nigger Cemetery"

In the Introduction, we noted the tendency of the following chapters to draw toward the pragmatic and the daily in the lives of English teachers. Here toward the end, in this penultimate chapter, we accelerate that drift. We explore an act that lodges very materially in English departments: *disposement*. The term is not self-explanatory. The word "disposement" passed out of the language in the seventeenth century. We justify our use in that the act of disposement is little discussed in English studies and has no received name. Yet it serves as a crucial step in a dynamics, also little discussed, which indeed English professionals practice every day of their professional lives: *diagnostics*.

The two terms bring with them two other concepts that also sit uneasily in English departments. One is *interpretation*. However it is defined, diagnostics must entail acts of interpretation. Yet literature teachers would rarely say that they "diagnose" works of art, even though most would say that interpretation lies at the heart of their craft. Meanwhile, writing teachers eschew interpretation. Student writing is not interpreted. Who has ever heard a composition teacher say, "I have a set of papers to interpret"? A student paper is read, marked, judged, graded, responded to, commented on, sometimes even diagnosed. Evidently, the notion of interpretation lies at the heart of a topic introduced in Chapter 1 that has run desultorily throughout this volume on authoring: the disciplinary attitude that allows writers such as Austen, Faulkner, Undset, and "Wordsworth"—but not students—to be authors. Famous authors are interpreted, student writers are read. It's time to focus on this disciplinary quirk.

Our fourth and last problematical term is *lame*. Diagnostics—the study and art of diagnosis—suggests an interpretative act that may end up quarantining the not-healthy from the healthy. Hence the dislike of the word "diagnosis" by many English teachers, who do not want to associate the subjects or even the subject positions of their discipline with bodily illness. But diagnosis can also distinguish the not-normative from the normative, or the eccentric from the central. In fact, we borrow *lame* from sociolinguist William Labov (1972), who meant by it a member of a clique, such as a street gang or a high school class, whose status in the group is marginal both socially and linguistically. Students themselves have their own term for lames—oddball, loner, weirdo, geek, gonzo, nut. They mean those who do not simply act eccentrically, but *are* eccentric. So do teachers have their terms for lame: bonehead, deficient, remedial, handicapped, challenged, basic. We choose Labov's term because in his original sociolinguistic sense it is non-pejorative. As we will see, in the dynamic vector that runs from diagnostics to disposement, naming students "lame" is a way to dispose of them so they do not have to be interpreted.

Diagnostics, disposement, interpretation, lame—the terms await further explanation. In the meantime, we lay our seven cards face up on the table.

- From the perspective of potentiality and singularity, the eccentric is the central.
- In one way or another, we are all lame.
- Every piece of student writing is a product of authoring and deserves to be read as such.
- Teachers don't just respond to student writing, they impose an interpretation that shapes response.
- Every piece of writing requires interpretation, no matter whether the author is student or famous.
- Interpretation disposes.
- The rub, and too often the tragedy, lies in the disposement.

LAMES

In higher education, there are lames in every class, where the polite term for them is eccentrics. One of ours wore a padlocked chain for a belt and sat front row center, cleaning his nails with the kind of knife more often used to bone fish. Another weighed 170 pounds, lifted weights for a hobby, and sulked in the back corner of her classroom, joining the discussion just once, to tell another student that his lifeboat theory of economic survival was a "pile of steaming pig dung." This chapter will study two other lames, Bob and Bill.

Why study lames? It's tempting to say that eccentrics—outliers, as statisticians call them—always test the mean. That strikes us as too easy and, in some cases, too reminiscent of the process by which certain non-desirables are declared beyond the pale and then *homo sacer*.[1] Instead, we will follow the premise of singularity that eccentrics consist neither of those outcast nor those casting them out, but simply everybody. As Wallace Stevens said, they are "the base of the design." Lames throw light into a very dark corner of our teaching profession. Our command of diagnostics has little progressed since one of Adams Sherman Hill's teachers first sat down in 1879 and determined from a one-hour impromptu essay on the topic of "Dueling in the Age of Queen Anne" or "The Style of 'Henry Esmond'" whether the student needed more instruction in writing before entering Harvard University. Indeed, it can be argued that the teacherly art of diagnostics may have actually declined since 1879, given the current popularity of computer programs performing the same function on student writing using algorithms that largely count and value only number of words and rate of solecisms.

This chapter will provide two examples of lame student writing and ask if there are better ways to go about diagnosing them. Please

---

1. For example, in a study to validate a new essay part of the 2005 SAT examinations, the College Board eliminated some "outliers" from their computations. The banned were five students whose scores on the essay were 2.5 standard deviations or more below the mean and whose scores on the SAT verbal part would have predicted something better on the essay part. The rationale for the banning was that it seemed "likely" that these students did not give their "best effort" in writing the examination essay (Norris et al. 2006, 7). But what if these five students were reacting to the essay requirement out of normal, non-deviational human drives, such as boredom, tiredness, or disgust at the silliness of the prompts? Their "best effort" may have entailed blowing off the essay. In Agamben's terms, the College Board has nullified the *bios* of the students by declaring them *homo sacer*, relegating them to a state of exception. And it has done so by disallowing their full potentiality, which includes the right to *not be*, to not apply their potential to a particular portion of a test. In our terms, the College Board—which for a living sells estimates of individual student potential—has also rejected the possibility that unpredictability is an essential ingredient of potentiality (see Chapter 7).

understand that these are *exempla* in the traditional sense, models of Every student, not descriptions of black sheep to be made an "example of." *From the perspective of potentiality and singularity, the eccentric is the central.*

BOB

Bob was a twenty-eight-year-old college student who found himself enrolled in the basic writing course of our department. He had been and, as it turned out, he continued to be a troublesome student. He had returned to college six times in eleven years at five different institutions. In total, he had passed seventeen courses and failed or withdrawn from sixteen others, and so many of the passes were in music performance and in self-help courses such as "Overcoming Shyness" that of the thirty-six semester hours he transferred to us, only three and one-third fulfilled any of our general education requirements.

With us, Bob had no intention of changing his ways. After eight weeks in basic writing, he had a verbal confrontation during class with his teacher about grades (she was giving him C's on his essays), and she remanded him to the writing center. After two meetings there, his tutor concluded that he was untutorable and sent him to the director of the center. Bob got into an argument with the director, accused him of "spiritual bias" (according to one account, called him a "religious pig"), was refused help permanently there, and was remanded to the director of composition. She read his file (which by now included the report that he thought his basic writing instructor had become enamored of him), refused to send him back to her, and remanded him to the chair of the department. After a twenty-minute conference with the chair, who later said he wanted to run out of the office after ten minutes, Bob was remanded one last time—to Rich.

Bob ended up in Rich's office possibly because Rich had an unsavory reputation of being able to get along with just about anybody. Bob and Rich, in fact, got along pretty well together. They conferenced off and on for a semester and a half, when Bob suddenly disappeared. As is customary in the tangential crossing of the life-histories of students and teachers (see Chapter 7), neither of us have seen Bob since. But we have thought about him.

Here is a characteristic two-paragraph passage from the first essay he wrote for his basic writing teacher. She had asked the class to "observe a photograph with meaningful, concrete description." Bob is describing a photograph in a liquor ad.

> The woman is typically gaudily dressed for a type of sincerely desperate woman, to go to the lengths of involving herself with gangsters just to be in the lap of luxury. She's listening intently with timid adoration as he explains himself or B.S. scheme, etc. Apparently, the woman appears to be deeply captivated by him.
>
> The aroma of burning candle and distinct booze encompass the air along with a mixture of two overly cologned people. Cigarette smoke, a substantial putridity to the combo either from smoke in the room or absorbed in their clothing from the outing they've just returned from considering how they're dressed.

Let's infer the system of diagnosis the teacher used to help Bob improve his writing. This is not hard to do, since she had commented on this particular passage heavily. She saw incorrect punctuation, sentence fragments, vagueness, obscurity, wordiness ("Appears . . . apparently"), and the inappropriateness and inconsistency of "B.S." and "combo." For improvement, she wanted Bob to "keep his reader in mind" and "work on phrasing."

She used what may be called the instrumental diagnostic frame, which takes writing as a machine whose purpose is to manufacture a product that will please the largest number of readers. She assumed that training in writing is comparable to training in the running of this complex machine. So she asked Bob to improve his operating technique ("don't rush," she wrote) and to make sure his product is acceptable: well polished ("work on phrasing"), readily consumable ("problems with style prevent your meaning from coming across"), and possessed of what advertising managers call unit impact ("be more consistent"). Bob, as we've seen, did not fit well into that diagnostic frame.

In that astonishing week's gamut, evidence for the diagnostic system of Bob's other mentors—well intentioned all—is more fragmentary, but several familiar schemes are not hard to detect. The writing center tutor for Bob used a skills diagnostic. This frame sees writing as a personal skill, like skiing or parenting, which is improved through desire for perfection, positive attitude, focus on task, and practice. Her lab reports complained that Bob avoided working at his writing with her. Instead he "crucified" his basic writing teacher, demeaned his own abilities ("I got D's in English in high school"), and talked about himself ("I'm 28 years old . . . I am a Christian"). She didn't say what she had him work on but was quite indignant in noting that, while Bob appeared to attend to her criticisms, he returned the next session only with objections to them. She concluded that Bob had a major skills deficit, a "poor attitude": "he is not only unwilling to try, he does not want to learn."

We'll have to skip the director of the writing center, since it is difficult to guess how Bob translated his diagnostic methods into the epithet of "religious pig." However, the two other administrators—the director of composition and the chair—clearly were acting in good faith within what may be called a solidarity frame. Writing is a social act with the end of achieving social equanimity through conventional behavior. Instruction in college writing proceeds by initiating the novice into the habitus or acceptable ways and manners of the academic community. The administrators' concern with Bob was primarily to find a guide who could perform such an initiation by means of a relationship that itself was socially acceptable—that, for instance, would not disturb sexual conventions (as they thought was doubtful with the basic writing instructor). Perhaps the administrators trusted in Rich's beard dignified with white, and his office paneled with last decade's composition textbooks.

It is axiomatic that when eccentrics fail instruction it is because *they* failed. They failed us. The two semesters with Rich suggested that with Bob the reverse was the case. These three evaluative methods— the instrumental, skills, and solidarity frames—did not well diagnose this particular lame. That is, whatever else they served, they would not serve to improve or further his subsequent writing experience. In a word, they disregarded his potentiality as a writer. For instance, his basic writing instructor had arranged her course in the running of the language machine to follow her idea that trainees must be introduced to the instrument gradually. She began with technically the simplest operations (description, report of personal experience, and summary) and then moved to the most complex (persuasion and interpretation of texts). But while Bob appeared to be inept with the beginner operations—as our passage seems to demonstrate—he showed more and more success with the advanced ones. The instrumental, with its focus on technique (for instance, on surface expression and consistency) just didn't fit his exuberant drive toward ideas.

The writing center skills frame, which found him uneager to learn, didn't fit Bob's contentious bent to learn on his own through resistance to mentors. And inserting Bob into a peacekeeping solidarity frame was like trying to put a cat held with one hand into a sack held with the other. In sum, the three diagnostics fit Bob's actual writing, but they didn't fit Bob—not the potential Bob. It's not that they address writing products to the exclusion of writing processes. They address the present to the exclusion of the future—Bob's future. They may be useful in evaluation and assessment, but not necessarily in diagnostics.

What is equally evident is that the primary ways of responding critically to student writing—dealing with stylistic technique, product consistency, personality deficit, and behavioral conventionality—are as interpretive as critical. *Teachers don't just respond to student writing, they impose an interpretation that shapes response.* If teachers want to investigate what teachers do when they read student writing and subsequently what they do with it, they might well look for their first clue to such interpretive frames.

BILL

Bob dropped so suddenly and completely out of sight that we have to speculate about any long-term effect of his mentors' diagnostic frames. Bill's usefulness here is that we know more of his subsequent history. He was definitely another eccentric—a loner with a history of emotional instability. In college he was very much on his own, with no parental home. When he wrote the following piece he was not a student, though exactly Bob's age, twenty-eight. His stint in college had been so uncongenial that he wasn't thinking of pursuing another degree. He had never held a job for longer than five or six months, owed money to support a child he had fathered out of wedlock, and had just experienced a nervous breakdown during which friends had to play cards with him every night to keep him in one piece.

Some of his history perhaps can be told by the fact that in the following sample, some untitled thoughts on "morals," the handwriting is so wretched it is a pain to decipher, and after a few more paragraphs the piece breaks off in mid-sentence. Here is Bill's start.

> I think publications in which we formally & systematically lay down rules for the behavior of people cannot be too long delayed. I will hardly express myself too strongly when I say that I consider such books as John Vincent

Peale's Jonathan Bach's, & those of the whole tribe of authors of that class as impotent [in? to?] all their intended good purposes, to which I wish I could add that they were equally impotent to all bad one. This sentence will, I am afraid, be unintelligible. You will at least have a glimpse of my meaning when I observe that our attention ought principally to be fixed upon that part of our behavior & actions which is the result of habits. In a [simple? strict?] sense all our actions are the result of our habits—but I mean here to omit those accidental & indefinite actions, which do not regularly & in common flow from this or that particular habit. As, for example: a heartbreaking story is related in *a mixed company*, relief for the sufferers proposed. The vain person, the self-centered person, the tight-fisted person etc. all contribute, but from from [*sic*] very different feelings. Now in all the cases except in that of the affectionate and good-hearted person, I would call the act of giving more or less accidental—I return to our habits—Now, I know no book [etc.].

As with Bob's piece, at first glance the instrumental, skills, and solidarity diagnostic frames seem to fit Bill's present writing. The machine jerks along with stubborn hitches in expression—sentence fragments, misspellings, mispunctuation, lapsus calami, and obscurity everywhere ("accidental & indefinite"?). Consistency is another problem, especially in register, with vacillation from formal ("systematically lay down rules") to colloquial ("tribe"), and in voice, with jarring switches from passive to first person to second person. As for his achieved literacy skills: that this introverted, gauche piece was penned by a twenty-eight-year-old with three and a half years of college is evidence enough that he suffers from some major writing deficits. And prescriptivist comments, such as "rules for the behavior of people cannot be too long delayed," question his ability to get along with any group.

But as also in Bob's case, these diagnostics do not fit the future Bill. The argument is not hard to make, considering that Bill is better known as William Wordsworth. He did write this piece, although we reworded six spots to disguise its eighteenth-century origin, and, given its execrable scrawl, we know of no scholar who has suggested Dorothy had any hand in it.[2] Scholars tentatively date its composition as spring of

---

2. For the full draft, see Wordsworth (1974, 103). Changes we have introduced in Wordsworth's manuscript to disguise its eighteenth-century origin: "people" for "men" (sentence one); "will hardly" for "shall scarcely" (sentence two); "John Vincent Peale's Jonathan Bach's" for "Mr Godwyn's Mr Paley's" (sentence two); "behavior" for "conduct" (sentence four); "heart-breaking story" for "tale of distress" (sentence six); "person" for "man" (sentence seven); "good-hearted" for "benevolent" (sentence eight).

1798. Within a semester's time, Bill will write the "Advertisement" to the 1798 *Lyrical Ballads*. Two years later will come the second edition of *Lyrical Ballads* with its famous "Preface," whose technical mastery, impassioned motivation, and appeal to reader solidarity few English teachers would find hard to fault.

Wordsworth's piece severely questions the evaluative frames of our profession in treating eccentric writers. If they don't work with Wordsworth, how can they work with Bob? It's no good to argue that we are comparing apples and oranges, or rather giants and pygmies— or that Wordsworth turned out to be a great writer—because we don't know how Bob turned out, or is going to turn out. And it's no good to argue that Wordsworth could well have used our professional critique—or that we don't care that he became famous; this piece is still poorly written—because the very qualities that our diagnostics locate as deficiencies turned out, in Wordsworth's case, to be vital strengths. For instance, the mingling of high and low registers became a central feature of his style. The awkward absolute construction of sentence six became a habitual syntactic frame on which he hung some of his most memorable phrases,

> Until, the breath of this corporeal frame
> Almost suspended, we are laid asleep
> In body, and become a living soul.

The switching back and forth from objective to first-person point of view become his most fruitful modality. His challenging of convention and his personal alienation become centers of power out of which he produced works that arguably have had the most cultural impact of any poet's since Shakespeare or Milton. Slim odds that any one of the eccentrics in our classes will turn out to be as great an artist, but if a great artist does show up in a college writing class, the chances are that she or he will be judged an oddball. In Wordsworth's case, the profession's current diagnostic frames simply could not recognize the amazing potentiality embedded in his fragmentary 1798 essay.

But we have not tricked our readers with giant Wordsworth just in order for him to charge the diagnostics of the profession with inadequacy.[3] We have used a literary figure because the literature side of

---

3. In *Rhetorical Traditions and the Teaching of Writing* (1984), C. H. Knoblauch and Lil Brannon similarly trick the reader with an unidentified passage from D. H. Lawrence's *Studies in Classic American Literature*. Their point is that writing teachers

our profession may offer a way to construct more adequate diagnostics. The prevailing wisdom assumes, of course, that the study of literature is the last place to look for answers to questions about pedagogy of composition, in part because scholars of literature often profess a certain disdain for composition students, teachers of writing, and pedagogy itself.[4] Their literary scholarship is also lacking in theory and practice of value-making, as Barbara Herrnstein Smith and others have shown. When it comes to pedagogy, most people assume that it is the composition faculty who may have something to teach their colleagues in literature.

Yet the reverse may be true with the theory and practice of diagnosis. Certainly literary scholars are not inclined to offer advice about writing improvement to the authors they are studying, since most of those authors are in the grave. But scholars have devoted avid and loving attention to their authors' growth in writing, which they can see especially well precisely because the authors are dead. Literary scholars have an advantage over writing scholars in that their authors do not tend to disappear from sight after the last day of class. Our argument is that any composition diagnostic needs a clear hypothesis about growth in writing upon which to base recommendations for improvement, and that the study of literature has a trove of such hypotheses.[5] That they apply as well to first-year students as to immortal writers seems a reasonable hypothesis of its own (see Chapter 1). "The Poet thinks and feels in the spirit of human passions," wrote Wordsworth in his Preface to the *Lyrical Ballads* two years after scribbling the fragmentary essay on morals. "How, then, can his language differ in any material degree from that of all other men who feel vividly and see clearly?" *Every piece of student writing is a product of authoring and deserves to be read as such.*

---

have model texts they want their students to match, models that do not necessarily fit accomplished, published texts. We have already noted, in Chapter 1, a parallel mismatch of student to working author with the act of composing.

4. Lionel Trilling once wrote that "Pedagogy is a depressing subject to all persons of sensibility" (1976, 3). On the other side, we won't mention the antipathy many composition teachers feel toward teachers and scholars of literature. Such is the schismatical and sometimes dysfunctional nature of English departments that this book would wish otherwise (see Chapter 1).

5. It bears stressing that the composition side does not lack scholars who demonstrate diagnostic readings of student writing, especially writing deemed "basic," as penetrating as the best interpretation by literature specialists of published authors. See, for just one example, Wall and Coles (1991).

LITERARY CONCEPTIONS OF GROWTH

Consider what Wordsworth scholars might see in the fragmentary "Essay on Morals," as they call it, that a typical composition teacher would not look for. In the first place, they would not focus on the lapses in expression, as would instrumental diagnosis. This is not just because they have Wordsworth's later stylistic mastery to excuse his earlier fumbling, but because they would habitually read first for content. A writing teacher reads "As, for example: a tale of distress is related in *a mixed company,* relief for the sufferers proposed," finds an obscurity, and attributes it to the sentence fragment and the poorly handled absolute construction. A Wordsworth scholar finds the obscurity, puzzles out the intended meaning, and relates it to late eighteenth-century methods of philanthropy and to the dramatic frame for many of Wordsworth's later poems, where a narrator tells a pathetic tale to a sympathetic listener ("The Ruined Cottage," for instance). The truly pitiful tale here is a composition teacher's vision of writing growth in which current expression counts for nearly everything and future progress amounts to little more than a decontextualized fantasy about reduction of mistakes, the sooner the better. The literary scholar envisions a writing growth in which ideas lead the way, gradually maturing and richly entangled in the historical milieu.

Or consider how the literary scholar replaces the composition teacher's concern for internal consistency with attention to biographical intertextuality. Wordsworth's comments on "accidental actions" (for example, impromptu alms giving) would loom as an ill-proportioned digression in any holistic evaluation, but a literary analysis would offer fruitful connections with other works in Wordsworth's oeuvre—for instance, "The Old Cumberland Beggar." The writing teacher may think of writing growth as a Christmas-tree string of polished perfections, as if a writer's development should be summed up in a portfolio of pieces all finished to "passing" quality. The literary scholar thinks of growth as a singular and complex pattern formed by the larger coherence of the writer's whole output, including diary entries, journal jottings, hastily drafted letters, and other unrevised scribblings. The scholar is not dismayed one whit by the fact that Wordsworth's "Essay on Morals" is a fragment.

Indeed, that incompleteness itself may easily be meaningful in terms of Wordsworth's growth. Edward Bostetter certainly would think so; his influential book on British romantic poetry, *The Romantic Ventriloquists* (1975), explores the curiosity that many of the major works of British romanticism were left unfinished. What compositionists automatically see as imperfections in writing, literary scholars habitually interpret as embryonic prefigurements of later accomplishments, or as conflicted nodes out of which emerge later artistic solutions. They would welcome the thought that the digression on philanthropy in the "Essay on Morals" shows Wordsworth—albeit clumsily—attempting a technique he later perfected, of following digressions or sallies or "excursions" of thought until they end up at the center of his being. Typically, literary scholars do not attribute imperfections, at least in juvenilia, to permanent deficits of character. Instead, their favorite image of an author's life-history recognizes imperfections as signs of encumbrances eventually surpassed, or of stifling mort mains—traditions or conventions—eventually transcended.

Which brings up a final way the study of literature offers a useful concept of growth. Writing teachers imagine conventions as an end toward which student writing should strive and as a standard against which student writing can be judged as imperfect or immature. Students of literature imagine conventions as a historical given sometimes out of which great writers struggle as from a quagmire. In short, they replace the touchstone of conventions with the catalyst of alienation, vanguardism, or originality. Now, as we point out in Chapter 8, the only part that originality plays in current composition diagnostics is the role of false tempter. There is not a single article in composition journals from the last ten years that speaks of originality as a major motive for students or an important attribute of student writing. Literary scholarship, especially the New Historicism, has its own doubts about absolute originality of literary enunciations. But they are constantly on the lookout for new turns in an author's oeuvre that may mark crucial steps in artistic growth. Read Wordsworth's "Essay on Morals" with a writing teacher's eye, and the interjection "This sentence will, I am afraid, be unintelligible" jumps out as a thrust of metadiscourse that breaches conventional decorum. To the eye of the Wordsworthian scholar, such an authorial intrusion might mark an early appearance of an idiosyncratic habit that Wordsworth elaborated into an original poetic genre of enormous influence, the self-reflective narrative (Richard H. Haswell 1970). What if one of Wordsworth's Cambridge dons—he called them "elders," comparing them not to Biblical patriarchs but to the tough-grained tree—had permanently squelched this habit?

Can these literary visions of growth be converted to diagnostics of student writing? It is a transgressive question. Many writing teachers would think that it commits them to some very suspicious acts of reading. But notice what happens when we read Bob's essay with a literary scholar's eye for growth. We set aside the puzzling assignment (to "observe [sic] a photograph with meaningful, concrete description") and the imperfections of the technique and the over-packed imagery, and we look for content or ideas that may prefigure later accomplishments. Quickly we see Bob's interest in psychological motivation and his understanding that human motives are complex ("sincerely desperate," "timid adoration"). Bob's compressed syntax now looks like an exuberance of conflicted ideas ("explains himself or B.S. scheme") that could be developed into a real strength. Two of his most awkward phrases, "typically gaudily" and "substantial putridity to the combo," now connect up and suggest a deep-seated and somewhat unconventional viewpoint—let's call it puritanical—that probably will grace any writing Bob will produce. And the simple question of what may be original here, or at least what may individuate Bob from the usual run of student writers, directs the attention to the way he enlivens a static photograph with implied emotional states and active verbs: "dressed," "explain," "listen," "captivate," "encompass," "absorb."

Such textual but growth-centered explanation generates recommendations for further work quite at odds with the advice Bob got from his teacher and his tutor. Follow your ideas (not work on expression). Let the ideas pour out (not avoid rushing). Pursue the contradictions you feel and see in the world (not be consistent). Adhere to your beliefs and develop them (not keep your reader in mind). Based on a perspective of singularity and potential, such diagnosis takes Bob not as an inept apprentice or lame misfit (his previous, assigned identities), but rather Bob as an ongoing authoring-agent. It does a better job in extending to Bob the rights of full authorship.

It also will do a better job of advancing Bob as a writer.

This was certainly not the diagnosis Rich first came up with in working with Bob, but it should have been. It took a month or so of sometimes frustrating conferences for Rich to learn enough about Bob to see that the above recommendations were exactly what he needed, and that anything else he would only resist. But as soon as Rich's traditional composition diagnostics were overcome by Bob's insistence that he be allowed the freedom to follow his own peculiar demands—and Bob was a very demanding person—suddenly he started writing in a way that would have convinced even his first four mentors that he was absolutely right in fleeing the basic writing course, at least as it was being taught. It did not fit his potential. Here is a paragraph from a paper Bob brought to conference, applying a chapter from Machiavelli to Soviet-bloc governmental policy (Bob and Rich met a few years before the fall of the Berlin Wall).

> As you can see, the Soviet Union's Marxist theology on life, together with man's supreme rule and capacity to govern himself through whatever means necessary, is vulgar foolishness. Not only are there rebellions within the leadership of the different countries, having attempted to "Elmer's-Glue" them all together with a tank and a machine gun . . . but there are rebellions within the rebellions, and rebellions to the rebellions against the rebellions. Makes a lot of sense, right? What a way to govern a land!

This passage, especially in its conservative adherence to the belief that humanism is the work of Satan, falls into a camp many might call cranky or eccentric. But that is the camp Bob occupies. He is finally writing from that heated center where words and ideas personally cohere, out of which personal change in writing will always arise.

DISPOSEMENTS (DISPOSITIFS) AND METADIAGNOSTICS

It may sound like all we are saying is that when we deal with cranks and oddballs in our classes, it is well sometimes to think of the great artists and their youthful eccentricities. But leaving it at that oversimplification cuts off further important questions. Teachers should not assume that what may work for eccentrics will necessary not work for the rest of our students and so continue with their usual practices. The standard diagnostic procedures definitely failed with Bob the singular misfit, but that does not mean they will then fit everybody else.

It also leaves unsaid the crucial point that literary scholarship provides only one of many explanatory frames of growth. It is true that literary scholars have a special interest in biography and history—both constituted in the author's act of becoming and in the reader's act of inferring from scattered evidence. Scholars are used to puzzling out pieces of literature as murky evidence of the future, of the author's potentiality or the works' promise. But as we say in Chapter 7, other disciplines have their own interests in the yet to be actualized. There is plenty to choose from: radical liberation through discursive critique, social demarginalization, racial identity formation, psychosocial actualization of the self through dialogic interaction with others, progression from novice to expert, normative shifts in the construction of life-histories, and many others. Can these visions of growth rehabilitate English profession diagnostics? Can comparison of them let us choose the best for our students?

The trouble is that, as Thomas Kuhn, Richard Rorty, Donald Davie, Richard Bernstein, and others have pointed out, there is no ultimate, principled way to choose from among interpretive frames or methods. Such schemes are incommensurable. To proceed along our course of inquiry requires a metadiagnostic, or at least a critique of diagnostics. Someone has said that Michel Foucault is a good "toolbox." Indeed, a good candidate for a metadiagnostic is his late concept of *dispositif.* Foucault's term helps us see that diagnostics is not a one-way street, but two-way: how we evaluate students and what the evaluation does with students influence each other. In legal terms, judgment leads to sentence, but also sentence leads to judgment.

Dispositif is variously translated as "deployment," "mechanism," "plan," "enforcement," "organization," or "apparatus"—no one of which seems satisfactory because the French term itself has so many meanings. This is why we take advantage of an English word that has long dropped out of common usage and translate Foucault's term as *disposement.* In French a *dispositif* may be an enforcement of a legislative ruling, a military plan of battle, an internal system by which a machine functions, a police dragnet or, most generally, a scheme to get something or do with something. So *dispositifs* range from the public to the mental to the biological to the legal to the material. Foucault appropriates this rich term to refer to the way society unconsciously controls and regulates itself in potent areas such as crime, sex, and learning. The way society goes about deciding that a certain act is "criminal" and deserves a certain sentence requiring a very specific and concrete method of punishment is, altogether, a *dispositif.*[6]

The key word is "altogether." For Foucault, a *dispositif* is not just the conception, not just the execution, not just the physical apparatus effecting the execution, but all these together, a unit. *Dispositifs* are instances of "power-knowledge" or "biopower" or "biopolitics" so

6. In Agamben's analysis, *dispositifs* would be the psychosocial framework, political regulations, and material means that convert a person from *bios* to *homo sacer* to *Schmattes.*

unified that power and knowledge or power and body cannot be separated—one existing only as a function of the other. Consequently,
dispositif cannot be translated just as "apparatus" (mechanical means)
or "deployment" (act) or "plan" (conception); it is all three together.
Therein lies the advantage of Foucault's concept of *dispositif* as a
metadiagnostic.[7]

Usually in English studies and English department instruction, *dispositifs* or disposements are tacit, and understudied as such. No better
place to look for black boxes in the profession. Letters of recommendation, grades, syllabi, tests, learning groups, gender frames, conceptions of academic voice, literary canons, standard interpretations of
canonical works, placement tests, cutoff scores on placement tests, theories of authorship, typologies of literary character, models of student
development, literacy-narrative assignments, axiologies of ethnicity,
subject positions, agendas for feminist political action, exchange values
for intellectual work, politicizations of the self, epithets of every ilk (to
confine the list to topics in the current book) are all disposements that
can be metadiagnosed as disposements.[8]

A composition teacher's diagnosis is clearly a kind of micro-dispo-
sement, with power lines stretching to macro-disposements, some of
which, unfortunately, may be the very ones Foucault himself analyzed,
such as criminality. A teacher may conceive of students "breaking" writing "rules" when they "commit" comma "faults" and assign them "pun-

---

7. Foucault had a cluster of synonyms and near-synonyms for his concept of *dis-
    positif*: *appareil, appareillage, mécanisme, mécanique, filtre, schéma, réseau, engrenage, tech-
    nique, tactique, machinerie, encadrement, procédé, procédure, processus, ruse, rouage, circuit,
    systéme, stratégie, agencement*. His characteristic use of *dispositif* makes its appearance in
    the middle of the 1975 original French edition of *Discipline and Punishment* (*Surveiller
    et punir: Naissance de la prison*, Chapter 2 of Part Two) and continues through the 1976
    original first volume of the *History of Sexuality* (*La Volenté de sauvoir*), but virtually dis-
    appears in subsequent volumes.

8. Take tests. Foucault's description of the method of quarantine applied by town
    authorities during a seventeenth-century plague provides one of the best operational
    definitions of what he meant by *dispositif*. The degree that the description could be
    applied to current mandated testing by computer in the United States is eerie. "This
    enclosed, segmented space, observed at every point, in which the individuals are
    inserted in a fixed place, in which the slightest movements are supervised, in which
    all events are recorded, in which an uninterrupted work of writing links the centre
    and periphery, in which power is exercised without division, according to a continu-
    ous hierarchical figure, in which each individual is constantly located, examined and
    distributed among the living beings, the sick and the dead—all this constitutes a
    compact model of the disciplinary mechanism [*dispositif*]" (*Discipline and Punish* 1990,
    197). Just substitute "passing, remedial, and the failed" for "living beings, the sick and
    the dead."

ishment" by making them "correct" them. That disposement includes not just the evaluation (the knowledge scheme) but also the announcement of guilt, the sentencing, the punishment, the demonstration of atonement, the public prediction of remediation, the private expectation of recidivism. And, let's not forget, the social contract by which the student believes what is being done to her or him is just (the power *dispositif*), as well as the physical means for all of this—the assigned classroom, the confessional teacher's office, the required technology to generate the required work (the material *dispositif*). All of this is diagnosis, and any metadiagnosis worth its salt will savor all of it and consider the interconnectedness of it all.

A FUTURE BOOK

A thorough metadiagnostic is potential for a future book. Too little is known about specific diagnostics now in operation. But even this brief excursion into the directions metadiagnostics might take makes salient two facts about current practice and brings us back to the issue of diagnosis and the lame student writer. One fact is that *interpretation disposes*. The ways some methods of interpretation dispose are hard to justify. Some teachers grade a paper, dispose it with the writer—a Dispose-All disposement (grind something up fine enough and it can be washed down the sink). Other teachers don't even look at the paper, dispose it among other students, let them critique it according to a criteria sheet—a deposition disposement (turn the evidence and judgment over to the lottery and the crowd, but first hand out stones). Other teachers collect papers one by one from a student and put them in a folder, dispose of the folder to other teachers at the end of the semester—a depository disposement (file a matter away so somebody else will have to deal with it). Student proposes, teacher disposes. *The rub, and too often the tragedy, lies in the disposement.*

Extreme cases of disposement, for sure—even Bob's basic writing teacher took more time. Still, when the instrumental, skills, and solidarity diagnostics do not work well it is because they tend to dispose of the student author prematurely. Chapter 2 only touches upon the amount of activity in the discipline geared for quick and economical disposal of students: placement exams, exit exams, general education requirements, ability tracking, remediation, grading, peer editing, personal computer labs. So much of our time is instrumentally designed to answer the pressing alpha-omega question of what to *do* with this student, right now, and so little designed to answer what to do *with* the student, however long it takes.[9]

Foucault would say our apparatus is analogous to the discipline-and-punish disposements of the legal system, where the law also prematurely washes its hands of the criminal, not before incarceration but before treatment. For example, English departments experimented with an early form of the portfolio method (sometimes called the "folder" method), where writing teachers discussed, one-on-one *with* the student, a collection of a student's writing gathered over long periods of time. This allowed both teacher and student to see improvements and then talk about future improvements. But historically this form of the portfolio soon modulated into an evaluation disposement where a few pieces are collected and separately judged for a grade or exit from a course—and voilá, another *dispositif* to *do* with students, and another possible perspective into writing growth closed off prematurely. The folder method treated each student as singular and attended to potential; the later portfolio method assigns identity to the student (that is, this student belongs to the category of "passing" students) and *does* with the student once and for all by producing a final grade for the course.

The second salient fact about interpretation and disposement is that there are and there will be no diagnostics free of social contingencies. Since in any disposement knowledge and power are mutually implicated, no complete act of diagnosis will exercise interpretation uncontaminated by the empowerments that teachers take on with the salary, and the presuppositions that teachers must entertain to interpret necessarily involve the posterior fate of their decisions. Just as cut-off scores on a placement exam sometimes are decided by the number of basic writing sections available, teacher interpretations are shaped by the time it takes to comment on them, the space available in the writing center, the odds that an oddball student will complain to the chair, the time left in the semester, and scores of other material and social hitches.

---

9. Adriana Cavarero (2005), following Hannah Arendt, argues that *being with*, or corporeal relationality, lies at the core of a politics that respects the uniqueness of people—a point useful for feminism, as we say in Chapter 11, and a clear path to that social praxis of potentiality and singularity we will call hospitality in the section that ends this book, "Hospitality and Alice Sheldon."

These contingencies make the direction teachers ought to move toward clear. It is pretty much the direction Foucault suggested in dealing with other disposements, such as sexuality. While given knowledge frames and power entitlements regulate sexuality, said Foucault, there still remain bodies and pleasures, toward which we all can move (1990, 157). Instruction in English is latticed with disposements, but there still remain interstices for growth and the pleasures of writing and reading. These are openings toward which we ought to move in our diagnostics as much as we can.

To do this, English professionals need to critique themselves as well as teach critique to their students. They need to understand better the diagnostics they now use and to appropriate growth frames from other disciplines. They need to pick and choose, reshape and create the diagnostics that work for their students. And no doubt they ought to discard any speculation about which diagnostic is the best for students. There is no "best" diagnostic, because there is no "best" student. We will have to individualize diagnostics because we and our students are singular. *In one way or another, we are all lames.*

THE STUPID AND THE CRAZY

By definition, interpretation addresses a puzzle, something that needs figuring out. We *respond* to a face with a familiar look, we *interpret* a face with an ambivalent look. This is why English teachers interpret "the work" of famous authors, but respond to "the writing" of student authoring. "Writing" is not puzzling—we think we already have it figured out. One situation in which we have it figured out is when all we do is rubricize the writing, hurriedly setting it up against a set of criteria, a standard of values, or an approved package of received interpretations. Once we try to read the singular student *through* the writing (the literal meaning of *diagnose*), and especially to imagine the potentiality of the student through the writing, to guess as through a glass darkly what the student will become, then the writing will reveal itself as a puzzle. Students will become quizzicalities, not just subjects for quizzes. *Every piece of writing requires interpretation, no matter whether the author is student or famous.*

Walt Whitman, who announced to the reading public that he was famous before the fact, abjured poets to "stand up for the stupid and crazy." Since he also commanded them to "devote your income and labor to others," we figure he may have had English teachers especially in mind. Let us create diagnostics that stand up for the stupid and crazy, but while we do it, let us also remember that we are all, students and teachers alike, a little stupid and a little crazy, and see if the diagnostics for lames may not help everybody grow in their writing. At the level of growth and pleasure in writing, that hypothetical horizon we assume somewhere beyond disposements, Bob and Wordsworth—two singular authors—can stand as equals. The compositionists who instruct Bobs may not believe it, and the scholars who study "Wordsworths" may not believe it, but Whitman knew it, and he said that all poets know it: "The poet sees for a certainty how one not a great artist may be just as sacred and perfect as the greatest artist."[10] Sacred and perfect, we would add, even when the potentiality of one not yet great has been predisposed as not great.

---

10. When the first version of *Leaves of Grass* appeared in 1855, Whitman wrote and placed three anonymous and glowing reviews of the book, including: "An American bard at last!" Both of our quotes are from the 1855 Preface to *Leaves of Grass*.

AUTHORING AND ALICE SHELDON

When you get through you can be a 10th rate writer like me.

Alice Sheldon

Interviewed by *Contemporary Authors* in 1982, Alice Sheldon revealed something of her "so-called writing technique."

> I mull over the story in my head, and in notes, until I have a complete visual-aural picture of everything; every scene, people, whether somebody hands another person something with their right or left hand, what people who aren't even mentioned are doing—everything pictured and heard. I'd say, like a movie, but films today are all cut and fancied and are art themselves: maybe like a very dull and complete documentary. Then when I have it all pictured, I tell the story, just as I would if it were a piece of life, in what I hope is a punchy way. (qtd in Locher 1983)

To balance her dismissive "so-called writing technique," she adds that "I've found that some other writers at least do it too."

Indeed, on occasion other authors describe something like the same style of composing. Joyce Carol Oates said that "By the time I come to type out my writing formally, I've envisioned it repeatedly" (Darnton 2001, 171). C. S. Forester, author of *The African Queen*, the Horatio Hornblower series, and a stack of other historical adventures, would have a mental picture of a new work, begin writing as if possessed, continue writing in a frenzy for weeks until the book was done, then send the manuscript off to the publisher and thereafter refuse to revise a word. Not only fiction writers, some of them, follow this method of internally composing much of a work before then copying it down. Stephen Jay Gould said, "I never write a second draft. I almost never shift a paragraph. I add something if something new comes up. But I'm a believer in the old-fashioned technique of outlining—that is, you don't sit down and write until you pretty much know how it goes" (Monastersky 2002, A17). The style may have to do with genre. Technical writer Barrie Van Dyck describes the authoring of certain kinds of banking documents as "first time final." The contents and the form are fully rehearsed ahead of time and all it takes is typing the piece out, with changes, if any, made along the way (Van Dyck 1980). Or the composing style may be personal. "I hate to revise. I would rather write a completely new essay than revise extensively a completed one," confesses much published compositionist Frank D'Angelo (Waldrep 1988, 50).

In part, the defensive tone ("so-called," "old-fashioned") in these author testimonies may owe to the good press multi-drafting and multiple revising has received for decades in English classes. It is hard to resist the appeal of legendary revisers such as Dylan Thomas, who could pen a hundred versions of a line before it finally rested in print. Even harder for English students to resist the line sung by a solid chorus of composition teachers (Frank D'Angelo was an apostate). As with collaboration (see Chapter 8), revision carries the clout of holy writ in textbooks and websites. The name of the game is inksheddings, freewrites, or mind dumps, followed by a draft, followed by peer and teacher critique, followed by second draft, followed by proofreading. In course syllabi, "paper due" has been replaced by "first draft due."

So what happens to students whose personal authoring style, as Sheldon's, prefers a long mental rehearsal followed by a first time final scribing?[1] This is not a question of a habit of composing that is necessarily immature or counterproductive. Research into authoring behavior indicates that a "think-then-do" strategy is ingrained with some students, associated with better quality writing, and stable over an undergraduate career (Torrance, Thomas, and Robinson 2000). Stephen Witte (1987) studied "pre-text," or what goes on in the heads of writers before they scribe text, and found some writers forming large chunks and then translating a good deal of it nearly verbatim. Muriel Harris (1989) discovered the presence of "one-draft writers" among undergraduates, good writers who "do all or most of the revising of those plans and pre-texts mentally, before transcribing," and these are not the kind of poor student writers "who—driven by deadlines, lack of motivation, insufficient experience with writing, or anxieties about 'getting it right the first time'—do little or no scratching out of what they have written" (178).[2]

---

1. Of course, Sheldon would rewrite stories when they came back from editors rejected or with revisions requested.
2. D'Angelo calls Harris' "one-draft" composing "Mozartian" or "premeditation composing," and notes that it was practiced by historian Edward Gibbons and phi-

As Harris makes clear, the central issue is not what portion of students are legitimately one-drafters (though it would be helpful to know what that portion is). Even if one-drafters form only one percent of functional writers, that one percent has their rights and legitimate ways of authoring. The central issue is whether current fads in writing instruction suppress, ignore, or neglect certain kinds of successful writing behavior—an issue we will explore in our final chapter.

As we have noted, Alice Sheldon was a oner. That eccentricity extended to her authoring. No writer ever felt more vulnerable. She said she would advise eighteen-year-old students that they too can write, "provided they peg their whole nervous systems out on a field of shards and cacti."[3] She had to take herself "by the scruff of the neck" to get to the typewriter and "that dear old familiar nausea" of composing, yet she found the blank sheet of paper that is about to receive a title for the first time "one of the most exciting things there is." She wrote her first published science fiction stories as a break from writing her dissertation. At age fifty-five, entering the peak of her productivity, with painful arthritis in her right hand, she took codeine and switched to an electric typewriter. For long bouts of writing, often from midnight to dawn, she might take small doses of Dexedrine. At age sixty-three, her identity as James Tiptree Jr. revealed, she impulsively burned manuscript notes, stories, and a novel in a wood stove, and later had to reconstruct them from memory.

All told, not a writer whose method of authoring we can recommend to students. But on what grounds do we have to discommend it? Even Sheldon's dissertation was published, in the prestigious *Journal of Comparative and Physiological Psychology*.

---

losopher Bertrand Russell (Waldrep 1988, 49).
3. This line and the epigraph are from an unpublished letter of Alice Sheldon's to Adam Frisch and used here with his permission.

14

AUTHORING NEGLECTED

Books are not absolutely dead things, but doe contain a potencie of life
in them to be as active as that soule was whose progeny they are.
                                        John Milton, "Areopagitica"

Chapter 7 ends with an emblem of the kind of English instruction this book defends. Two people are imaged,

> a novice reader-writer and a mentor reader-writer. Between them stands a piece of text—unfinished draft or widely published masterpiece, it matters not. The text is now public, and has had or may have lasting importance to one or both of them. The two seem to be asking: What do we do with this piece next?

We call this the "life-course emblem of teaching" because it allows in the potentiality and singularity of both the student and the mentor. Potentiality and singularity are vital elements of real-world authoring, as we show in Chapter 1, "Authoring Accepted." How does the scene change in English department courses when authoring is neglected?

Here is the diabolical inversion of the life-course emblem of English teaching. Two people sit with a piece of writing between them. One of the two has authored it, and it is now a public document. Although to the non-author the piece will have no lasting importance, he or she has complete power over it. Nor does the non-author have genuine interest in what the author might say, especially about the authoring of the document. The non-author is merely asking: What shall I do with this piece? The decision will alter the life-course of the author, who can only wonder: What is going to be done to my piece? If you would like, although this is not essential to the emblem, picture the space as reduced in elbow room, deprived of windows, and stripped of adornments, except for one stark, ritualized symbol of authority barely visible on the wall. Dante would have located this room in the outer ring of the Seventh Circle of Hell, occupied by those who have done violence against property.

Surely it is not right to locate this room, even metaphorically, in current English departments. Yet on second thought we have to acknowledge certain practices that lie not far from it. Think of isolated ACT readers who must concentrate only on the essay in front of them and decide a score for it, although it is a score that may deny the author entrance into mainstream English courses or even into college—an essay the reader will probably not remember the next morning. Think of an English teacher in a faculty office with a student, both staring at a paper written by the student, the teacher preparing to defend the grade on it by contrasting the student's interpretation with a canonized one. (That is a reproduction of George Vertue's engraving of Alexander Pope on the wall.) Think of a "document instructor" employed in a system that has periodically appeared and disappeared in United States colleges for over a century, preparing to give a grade to a paper written by an unknown student taught by an unconsulted teacher. In fact, an English department utilizes many *dispositifs* that, whatever else they are intended to do, suppress the pleasures, agonies, and rights of authoring.[1]

This final chapter looks at what happens when authoring is bracketed, neutralized, or denied in English courses. By way of conclusion to this book, the chapter again focuses on the capability and nature of authoring we have called potentiality and singularity. The chapter may make those English professionals bristle who over the past decades have directed much energy toward bringing experiences of the student reader and student writer back into legitimate play in the classroom—especially those experiences termed ethnicity, gender, and social class, but also nationality, region, age, and mother tongue. However, other student experiences such as potentiality and singularity have largely been left by the wayside.

Some reasons for the neglect are evident. An instructional agenda that cheers on the student's membership in an ethnic group, for instance, understandably may emphasize group performance and group identity over the potentiality and singularity of single members. To launch a campaign to eradicate social bias or stereotyping,

---

1. As we say in Chapter 1, it is surprising that the neglect of authoring seems most set among the compositionists of the English department. Richard Larson, who edited *College Composition and Communication* from 1979 to 1986, testifies that "I have not heard many readers of written texts inquire, while interpreting or judging a text, by what process it came into being, and whether that process was or was not wisely adopted or felicitously pursued" (Waldrep 1988, 112).

the agenda may construct a centrist group voice that erases outlying voices, thereby furthering the entrenchment of bias and stereotyping. Other reasons for authoring's neglect in English departments may be more cryptic, as this chapter hopes to make clear. At root, we argue, lies a power struggle between student and teacher that the teacher will always lose.

Following our quirky bent, this chapter takes up a border official from Perú, a concept of *secret* from Derrida, a more recent concept of *gesture* from Agamben, a group of student and teacher participants from a research experiment, a cohort of middle school and college students from another, and an avatar from the marriage of George and William Butler Yeats. Throughout, our attention is upon the neglect of authoring, but our hopes are upon its acceptance. We want to end this book with the thought that English professionals should and can teach and interpret with the expectation of the unexpected, the eccentric, the singular, and the potential, thereby encouraging the only authoring worth learning and worth reading.

¿QUÉ GUERRA? WHAT WAR?

Rich once experienced the diabolical inversion of authoring, not as an emblem but as a reality. It happened in a room that certainly belongs in the Seventh Circle of Hell, although it is the hell more of Solzhenitsyn than Dante.

At the start, let's allow that a transit visa is a piece of authoring, if a minimal one, since the signature on it has been inscribed by the bearer of it. Also it should be acknowledged that the sad straggle of houses named Macará—an isolated and little-used crossing where on occasion travelers leaving Ecuador hand over their visas to Peruvian state apparatuses such as consulate, customs, and civil guard for permission to enter Perú—lies on the border between Ecuador and Perú or it does not. In 1969, when Rich drove down out of the central Ecuadorian Andes into Macará with his visa, the border was disputed and had been and would be again a matter of armed conflict between the two countries. Perhaps this was one reason why the Peruvian consul in Macará took a second look at Rich's visa—multiple-entry, good for four years—which had been issued to him by the Peruvian ambassador in Quito. The minor border consul then took a second look at Rich, and said, "Ésta visa no existe"; this visa doesn't exist. Then in English he said, "Come with me."

He took an alarmed Rich to a back room that had just enough space for a desk, a chair behind it, a chair in front of it, and nothing on it but an ink pad and ink stamps. A portrait of Peruvian President Fernando Belaúnde leaned out from the pitted wall—ex-President Belaúnde, actually, since he had been ousted the previous year by a leftist military coup. Some right-wing supporters of Belaúnde had kept his portrait on surly display. The consul looked rather like the portrait—squarish, soiled, and two-dimensional. He revealed nothing behind his gaze. He was wearing a faded jacket of the Guardia Civil del Perú. The shoulders had paler spots where insignias had been removed. Placing the visa open on the desk between himself and Rich, he asked in Spanish, "Why have you come to the War?"

Rich's Spanish was just sufficient to make out this question, and his political knowledge of the region just sufficient to realize that "la Guerra" might refer to something potentially more dangerous to him than an ongoing border squabble. More than Ecuador's claim to a few million hectares of desert-like bush, Perú was preoccupied by the Communist threat. Two years earlier, Che Guevara had been killed in neighboring Bolivia, presumably intent on fomenting revolution. Rich thought of a three-day drive back to Quito over Andean dirt and cobble roads devastated by an early rainy season. In a panicky mélange of English and broken Spanish, he responded that he knew nothing about any war. "¿Qué guerra?" he asked. He was just a tourist. The consul sat there without expression. Then he asked a question for which, to this day, Rich has been unable to form a reasoned response: "¿Y sus botas?"

The consul pointed at Rich's L. L. Bean hiking boots. For a moment Rich was speechless in either Spanish or English. What did he mean, "And your boots?" Was the man saying that tourists don't wear such kind of footwear and that Rich's boots were proof he was secretly a Communist guerrilla hoping to enter Perú with a falsified visa? Actually, more likely he was just asking for a bribe, an exchange of Rich's boots for a signature and a stamp of "ENTRADA" on his visa—an interpretation that occurred to Rich not until hours afterward. He reiterated his childish Spanish, "Soy sólo una turista, nada más, nada más." The consul considered him in silence. Then abruptly he chose a stamp and printed "INVÁLIDA" across Rich's multiple-entry visa, issued him a basic three-month tourist visa, and sent him across the Macará river into the desolate, dry forest of northern Perú.

Can authoring have been denied more completely? The issue was narrowed down to one thing, the fate of a text. The author just wanted the text to pass muster. The reader just wanted the text to extract some money out of the author. There was no useful communication between the writer and the reader, and the reader's interest in the writer was spurious, just a levering of authority to make the text work for him. The singularity and potentiality of the writer had no bearing upon the text, nor did any of their attributes that this book has explored: creativity, sustainable learning, authorial voice, life-course growth, multiple interpretation, character, unpredictability, motivation, individuation, dignity of self, recentering, originality, self-agency. The reader ended up by rewriting the text in a way that stamped the writer even more into a stereotype—into just another dumb tourist from the United States passing through.

THE SECRET AND THE GESTURE

At the heart of the Peruvian consul's lack of attention to authoring lay two blindnesses that deserve some further thought. One of the curiosities of the event was his unquestioning acceptance of the signature on Rich's visa. A signature can be inscribed with widely differing intents— pride, expediency, indecision, hope to deceive. But there is one aspect of signing a document that remains the same, its taking part in an irresolvable contradiction, an aporia. For the signing is a single, unique act in time, never to be repeated, and the signature is a piece of language whose worth lies in its iterated reading over time. How can the same act be both singular and multiple? Jacques Derrida calls this timeless moment in time, when the two contradictory sides of the aporia join, the *secret*. He says we must accept and cannot accept "this iterative identification which contaminates the pure singularity and untranslatability of the idiomatic secret" (1995, 140). It is *secret* because it is unknowable, inexplicable by any mode of analysis: religion, philosophy, ethics, politics, law, psychology, psychoanalysis, physics, metaphysics, phenomenology (24-27).

Scattered over a number of his works, Derrida has applied the concept of the secret to religious mysteries, which cannot be spoken without being destroyed but must be spoken by the initiate; to social duty, which can function only as a rule or norm but cannot be responded to out of a sense of duty; to secrets themselves, which must be known privately but can't be known privately (how can one keep a secret to oneself?). But essentially all these instances of secret originate in the aporetic hiatus that lies in the production of language, when singular experience is transmuted somehow to non-singular, iterable words. What the consul blindly denied—he had to deny it, or else his job in validating visas would be impossible—was the inexplicability that lies in the center of the act of signature. Even Rich could not explain, much less defend, his own singular moment of signing, just as the consul could not explain the contradictory gap that stood between his once-only (once only!) stamping (stamping!) of INVÁLIDA on Rich's visa.

In acts of authoring there is always, there has to be, an originary secret. No author can understand all of why he or she writes, not during the act of it or afterward. Something ineffable takes place. This English teachers naturally deny. Their job is explication, and anything inexplicable is alien to them. Hence their final resort to the text, in both literature and composition. Also, in the end, their job is to explicate the student, for evaluation. Yet no matter how much a teacher asks students to divulge and disclose, they finally cannot tell everything about their authoring. Why would they know that secret? How can they resolve a contradiction the philosophers cannot?

There is a second curiosity about the consul's blindness to Rich's authoring of his visa. Why didn't he consider, or even acknowledge, the risk Rich understood he would be running when he had signed his name and thereby authored and authorized his four-year, multiple-entry visa? By the same token, why had Rich handed over his visa to the consul in that isolated border town of Macará? Why was he willing to follow it into the ominous, scabrous back room?

The same year that Rich stood before the consul and handed over his visa, 1969, Michel Foucault stood before the Société Française de Philosophie and delivered his famous lecture, "What is an Author?" Just as Rich as an author disappeared in the consul's eyes, every author, argued Foucault, disappears as soon as his or her work is penned and is turned over to the apparatuses of power, the social and linguistic ways of interpretation. The author is gone and only the "author-function" remains, in which the author is notable only by "the singularity of his absence." Recently, in an essay entitled "The Author as Gesture" (2007, 61-72), Agamben has amended Foucault's notion of the author-function. Agamben argues that ethically something of the authoring beyond the author-function does remain in the text. In the act of writing, an act which Agamben agrees irrevocably casts it into the mechanisms of power, the author has made a decision to do just that, give it up to the apparatus, and that decision remains with the text, remains as an irreducible part of the text. In the inscribing, the author has inscribed the risk of inscription, the risk of consigning one's authoring to the "author-function."

Agamben's point is not mere philosophy. Certainly, the living author is not bodily present in the written text, but it is the living author, not the text, that can be indicted or sued for what the text says. Rich's body was absent from his signature on his visa, but if the visa had been deemed fake it would have been his body that suffered the real hell of a jail in Macará, Ecuador. What is an author? "The author," says Agamben, "marks the point at which a life is offered up and played out in the work" (2007, 69). This writing of personal risk and liability into the text Agamben calls *gesture*. "A life is ethical not when it simply submits to moral laws but when it accepts putting itself into play in its gestures, irrevocably and without reserve" (69). The bodily associations with the term are not accidental, as we note with authorial offerings in Chapter 10.

The "author as gesture" in Agamben's sense is routinely disregarded in English classes. Composition teachers don't like to think of the risks a student takes in submitting his or her work to the *dispositifs* of their courses—for instance, to the scrutiny of peer students, the judgment of a "document instructor," or the quasi-legal mechanisms by which an institution deals with plagiarism. Instead, their courses conceptually focus on the benefits that accrue from composing essays and receiving feedback on them—benefits that must be based evaluatively on the texts, not potentially on the authoring of them (see Chapter 2). Nor do literature teachers like to think of students taking personal risks in interpreting the texts of the great authors, even though that rewriting must make its own authorial gesture. Probably literary historians do the best job of acknowledging the reality of authorial gestures. For instance, it is hard to evoke Wordsworth, even "Wordsworth," without thinking of the personal character damage he suffered from the critics of his day. But typically, the literature course will put more stress on the historical fortunes of the work or on the response of readers than on the risks of the author.

Derrida's *secret* and Agamben's *gesture* mark opposite ends of an axis of authoring we consider in this chapter and in this book. The power of the secret is that there is something in authoring that can't be said (a power inherent in singularity); the power of the gesture is that there is something in authoring that can't be unsaid (a power inherent in potentiality). Are these powers student authors have that teachers would like to deny? Over these powers, are students and teachers unconsciously at war? ¿Qué guerra? What war?

AUTHORIZING BIAS BY DENYING IT

This book has sketched a number of routes teachers follow in neglecting student authoring. Teachers exclude writing behavior they see as eccentric because it does not fit centric, even stereotypic, gender behavior (Chapter 3). They ban certain gendered modes of thinking or patterns of style (Chapter 4). They restrict the variety of individual voices by imposing a unitary academic voice (Chapter 5). They exclude marginal or unorthodox kinds of authoring (Chapter 6). They exclude life-course practices in authoring that can't be squeezed into the ten-week or fifteen-week course (Chapter 7). They suppress singular, private offerings in student authoring in order to promote generalized public agendas (Chapter 10). They squelch aspects of student authoring that do not chance within current discourse conventions or diagnostic frames, aspects which energize potentials necessary to the students' growth (Chapter 13). As we point out in Chapter 1, there are many ways English teachers construct students merely as writers, not as authors, such as grading their writing rather than appreciating it, or ranking it rather than interpreting it, and, as Peter Elbow (1993) and many others show, these ways continue to be lamented by the profession because they continue.

One route of authorship denial, however, needs to be mapped more fully. It is a route followed by teachers, especially composition teachers, and it traverses some ugly country. Caught up in a dynamic of authoring neglect, teachers begin by imagining themselves free of bias, and end by forcing their students to practice bias. This unconscious scapegoating—choosing students as a sin offering—probably hides under more cloaks than as English teachers we know or care to think about. But we have clear evidence for at least one kind. It can be hidden in the standard pedagogical sequence in which students write, teacher evaluates the writings, teacher recommends revisions, and students rewrite. Our inside view of this sequence was allowed by the protocol of the gender research study described in Chapters 3-6.

It may be remembered that the protocol set an order of tasks for participants. Students and teachers of English, half male and half female, were first asked to read a student essay, then to evaluate it, then to offer suggestions to the student author for revision. Only then were they asked questions about gender and response—what clues in the writing indicated the sex of the writer, and whether the writer's sex should influence a teacher's judgment about the writing. One of the salient findings of this study was that nearly all participants insisted that the writer's sex should never influence a teacher's judgment and, at the same time, nearly all participants showed that the sex of the author thickly infused their reading. They declared themselves rid of gender bias, and they demonstrated themselves riddled with it. Of more pertinence here, however, is the way that the bias "played out" (in Agamben's sense) in their evaluation of the writing, and especially in their recommendations for revision. In a word, our responders denied they are biased, they formed their evaluation in tune to bias, and then they would ask the student to commit the bias.

This dynamic can be illustrated with six of the teacher participants. In each, note how the gender clue seen in the writing then underlies the evaluation of the writing and then connects with the recommendation for revision.

Participant	Author of essay	Gender clue	Evaluation	Recommendation for revision
Teacher 7	Kevin	female thinking is somewhat circular, their writing is repetitive	the writer was caught in a loop and couldn't get out of repeating himself	he should sit down, really organize his thoughts, and pin down some sort of organization
Teacher 11	Victoria	"load of bull" is masculine	"load of bull" is colloquial and not appropriate given the topic of Plato	remove the phrase "load of bull" from the essay
Teacher 13	Kevin	males need to rationalize, split hairs	too much second-guessing	try writing with more confidence
Teacher 15	Victoria	with females emotion gets in the way of logic	the assertion about conflict in law is sort of a value judgment; the essay lacks a distinction between emotional and logical methods	qualify more and consider assumptions

Teacher 18	Kevin	men will be skeptical or critical of advice and reject it even after verifying its validity	the essay needs more thought about statements concerning whether the writer listens to others or not	he should ask himself if he listens to professors and if maybe he didn't understand Plato
Teacher 26	Victoria	females lack self-reliance	the essay needs to take a stand regarding what the author is talking about	take a stand regarding what she is talking about and give examples of her own personal values

So Teacher 7 believes—on no documented evidence we know of—that females are circular thinkers and repetitive writers, then finds those traits in Kevin's essay, and then would make Kevin rewrite his essay in a more logical, orderly way, thereby reinforcing the stereotype that females are illogical and wordy. Teacher 11 believes—on no documented evidence we know of—that females do not use rough language, and then finds rough language in Victoria's essay, then would make her remove it, thereby reinforcing the stereotype that females talk and write in a delicate way. Comparable self-fulfilling prophecies can be found in most of the transcripts of the sixty-four research participants. Unacknowledged bias is passed on, as in a Tiptree science fiction story, like an alien spore carried by an unsuspecting human host.

The participants would not have traveled this road if from the start they had treated the authoring of Victoria and Kevin with more attention and respect. It will be remembered that Kevin, when told readers had found his essay too "feminine," said personally he didn't believe in that "macho stuff." Victoria pointed to the phrase "load of bull" in her essay and said, "That's me!" Even if the stereotypes taken by the teachers as true turned out to be true, it would be no excuse to use them for diagnosis and treatment, for an author has every right to write against the grain. Not one of the readers mentioned the singularity of Victoria or Kevin, much less proposed that fact as a rationale for revision. And, as will also be remembered, only one of the sixty-four readers set the individual potentialities of Kevin and Victoria ahead of conventional proprieties and would have asked them, "How do you propose to express yourself?" (Chapter 4).

Nor did any note that at the heart of Victoria's and Kevin's acts of composing lay (as it would at the heart of any of their revisings) a Derridean secret that no evaluation or diagnosis can analyze or even access—an ineffable point where singular experience transmutes to language, transmutes to iterable trace, whether that trace be a living thought or a dead stereotype. None mentioned as part of their evaluation, and therefore as part of their diagnosis, the authorial gestures of Kevin and Victoria, gestures both made when they wrote in class for their teacher, and remade when they agreed to let their essays be used for our experiment in reading; gestures that inhered in their essays and, as Agamben argues, signaled that as authors they would take on the risk of whatever interpretations lay in the offing—even self-aggrandizing or stereotypical ones. Though not, we argue, ones that would ignore the significance itself of the gestures. That secret and that gesture, of course, still inhere in the essays of Victoria and Kevin, and override any neglect of their authoring.

THE AUTHORING OF READING: EMBERS IN THE ASHES

The act of reading is an act of authoring, as everyone since Louise Rosenblatt and Wolfgang Iser admits. Readers exercise their potentialities with the self-furthering works they choose to read, with the works that they choose not to read or that they discontinue reading, and with the ways they read the same work differently after a passage of time. Readers show their singularities with the way they take in language (as eye-tracking studies demonstrate), with the unique autobiography-shaped interpretations they construct, and with the idiosyncratic libraries of works read and works kept that they build along and in step with their singular life-histories. Reading is an act of authoring in the way it repeats Agamben's gesture. Although the readers do not enter bodily into the work, they become bodily liable to their interpretation of the text, as anyone knows, for instance, who has jumped on a subway car guided by vague directions from strangers. Readers testify to their readings and, as Agamben says, "repeat the same inexpressive gesture the author used to testify to his absence in the work" (2007, 71). It is, he argues, the synonymy of reading and authoring that sets the limits to legitimate interpretation, that limit being the border where the reader "encounters in some way the empty place of what was lived" (72). Similarly, reading also repeats Derrida's secret. In some ways, Derrida argues, literature is the most compelling example of the secret, of the absolute aporia of singular presence and non-singular language. Literature "stands in place of the secret" because just as the writer can never explain or even access that gap, as readers we singularly experience the presence of the gap through the indeterminacy of the language, and this "keeps our passion aroused" (1995, 27-30).

The ways English teachers neglect the authoring of literary works hardly need repeating. They impose a literary canon on students with little thought about the effect it might have on the students' continuing to read beyond the canon. They may talk the talk of singularity and creativity of individual interpretations, but on test and in term paper they rarely look beyond an understanding of established or authoritative interpretations. Their focus is upon the texts studied, and they have little interest in the way student readers might commit themselves to the texts, might feel liable for their interpretations. And despite the lip service paid to Derrida, one hears little in the classroom about the ultimate ineffability of the literary work or the passion of the literary reader. What does bear repeating about this neglect of authoring in reading, however, is its effect on students. What happens to students over the years, in school and in college, when their teachers persist in treating the act of reading as if it were only a teacher-prescribed act of translation, and not a student-sponsored act of creativity?

Perchance, does the love for reading—Derrida's "passion aroused"— more and more get stifled? Some evidence for the answer comes from a study we helped conduct in Texas, not far from the border with Mexico—evidence all the more interesting because it is based on the students' own opinions and words.[2] The researchers canvassed about one hundred ninth graders and about one hundred first year college students, all living in the same county. The participants filled out a questionnaire asking them to detail the amount and kind of reading they did on a weekly basis, distinguishing between that done at their teachers' behest and that done on their own urging. After they finished the questionnaire, they were asked to write impromptu a personal history of their reading. It was this second task that proved the more enlightening to the researchers.

The questionnaire divulged once again the kind of information about student reading that has been found by researchers for over half a century. Students spend more time on self-sponsored reading than

---

2. This unpublished investigation was conducted in 2000 at Calhallan High School and Texas A&M University Corpus Christi, in Nueces County, Texas, by Annette Arkeketa-Rendon, Christy Cattana, Rich Haswell, Kim Picozzi, and Jack Stubblefield. A sixth investigator dropped out of the project after it was completed but before it could be written up.

school-sponsored, although the percentage drops from ninth graders (80 percent) to first-year college students (60 percent). The self-chosen genres are the predictable sorts that discourage English teachers—well, some English teachers: magazines, mysteries, science fiction, romance, horror, inspirational books, how-to books, Internet fiction. Fewer college students report reading in all of these genres, with the most substantial drop in horror (from 63 percent of school participants to 19 percent of college). Not surprisingly, the estimated pages per week spent in self-chosen reading also drops (from 90 pages in school to 51 in college), and rises in teacher-chosen reading (from 73 in school to 90 in college). There are some surprises. More than a third of both groups report reading poetry (and more than a fourth writing it). Nearly a fifth of college females report reading science fiction. Alice Sheldon lives on, as James Tiptree Jr. And though it will not surprise anyone who has read this far in this book, the personal lists of works read show how singular reading habits and predilections are, even of ninth graders (the eccentric is the base of the design).

It is the stories the students told about their history of reading, however, that may open the eyes of English teachers. Here we will stick to the first-year college students, since their lifestories are longer. There was the plot of I-learned-to-read-from-X, with parents being the X three times more often than teachers, with mothers twice as often as anybody else, and with siblings and friends hardly ever. There was the story of I-always disliked-reading ("I always thought reading was something you did when you get old and lonely"), and I-liked-reading-though-my-friends-did-not ("reading was for losers").

But overarching all was a war between two conflicting narratives, like the struggle of the good angel and the bad angel over the student soul. One, the good angel, is the archetypal comedy of I-am-reading-more-and-more, in all of its varieties, such as reading-was-something-I-learned-not-to hate, I-beat-the-odds (dyslexia, for instance), and I-was-rescued-by-a-benefactor (teacher or friend). The other, the bad angel, is the tragedy of I-once-loved-to-read-and-then-lost-it. The culprit varies, from internal nature, lack of time, competition with movies and TV, competition with life and friends. Most often by far, though, the culprit is school and college. In easily the most common history of reading among these participants, in what might be called Gresham's law of literacy, bad academic reading drives out good personal reading. Sometimes it is line-by-line exegesis of *Macbeth* in the ninth grade, sometimes the dry-as-dust technical language of textbooks, sometimes the accumulated weight of course reading assignments that, week by week, simply smother any time for pleasure reading.

> When I was younger I loved to read. I was always reading. But as the years have gone by, I've been required to read so much I have lost interest in it. I already see my little sister doing the same. Now my current reading habits basically are just reading for my classes, since three of my classes assign one full chapter and extra reading in my viewpoints book. I really have started to hate reading. It's pretty bad. I don't even read the newspapers any more.

This is not the exceptional or the minority account. The school-has-destroyed-my-pleasure-in-reading plot outnumbers the school-has-improved-my-reading plot six to one.

English teachers can take heart—well, some of them—from a sub-plot that emerges in about one-third of these college-student literacy narratives. It might be named the embers-in-the-ashes story. School demands have burned out the love of reading, but buried in the ashes lie some embers that, after school is over and the degree earned, might be breathed back into flame.

> In high school my reading habits changed from loving to read to reading being a drag, because of the mass amounts we'd have to read in a short period of time. I suppose once I get a chance to sit down and read for fun again, I'll enjoy the talent I have, as many others do, for reading.

> The reading that I do all pertains to education. I started reading when I was 3.5 years old in a Montessori school. Back then I looked at reading as fun; now I just consider it a chore. Hopefully, one day I will regain the fundamental of enjoying to read!

> Pleasure reading really left the picture in high school. I was bombarded with book after book. From *Animal Farm* to *Billy Budd* and my personal favorite (sarcastic) *1984*, I simply grew to hate the written word. I felt that I was always being pressured to finish, and I was, because of the test date. The tests who test exact detail and I, of course, always read for content. I do have to say, though, all it takes is a good novel to capture my attention. I think that's why I look forward to Christmas.

The authoring entailed in reading is hard to suppress. In the long struggle of teachers and students over reading conditions, the ultimate power belongs to the students. They wage a guerrilla strategy of attrition. They know that, however powerless they are in school, they can outlast their teachers. During a semester, it is only a fifteen-week wait. If students lie low long enough, eventually every teacher will retreat from their lives.

INTO IDEATIONAL SPACE

This is a struggle teachers don't have to lose, because it is one in which they do not have to engage.

In the Introduction we mentioned our sense of being boxed in by the terms currently in favor in the discipline of English and our aim to find out where a redirection of attention might take us. Our three déclassé terms—authoring, potentiality, and singularity—took us in more directions and to more places than we first imagined. In authoring, potentiality and singularity turn out to be interconnected. For instance. human language potentiality exercises and maintains itself by producing new and singular discursive actualizations.

Moreover, the two terms align themselves in parallel ways. This can be seen by listing some of the dimensions covered in preceding chapters and noting the way that the potentiality/singularity nexus consistently gravitates toward Column B, and the performance/identity nexus—the current disciplinary correlative to potentiality/singularity—toward Column A.

Disciplinary dimensions	Chapter	A	B
Guiding terms		Performance/Identity	Potentiality/Singularity
Author interview	1	no essential relationship to interpretation of the work	author's unique intentions are part of the work
Experience of authoring	1	little relevance to social context or critical evaluation	sense of personal potential and uniqueness are essential to writing
Letters of recommendation	2	record of past work	prediction of future work
Grading	2	on work done	on future promise
Brain functioning	2	storehouse	recategorization
Language functioning	2	access to learned lexicon and syntax	transformative production of unique utterances

Writing groups	2	adaptation to other members	construction of novel ideas
Composing	2	imitative or bounded	creative or open-ended
Course learning	2	course stopped	sustainable life long
Gender framing	3	stereotypical labeling	acceptance and adaptation
Gender shaping	4	tailoring by readers	gendership by writers
Voice	5	single and academic	multiple and authorial
Interpretation	6	canonical	creative or sui generis
Reading instruction	6	directive	maieutic
Student change	7	academic-course mastery	life-course growth
Evaluation	7	single dimension	multiple dimension
Pre-instructional assessment of student	7	predictable	unpredictable
Pre-instructional qualification of student	7	readiness	motivation or interest
Authorship	8	non-autonomous	singular
Collaboration	8	collectivist	individuated
Self	8	socially constructed	uniquely constructed
Motivation to write	8	from a sense of social identification	from a sense of self-uniqueness
Literary character	9	type	one of a kind
Character dignity	9	social clout	independence
Growth of self	9	decentering the egotistic	recentering the overly socialized
Literacy narrative	10	cultural	lifestory
Ethnicity	10	group affiliation	shatterbelt
Identity	10	subject position	self-determination
Act	10	performance	self-agency
Feministic action	11	identity or group politics	one-on-one interaction
Discourse value	12	exchange value	sustainability
Politicization	12	self-loss	self dignity
Naming	12	epithet	personal name
Assessment	13	disposement	diagnosis
Sorting	13	rubricization	interpretation
Point of inscription	14	lost	secret
Authorial presence in published work	14	disappearing act	lasting gesture

Horizontally, the poles of these dimensions are not mutually exclusive. These dimensions are psychological or social vectors, not dualities, not hermeneutic or deconstructive aporia. All we are suggesting is that, given the nature of college-age students and their literary and compositional predilections, and given the structure and dynamics of academic institutions and their curriculums, and given the pendulum swing that the English profession has taken in the last thirty years, English professionals might do well for their students and themselves, might break down some of the unspoken conflicts that turn students and teachers away from one another, were they to gravitate toward Column B.

Vertically, though, is it possible to generalize Column A and Column B? Are we looking at age-old contrasts between conformity and rebellion, constraint and freedom, product and process, group and member, collectivism and autonomy, tradition and utopia? Perhaps something of all of these ancient struggles inheres in the differences between Column A and Column B, including even more fundamental oppositions: between stability and change, or between the whole and the individual part. Other areas suggest other alignments: in religion, legalism and antinomianism; in psychology, the nomothetic and the idiographic; in politics, conservatism and liberalism.

A	B
Performance/ Identity	Potentiality/ Singularity
conformity	rebellion
constraint	freedom
product	process
group	member
collectivism	autonomy
tradition	utopia
stability	change
whole	part
legalism	antinomianism
nomothetic	idiographic
conservatism	liberalism

Perhaps we are asking too much of single members of the profession. Maybe we two members of the profession are just siding on one side of polarities so fundamental to human nature they can't be wholly elected at will.

These namings could go on forever, out into interplanetary ideational space. Let us just say that they are like the life-course emblem of authoring in Chapter 7, ideals toward which this book recommends English teachers strive.

And return once again to Earth.

AUTHORING'S AVATAR

Our professional earthly manifestations of the ideal range, up from the diabolic inversion Rich experienced in Macará through an ever-growing number of encounters over time between authors and readers, students and teachers, texts and scholars, each encounter unique, each complex. Derrida and Agamben help us respect their absent gestures, ungraspable secrets, and stranger-than-fiction unpredictabilities.

Once in a bar aboard a Caribbean cruise ship, Jan gave a scholarly talk on Yeats. It was the annual convention of the American Conference for Irish Studies, and the ship was about fifty miles west-northwest of Nassau, Bahamas. The bar was the only room Carnival could offer suitable for academic gatherings, and early morning the only time the bar was not open for non-academic business. With the bar counter as her podium, Jan faced the mystic-blue waters of the Caribbean. The blaze of morning light pouring through the windows rendered the tables full of attentive scholars dark and faceless. Her talk challenged a scholarly misreading of some poems in the Yeats canon by disclosing the early history of their authoring buried in the Automatic Script. As Chapter 6 recounts, the Automatic Script is George and William Butler Yeats's record of their conversations with the spirits.

One of the poems was "A Prayer for My Son," which provided Jan an opportunity for some humor. At one time the spirit voices had convinced W. B. that of all people in the world the Avatar, the New Messiah or leader of the coming millennium, would be his first-born child. George, the medium for the spirit voices, happened to be pregnant at the time. When the baby turned out to be a girl, W. B.'s conviction suffered only a temporary setback. Their second child soon followed, a son they named Michael. How long W. B. believed that Michael was the Avatar, if he ever really believed it, is not easy to document.

Now all this was news to most of the academics seated around their bar tables, even to most of the Yeats scholars among them, since the volumes of the Automatic Script were still being published. Dutifully, the audience found the story funny enough. Jan did not find it funny, however, when at the end of her talk she saw a co-director of the conference escorting two people to meet her, an older couple in good Irish wool suits, and they turned out to be seventy-five-year-old Michael Yeats and his wife Gráinne.

What the Avatar said to Jan can be appreciated only by retelling some information about his parents that he had just heard in Jan's talk. As Chapter 6 details, it is a story of authoring in all of its complications. And the complications of authoring, this book finally wants to say, are something English teachers could well never forget.

In her talk Jan took on scholars who have argued that Yeats accepted violence as a necessary prelude to social and political change, and that he even promoted a poetics of hatred. In certain poems, especially "The Second Coming" and "Leda and the Swan," and in the closing chapter to *A Vision*, they have found a "bring-it-on" mentality from a preemptive poet hungry for violence for its own sake. The violence, they argued, was integral to Yeats's cyclic vision of history. He believed that the birth of civilizations is imprinted with chaos, brutality, and terror, and just as the classical millennium disintegrated in violence, the Christian one will see the same anarchic end. Jan's counterargument was that the Automatic Script, which served as an initial authoring of these texts and of this vision of history, set forth a quite different rationale behind Yeats's acceptance of end-times. The spirits had told George and W. B. that there would be a "loss of control" and a "sinking in upon the moral being" (Yeats 1978, 180), but the disorder would be counteracted by the arrival of a new Master or Messiah.[3]

---

3. In January 1918, the Yeatses began exploring a theory about the next leader, that he will follow Buddha (master of the Classical millennium) and Christ (master of the Christian millennium). The next Messiah, called the Avatar in the scripting after June 6, 1918, will come ten generations after Christ and will signify a new religious idea (*YVP3* 260). Lunar in nature, the Avatar will demand worship not of the one God, but of divinity as found in the many (461), but he will *not* be a "creator of differences, subordination & Mastery" (*YVP2* 155). The Avatar will encourage personality instead of character, thus spawning unity through diversity (*YVP3* 69). When will this new age occur? Somewhere between the years 2000 and 2100, the spirit-guides reveal (*YVP1* 482). Already the Christian age is on the wane, and for those such as the Yeatses, enlightened in the cyclic upheavals of history as outlined by the spirits, there is work to be done to ensure that the way is "made" and "not hewn by force" (111). Despite

The Automatic Script records that W. B. determined to learn more about this Avatar. The spirits reply that the New Messiah will be a male child from the "fifth generation" of a family associated with the mountain of Ben Bulben. After asking thirty separate questions about the identity of the Avatar, W. B. clarifies for himself what the spirits have been telling him for several pages:

> You mean that a spiritual being is about to manifest not necessarily through one two or 3 people, perhaps through many, & that the completion of this philosophy through self & medium [W. B. and George] is part of this being's work. (70)

The spirits answer: "Yes." That is, the dialogues conducted among W. B., George, and the spirit-guides will prepare the way for the new Avatar. Moreover, this new Messiah will be *their* physical child, a son born to them and marking the fifth generation of the Yeats family which has grown up near the mountain of Ben Bulben (*YVP3* 83, 338).

This information is passed on to the Yeatses on September 24, 1918. George gives birth five months later, on February 26, 1919, to a daughter. It must have been disappointing, but the spirits tell them that their daughter is the project of daimonic design (*YVP2* 255). In fact, she is "a form of the Avatar," but a passive form. The active form of the Avatar is yet to be born (255, 335). Finally, in August 1921, a son is born. He is christened Michael but in the Automatic Scripts given other names by his parents: Initiator, Messiah, Master, Avatar, Black Eagle, Fourth Daimon (255). Like all namings (see Chapter 12), Michael's name was a true act of authoring.

All this, however, remained strictly private. When W. B. published the first version of *A Vision* in 1925, he had erased the concept and story of the new Avatar. After the rapture of discovering their role in history, he backed away from any claims about his role in the end-times of the Christian age, perhaps with misgivings about publishing his mystical vision to the plodding, rationalistic, materialistic world. For more than half a century, the automatic script papers remained largely a family secret, accessible to only a very few scholars.

In the terms of our book, did William Butler Yeats *not-write* about his authoring of the Avatar to protect his own potentiality as an author?

---

turbulent beginnings, the new reign should be welcomed as one of love and understanding (112).

And did he also not-author to protect the potentiality of his son? Had he ever told his son? Reasonable questions even seventy-five years after the Avatar's birth and on a Caribbean Carnival cruise, but not ones that had entered Jan's head until she was shaking hands, astonished almost speechless, with Michael Yeats, the Avatar himself. How angry was he? As it turned out, Michael Yeats's response to Jan's talk was itself an act of potentiality, at least if there is any truth in our contention that one of the hallmarks of potentiality is unpredictability.

Michael said that the Avatar story was not news to him, that his friend and Yeats scholar George Harper had told him years ago. "I'm not interested in it," he said. "That was my father's business." "But there was a poem he wrote about me," he added, "that I wish he had never published."

Then he switched topics and said he was very much looking forward to the next session, because someone was talking about the failure of a plan to train emigrating young Irish women as schoolteachers (women who in Canada, however, could get jobs only as housemaids), and he feared that the scholar had misconstrued the facts. Michael Yeats was telling Jan that for all of his parents' efforts to prophesy the life of their son, Michael Yeats authored his own life.

In "A Prayer for My Son," written when Michael was a babe in arms, W. B. likens his son to Christ and pictures him becoming a famous poet like his father. In real life Michael took a different route. It seems his parents kept his childhood free from knowledge of his destiny as Avatar. In fact, according to his memoir, *Cast a Cold Eye* (1998), his childhood involved little to no intimate contact with his famous father, whom he refers to as "the poet" (1). Born in 1921, when W. B. was fifty-six years old, Michael and his sister, Anne, were deprived of ordinary family life, in part by a father who had no idea how to deal with small children, in part by a mother who protected her husband from any distractions from his work (3, 30). W. B. could not compose with anyone in the same room, even with a sleeping child in his cradle, even with George silently knitting.[4]

---

4. The well-known photograph of W. B. and his two children in a field at Thor Ballylee suggests a close and loving moment, but in fact the family circle was staged by Michael's mother, who had asked a photographer to take pictures of the tower. Spying her husband off by himself with a book, she herded the children to his side. Dutifully, W. B. placed the book on the ground, spine-side-up so as not to lose his place, and posed for the camera. Once the photograph was taken, he resumed his reading (M. B. Yeats 1998, 3). While Michael refers to his father as "remote and distant," he also

At the age of six, Michael was sent to school in Switzerland for three years. At the age of ten, he returned to the family in Dublin. First he was tutored by a governess, then enrolled in a series of local schools before enrolling at Trinity College in 1939, where he met Gráinne Ní Éigeartaigh through their mutual involvement in the Gaelic Society. Also while at Trinity he joined the Fianna Fáil party, a step that began his political career, first as an Irish Senator and then as an elected representative to the European Parliament. He devoted forty years to public service. He chose not to philosophize or revolutionize civilization, but rather to contribute to the growth of his country. As he reflects on his years of political involvement, he identifies important changes for which he fought: a decline in the dropout rate of Irish school children, a decline in emigration, an increasingly educated labor force, an expanded role of women in politics, and the fostering of the Irish language in schools. If, as he says, "politics is the art of the possible" (60), then Michael Yeats is an artist in his own right.[5] His refusal to author his father's kind of authoring was part of the political life that he authored for himself.

The decision of George and W. B. not to tell their son about the spirits' prophecy, or not to have him find out through any publication, is an authorial gesture of their own, an act of potentiality to not-do. "A Prayer for My Son," in fact, shows the real dangers had they done so. It was the poem Senator Yeats—we should give him his due title—wished his father had never published. While he was attending preparatory school at St. Columba's College, his schoolmates had unearthed the poem. They soon learned that to enrage the poet's son, all they need do was recite the first four lines:

> Bid a strong ghost stand at the head
> That my Michael may sleep sound,
> Nor cry, nor turn in the bed
> Till his morning meal come round.

After incessant teasing, the verses were shortened to "Bid a strong ghost" and eventually to the initials BASG, sufficient to drive Michael

---

remembers him as "full of vivacity and humor," particularly when as a young adult Michael would engage him in political conversations (28).

5. In what may or may not be an equivalent thought, his father had asked, "What is rhetoric but the will trying to do the work of the imagination?" (1961, 215). It was a line Alice Sheldon had pinned above her worktable.

into a fury (20-21). Years later, in his memoirs, Senator Yeats gave some advice to poets: "If you must write poems about your children, do not publish them until they have left school" (21). The momentary confusion in pronoun antecedence may have been deliberate. Parents do publish their children.

Let's put it another way. There is an avatar in authoring. Agamben might call it a gesture, Derrida a secret, and this book a singular potentiality that leads to unpredictable (because singular) potentialities. Some originary (because singular) power in an act of authoring will manifest itself later, always in new ways. Consider the gesture of W. B. in "A Prayer for My Son." We don't know his intent, but we do know some of the risks he took in writing it and turning it over to the vicissitudes of the reading public, because those risks inhered in the poem and, avatar-like, manifested themselves later—through readings that are authorings themselves, that make gestures of their own, and run their own progenitive risks. In authoring the poem, W. B. risked the use of it by the boys at St. Columba's College in the baiting of Michael's fury. W. B.'s authoring takes the risk that his son will characterize the work as a poem of "maudlin sentimentality" (20), as Michael's authoring takes the risk that any reader of his memoirs will use those words to not read the poem or to read it with a cold eye. W. B.'s authoring takes the risk of scholar-critics seizing on the imagery of armed guardian angels and the flight of the Mary and Joseph to Bethlehem to argue that the poem celebrates millennial violence, just as those scholar-critics take the risk of their own readers reading, believing, and acting on that interpretation.

And in writing "A Prayer for My Son," W. B. took on the risk, unpredictable as it would have been to him, of Jan reciting the last lines of the poem to his son, seventy-five years later, in a bar on a ship midmorning in the Caribbean Sea.

> A woman and a man,
> Unless the Holy Writings lie,
> Hurried through the smooth and rough
> And through the fertile and waste,
> Protecting, till the danger past,
> With human love.

Even Michael's twelve-year-old school chums could see that these lines compare George, W. B., and Michael with Mary, Joseph, and Jesus. Jan selected them, however, as a way of ending her presentation because they reminded her that, however inexplicable W. B. and George's mystical prophecy might seem, they were after all human parents who raised and loved a human son. In authoring her reading, Jan took the risk—improbable as it would have seemed to her at the time—of Senator Yeats's reaction, no differently than his bullying schoolmates did in their reciting of the poem's first lines. Michael Yeats died in January of 2007. The Avatar was real, in some ways as real as the avatars computer users create on the screen, in other ways more real.

When Jan met the living Michael Yeats, she felt the Automatic Script texts come alive in a new way. She better understood the serious intent and studious search of its authors, George and William Butler Yeats, who in that process bequeathed us not only a text but a living gesture in the form of a dedicated statesman. And bequeathed a lesson. Never forget that the texts we read, research, and teach involve real people who may walk into our lives and hold us accountable. Never forget that the classroom texts we require our students to author run the same risks as those shouldered by any other author in any other real world.

"The author marks the point at which a life is offered up and played out in the work" (Agamben 2007, 69). Agamben's sentence bears repeating, since it comes as close to a summary of this book as we can find. Our emphasis would be upon the word "life." Authoring doesn't die with the scribing of a text or with the reading of it. When authors relinquish their writing to the apparatuses of the world, they never let loose of it. When students (authors) relinquish their essays (writing) to their teachers and fellow students (apparatuses of the world), their text is still alive (they never let loose of it). Our prayer for once, future, and present English teachers is that they never let loose of that living complexity.

ENVOI
Hospitality and Alice Sheldon

In the end, all books are written for your friends.
Gabriel García Márquez

We can't take leave without noting, for our English colleagues and for their students, that socially and culturally the way authors manage both to safeguard their authorings and to relinquish them to the apparatuses of the world is through hospitality.

We mean hospitality in the old sense, the welcome and befriending of strangers, the cultural and religious codes that used to be (and sometimes still are) exercised on the byroads and backstreets, providing travelers with rest, food, and lodging. Rules governing the traditional relations between guest and host included swapping of information, unspoken assumption of social equality, unspoken assumption of the equal validity of differing customs, and a respect for privacy. The host would never ask the guest's name, but rather wait until it was freely given. In Chapter 1, it may be remembered, hospitality was listed as one of the phenomenological traits of authoring, the feeling of working authors that their future readers must be given a stranger's welcome. In the end—although Agamben would say the *gesture* does not end—authoring is a hospitable extending of the hand to unknown others.

When most people write, they assume that the results of the act somewhere will be invited in, or conversely that their work in words will serve as a friendly, if temporary, abode for reader-strangers. As Virginia Woolf put it, writers must find "some means of bridging the gulf between the hostess and her unknown guest on one hand, the writer and his unknown reader on the other" (1950, 110). In this book's terms, to the degree that authoring is a praxis happening within a social and cultural surround, that context always takes the shape of hospitality conventions, which embrace the singularity and the potentiality of both host and guest. Hospitality is the pragmatic or social means by which authors broadcast to the world.

All the scenes exploring the neglect of authoring in the previous chapter show hospitality present, pending, or missing. The Peruvian consulate might have invited the traveler into his country with more grace and less deceit. One manifestation of Derrida's "secret" is the password or shibboleth that tests the entrant and bars the unwelcome. Agamben's "gesture" is the decision of authors to chance their work at unknown doors. The readers of Victoria's and Kevin's essays might have better respected the individual differences of those author-strangers. English teachers might better respect the differing reading habits of the students who enter the gates of their academy. And aboard the no-man's-land of a cruise ship, Jan realized that there is a basic hospitality that should be exercised in the most erudite and exotic lodgings of scholarship. The act of hospitality, with all its social rules governing host-guest relations, inheres in the sociability of writer-reader relations.

In her works and in her life, hospitality haunted author Alice Sheldon like a half-remembered dream. The ancient host-guest codes underlie many of her tales. Often disregard or breach of the codes leads to tragic clashes between humans and between humans and aliens. In *Houston, Houston, Do You Read Me?* three male astronauts are rescued from their disabled craft and taken aboard another run entirely by women from a future female-only Earth—women who appear friendly ("their reception couldn't be more courteous"), but eventually put the men to death after learning of their gender-dominating sex drives by surreptitiously administering truth-telling narcotics to them. In "A Momentary Taste of Being" humans test life-forms on a newly encountered planet to see if it is livable and discover that humans are spermatozoa and the aliens are ova of a greater being—a discovery that envisions all of them as trapped in the essential inhospitality of mere biologic life, "hostile or smiling, suffering each in his separate flawed reality." But in "With Delicate Mad Hands" genuine hospitality occurs when the dying female narrator meets a welcoming alien on his planet and for the first time in her life finds an unoppressive relationship—an encounter celebrated by the other natives and retold as expressive of "the love of all that is alien." And in "Come Live with Me" human explorers acquire alien symbiotes, and together both learn to reject acts of manipulative hospitality and to perform acts of generous hospitality in order to return the symbiotes to their original home planet and to write a history of their race.

So in Sheldon's fiction, genuine hospitality leads to authoring. In her life, she found that authoring led to hospitality. For her, being allowed into the club of science fiction writers was like being invited as a stranger into a friendly home. As she described the experience to her academic advisor and friend Rudolf Arnheim, she had been "profoundly dispirited, alienated" and then was suddenly welcomed into a social network that followed the old hospitable ways, a "Camelot-world . . . each new friend *listening*, and oneself *listening*. . . . One corresponds with strangers, old, young, male, female, without caution or disguise, and without false needs" (Phillips 2006, 244).

In 1976, when she was sixty-one and fans and an editor blew her James Tiptree Jr. cover, she suffered a deep violation of the ancient code of hospitality where, as we say, the host never asks or questions the name of the guest. Sheldon's pseudonym or anonym was rooted deep in her psyche, and her images for its violation were bodily. She felt the violation as a fear, a fatigue, a death, a disembodiment. But perhaps the most poignant image is one she sent in a letter to fellow science fiction writer Joanna Russ: "I feel as if some microphone had gone dead on me" (361). Suddenly she no longer had a voice that would serve in an arena larger than a small room. What to others may have appeared an affectation or a feminist ploy, just a *nom de plume*, to her served as a vital stock for authoring. It was the secret gesture—singular, potential—without which she could not risk transmitting her writings to the world.

When Arnheim learned from Sheldon of her loss, he wrote back to his old student, "Good. You cannot live in permanent identity crisis" (379). No doubt he knew he was putting on a brave face and that finally teachers, even the few with his psychoanalytic astuteness, cannot solve their students' identity crises. Of course, most of our students are not Alice Sheldons. But some are. And all have unique identities that, in crisis or not, we need to welcome, not turn away at the classroom or office door. What do we say to them? The answer, if and only if it has potential, will be unpredictable. And if and only if it turns out singular, it will be useful. And if and only if it is an act of genuine hospitality, it will be ethical.

REFERENCES

Agamben, Giorgio. 1993. *The coming community.* Translated by Michael Hardt. Minneapolis, MN: University of Minnesota Press.

———. 1995a. *Homo sacer: Sovereign power and bare life.* Translated by Daniel Heller-Roazen. Stanford, CA: Stanford University Press.

———. 1995b. *Idea of prose.* Translated by Michael Sullivan and Sam Whitsitt. Albany, NY: State University of New York Press.

———. 1999a. *The man without content.* Translated by Georgia Albert. Stanford, CA: Stanford University Press.

———. 1999b. *Potentialities: Collected essays in philosophy.* Translated by Daniel Heller-Roazen. Stanford, CA: Stanford University Press.

———. 1999c. *Remnants of Auschwitz: The witness and the archive.* Translated by Daniel Heller-Roazen. New York: Zone Books.

———. 2007. *Profanations.* Translated by Jeff Fort. New York: Zone Books.

Ahmad, Aijaz. 1992. *In theory, classes, nations, literatures: Postcolonial literature.* New York: Verso.

Alcoff, Linda. 1988. Cultural feminism versus post-structuralism: The identity crisis in feminist theory. *Signs: Journal of Woman in Culture and Society* 13 (3): 405-36.

Allport, Gordon. 1960. Uniqueness in students. In *The goals of higher education,* ed. Willis D. Weatherford, 57-75. Cambridge, MA: Harvard University Press.

Anderson, Charles M., and Marian M. MacCurdy. 2000. Introduction. In *Writing and healing: Toward an informed practice,* ed. Charles M. Anderson and Marian M. MacCurdy, 1-22. Urbana, IL: NCTE.

Arendt, Hannah. 1958. *The human condition.* Chicago, IL: University of Chicago Press.

Aristotle. 1953. *Generation of animals.* Translated by A. L. Peck. Cambridge, MA: Harvard University Press.

———. 1997. *Poetics.* Translated by Malcolm Heath. New York: Penguin.

Barritt, Loren, Patricia T. Stock, and Francelia Clark. 1986. Researching practice: Evaluating assessment essays. *College Composition and Communication* 37 (3): 315-27.

Barthes, Roland. 1953. *Le degré zéro de l'écriture.* Paris: Le Seuil.

———. 1981. *Camera lucida: Reflections on photography.* Translated by Richard Howard. New York: Hill and Wang.

Bartholomae, David. 1986. Inventing the university. *Journal of Basic Writing* 5 (1): 4-23.

Battaglia, Debbora. 1995. Problematizing the self: A thematic introduction. In *Rhetorics of self making,* ed. Debbora Battaglia, 1-15. Berkeley, CA: University of California Press.

Bell, Susan E., C. Suzanne Cole, and Liliane Floge. 1992. Letters of recommendation in academe: Do women and men write in different languages? *The American Sociologist* 23 (3): 7-22.

Bem, Sandra Lipsitz. 1993. *The lenses of gender: Transforming the debate on sexual inequality.* New Haven, CT: Yale University Press.

Benhabib, Seyla. 1990a. Afterward: Communicative ethics and current controversies in practical philosophy. In *The communicative ethics controversy,* ed. Seyla Benhabib and Fred Dallmayr, 330-69. Cambridge: MIT Press.

———. 1990b. Hannah Arendt and the redemptive power of narrative. *Social Research* 57 (1): 167-96.

————. 1992. *Situating the self: Gender, community and postmodernism in contemporary ethics.* New York: Routledge.

————. 1995. Subjectivity, historiography, and politics: Reflections on the "feminism/postmodernism exchange." In *Feminist contentions: A philosophical exchange*, ed. Seyla Benhabib, Judith Butler, Drucilla Cornell, and Nancy Fraser, 107-25. London: Routledge.

————. 1999. Citizens, residents, and aliens in a changing world: Political membership in the global era. *Social Research* 66 (3): 709-25.

Bennett, Tony, Lawrence Grossberg, and Meaghan Morris, eds. 2005. *New keywords: A revised vocabulary of culture and society.* Oxford, England: Blackwell.

Berthoff, Ann. 1999. *The mysterious barricades: Language and its limits.* Toronto: University of Toronto Press.

Birkerts, Sven. 1994. *The Gutenberg elegies: The fate of reading in an electronic age.* London: Faber and Faber.

Bloom, Harold. 1970. *Yeats.* New York: Oxford University Press.

Bondi, Liz. 1993. Locating identity politics. In *Place and the politics of identity*, ed. Michael Keith and Steve Pile, 84-101. New York: Routledge.

Booth, Wayne. 1961. *The rhetoric of fiction.* Chicago, IL: University of Chicago Press.

Bostetter, Edward E. 1975. *The romantic ventriloquists: Wordsworth, Coleridge, Keats, Shelley, Byron.* Seattle, WA: University of Washington Press.

Bourdieu, Pierre. 1977. *Outline of a theory of practice.* Translated by Richard Nice. Cambridge, England: Cambridge University Press.

Brennan, Teresa. 1996. Essence against identity. *Metaphilosophy* 27 (1-2): 92-103.

Brodkey, Linda. 1989. On the subject of class and gender. *College English* 51 (2): 125-41.

————. 1996. *Writing permitted in designated areas only.* Minneapolis, MN: University of Minnesota Press.

Brooks, Neil, and Josh Toth, eds. 2007. *The mourning after: Attending the wake of postmodernism.* Amsterdam: Rodopi.

Brooks, Peter. 1984. *Reading for the plot: Design and intention in narrative.* Cambridge, MA: Harvard University Press.

Brown, Charles N. 1985. James Tiptree rebounds. *Locus*, no. 296: 4-7.

Burkitt, Ian. 1992. *Social selves: Theories of the social formation of personality.* London: Sage.

Butler, Judith. 1990. *Gender trouble: Feminism and the subversion of identity.* New York: Routledge.

————. 1995a. Contingent foundations: Feminism and the question of "postmodernism." In *Feminist contentions: A philosophical exchange*, ed. Seyla Benhabib, Judith Butler, Drucilla Cornell, and Nancy Fraser, 35-57. London: Routledge.

————. 1995b. For a careful reading. In *Feminist contentions: A philosophical exchange*, ed. Seyla Benhabib, Judith Butler, Drucilla Cornell, and Nancy Fraser, 127-43. London: Routledge.

————. 1997. *Excitable speech: A politics of the performative.* New York: Routledge.

————. 2001. Subjectivity, historiography, and politics: Reflections on the "feminism/postmodernism exchange." In *Postmodern debates*, ed. Simon Malpas, 110-16. New York: Palgrave.

Cameron, Deborah. 1985. *Feminism and linguistic theory.* New York: Macmillan.

————. 1995. *Verbal hygiene.* Toronto: Routledge.

————. 1996. The language-gender interface: Challenging co-optation. In *Rethinking language and gender research: Theory and practice*, ed. Victoria L. Bergvall, Janet M. Bing, and Alice F. Freed, 31-53. New York: Longman.

Cameron, Deborah, and Jennifer Coates. 1988. *Women in their speech communities: New perspectives on language and sex.* New York: Longman.

Caminero-Santangelo, Marta. 1996. Multiple personality and the postmodern subject: Theorizing agency. *Literature / Interpretation / Theory* 7: 63-86.

Carson, Barbara Harrell. 1996. Thirty years of stories: The professor's place in student memories. *Change* 28 (6): 11-17.

Caspi, Avshalom, and Brent W. Roberts. 1999. Personality, continuity and change across the life course. In *Handbook of personality: Theory and research*, ed. Lawrence A. Pervin and Oliver P. John, 300-26. New York: Guilford Press.

Cather, Willa. 1913. *O pioneers!* Boston, MA: Houghton Mifflin.

Cavarero, Adriana. 2000. *Relating narratives: Storytelling and selfhood*. Translated by Paul A. Kottman. London: Routledge.

———. 2005. *For more than one voice*. Translated by Paul A. Kottman. London: Routledge.

Chandler, Michael J. 1975. Relativism and the problem of epistemological loneliness. *Human Development* 18: 171-80.

Chaudhuri, Una. 1997. *Staging place: The geography of modern drama*. Ann Arbor, MI: University of Michigan Press.

Chodorow, Nancy. 1978. *The reproduction of mothering: Psychoanalysis and the sociology of gender*. Berkeley, CA: University of California Press.

Clines, Francis X. 1983. Poet of the bogs. *New York Times*, March 13. http://www.nytimes.com/books/98/12/20/specials/heaney-bogs.html.

Cobbett, William. 1912. *Rural rides*, vol. 1. London: J. M. Dent & Sons.

Coles, Robert. 1989. *The call of stories: Teaching and the moral imagination*. Boston, MA: Houghton Mifflin.

Connors, Robert J., and Andrea Lunsford. 1993. Teachers' rhetorical comments on student papers: Ma and Pa Kettle visit the tropics of commentary. *College Composition and Communication* 44 (2): 200-23.

Couser, G. Thomas. 1989. *Altered egos: Authority in American autobiography*. New York: Oxford University Press.

Crowley, Sharon. 1985. Writing and writing. In *Writing and reading differently: Deconstruction and the teaching of composition and literature*, ed. G. Douglas Atkins and Michael J. Johnson, 93-100. Lawrence, KS: University Press of Kansas.

Culler, Jonathan. 1975. *Structuralist poetics: Structuralism, linguistics, and the study of literature*. Ithaca, NY: Cornell University Press.

Cullingford, Elizabeth. 1991. Venus or Mrs. Pankhurst: Yeats's love poetry and the culture of suffrage. In *An annual of critical and textual studies*, vol. 9, ed. Richard J. Finneran, 11-29. Ann Arbor: University of Michigan Press.

———. 1993. *Gender and history in Yeats's love poetry*. Cambridge, England: Cambridge University Press.

Darnton, John, ed. 2001. *Writers on writing: Collected essays from the New York Times*. New York: Henry Holt.

Day, James M., and Mark B. Tappan. 1996. The narrative approach to moral development: From the epistemic subject to dialogical selves. *Human Development* 39: 67-82.

Dean, Eric T., Jr. 1997. *Shook over hell: Post-traumatic stress, Vietnam, and the Civil War*. Cambridge, MA: Harvard University Press.

de Certeau, Michel. 1984. *The practice of everyday life*. Translated by Steven F. Rendell. Berkeley, CA: University of California Press.

Defense Advanced Research Projects Agency (DARPA). Information Awareness Office. 2002. http://www.darpa.mil/iao/.

Deleuze, Gilles, and Félix Guattari. 1989. *A thousand plateaus: Capitalism and schizophrenia*. Translated by Brian Massumi. Minneapolis, MI: University of Minnesota Press.

de Montaigne, Michel. 1958. "Sur des vers de Virgile," III. *Essais*. Translated by Donald Frame. Stanford, CA: Stanford University Press.

Derrida, Jacques. 1995. *On the name*, ed. Thomas Dutoit. Translated by David Wood, John P. Leavy Jr., and Ian McLeod. Stanford, CA: Stanford University Press.

————. 1977. Signature event context. Translated by Samuel Weber and Jeffrey Mehlman. *Glyph* 1: 172-97.

Ede, Lisa, ed. 1999. *On writing research: The Braddock Essays, 1975-1998*. Boston, MA: Bedford/St. Martin's.

Ede, Lisa, and AndrEea A. Lunsford. 2001. Collaboration and concepts of authorship. *Publications of the Modern Language Association* 116 (2): 354-69.

Edelman, Gerald M. 1987. *Neural Darwinism: The theory of neuronal group selection*. New York: Basic Books.

————. 1989. *The remembered present: A biological theory of consciousness*. New York: Basic Books.

————. 1992. *Bright air, brilliant fire: On the matter of the mind*. New York: Basic Books.

————. 2004. *Wider than the sky: The phenomenal gift of consciousness*. New Haven, CT: Yale University Press.

Egendorf, Arthur. 1986. *Healing from the war: Trauma and transformation after Vietnam*. Boston, MA: Shambhala.

Elbow, Peter. 1973. *Writing without teachers*. New York: Oxford University Press.

————. 1987. Closing my eyes as I speak: An argument for ignoring audience. *College English* 49 (1): 50-69.

————. 1993. Ranking, evaluating, and liking: Sorting out three forms of judging. *College English* 55 (2): 187-206.

————. 2007. Voice in writing again: Embracing contraries. *College English* 70 (2): 168-88.

Elias, Norbert. 1991. *The society of individuals*. Oxford, England: Basil Blackwell.

Ellmann, Richard. 1979. *Yeats: The man and the masks*. New York: Norton.

Emig, Janet A. 1971. *The composing processes of twelfth graders*. Urbana, IL: National Council of Teachers of English.

Eshelman, Raoul. 2000. Performatism, or the end of postmodernism. *Anthropoetics* 6, no. 2. http://www.anthropoetics.ucla.edu/ap0602/perform.htm.

Faulkner, William. 1936/1986. *Absalom, Absalom!* New York: Random House.

Feldman, Carol, Jerome Bruner, David Kalmer, and Bobbo Renderer. 1993. Plot, plight, and dramatism: Interpretation at three ages. *Human Development* 36: 327-42.

Fellows, Mary Louise, and Sherene Razack. 1994. Seeking relations: Law and feminism roundtable. *Signs: Journal of Women in Culture and Society* 19 (4): 1048-83.

Fey, Marion H. 1992. Building community through computer conferencing and feminist collaboration. *ERIC Document Reproduction Service*, ED 351683.

Fillmore, Charles J. 1989. Grammatical construction theory and the familiar dichotomies. In *Language processing in social context*, ed. Rainer Dietrich and Carl F. Graumann, 17-38. Amsterdam: North-Holland.

Finke, Laurie. 1992. *Feminist theory, women's writing*. Ithaca, NY: Cornell University Press.

Fisher, William, III. 1993. Ideology and imagery in the law of slavery. *Chicago-Kent Law Review* 68 (3): 1051-83.

Flanagan, Owen. 1996. *Self expressions: Mind, morals, and the meaning of life*. New York: Oxford University Press.

Foley, Neil. 1997. *The white scourge: Mexicans, Blacks, and poor Whites in Texas cotton culture*. Berkeley, CA: University of California Press.

Forster, E. M. 1927/1954. *Aspects of the novel*. New York: Harcourt, Brace, and Company.

Foster, Don. 2000. *Author unknown: On the trail of Anonymous*. New York: Henry Holt.

Foucault, Michel. 1979. *Discipline and punish: The birth of the prison*. Translated by Alan Sheridan. New York: Vintage Books.

————. 1976. *La Volonté de savoir*. Paris: Editions Gallimard.

————. 1975. *Surveiller et punir: Naissance de la prison*. Paris: Editions Gallimard.

————. 1990. *The history of sexuality (Vol. 1): An Introduction*. Translated by Robert Hurley. New York: Vintage Books.

François, Frédéric. 2006. *Rêves, récits de rêves et autres textes: Essai sur la lecture comme expèri-ence indirecte*. Limoges, France: Lambert-Lucas.

Frank, Arthur. 1995. *The wounded storyteller: Body, illness, and ethics*. Chicago, IL: University of Chicago Press.

Freeman, Mark. 1997. Why narrative?: Hermeneutics, historical understanding, and the significance of stories. *Journal of Narrative and Life History* 7 (1-4): 169-76.

———. 2001. From substance to story: Narrative, identity, and the reconstruction of the self. In *Narrative and identity: Studies in autobiography, self, and culture*, ed. Jens Brockmeier and Donald A. Carbaugh, 283-98. Amsterdam: John Benjamins.

Friedman, Susan Stanford. 1995. Beyond white and other: Relationality and narratives of race in feminist discourse. *Signs: Journal of Women in Culture and Society* 21 (1): 1-49.

———. 1998. *Mappings: Feminism and the cultural geographies of encounter*. Princeton, NJ: Princeton University Press.

Fulkerson, Richard. 1990. Compositional theory in the eighties: Axiological consensus and paradigmatic diversity. *College Composition and Communication* 41 (4): 409-29.

Fuss, Diana. 1989. *Essentially speaking: Feminism, nature and difference*. New York: Routledge.

Gabora, Liane. 2005. Creative thought as a nonDarwinian evolutionary process. *Journal of Creative Behavior* 39 (4): 65-87.

Gardin, Bernard. 2004. *Langage et luttes sociales*. Limoges: Lambert-Lucas.

Garnes, Sara, David Humphries, Vic Mortimer, Jennifer Phegley, and Kathleen R. Wallace. 1996. *Writing lives: Exploring literacy and community*. New York: St. Martin's Press.

———. 1999. Writing lives: The collaborative production of a composition text in a large first-year writing program. In *(Re)visioning composition textbooks: Conflicts of culture, ideology, and pedagogy*, ed. Xin Liu Gale and Fredric G. Gale, 249-66. New York: State University of New York Press.

Gee, James Paul. 2002. Identity as an analytic lens for research in education. *Review of Research in Education* 25: 99-125.

Geertz, Clifford. 1983. *Local knowledge: Further essays in interpretive anthropology*. New York: Basic Books.

Gergen, Kenneth. 1991. *The saturated self: Dilemmas of identity in contemporary life*. New York: Basic Books.

Gilead, Amihud. 2003. *Singularity and other possibilities: Panenmentalist novelties*. New York: Rodopi.

Gilson, Etienne. 1965. *The unity of philosophical experience*. New York: Charles Scribner's Sons.

Gilyard, Keith, and Elaine Richardson. 2001. Students' right to possibility: Basic writing and African American rhetoric. In *Insurrections: Approaches to resistance in composition studies*, ed. Gary A. Olson, 37-51. Albany, NY: State University of New York Press.

Gloege, Martin E. 1992. The American origins of the postmodern self. In *Constructions of the self*, ed. George Levine, 59-80. New Brunswick, NJ: Rutgers University Press.

Goebbels, Joseph. 1998. From Goebbels diaries. In *Cybrary of the holocaust*. http://remember.org/witness/links.sp.goeb.html.

Greene, Graham, and Marie-Francoise Allain. 1983. *The other man: Conversations with Graham Greene*. New York: Simon and Schuster.

Halliday, Michael A. K. 1978. *Language as social semiotic: The social interpretation of language and meaning*. London: Edward Arnold.

Hallock, Daniel. 1998. *Hell, healing and resistance: Veterans speak*. New York: The Plough Publishing House.

Harper's Magazine. 2009. Known Knowns. June.

Harris, James. 1751/1968. *Hermes; or a philosophical enquiry concerning language and universal grammar*. Menston, England: Scolar Press.

Harris, Muriel. 1989. Composing behaviors of one- and multi-draft writers. *College English* 51 (2): 174-91.

Harste, Jerome C., Kathy Gnagey Short, and Carolyn L. Burke. 1988. *Creating classrooms for authors: The reading-writing connection*. Portsmouth, NH: Heinemann.

Haswell, Janis Tedesco. 1997. *Pressed against divinity: W. B. Yeats's feminine masks*. DeKalb, IL: Northern Illinois University Press.

———. 2005. The healing that peace did not bring: Second generation studies of the Viet Nam war. *Journal of Teaching Writing* 22 (1): 1-27.

Haswell, Janis, Richard H. Haswell and Glenn Blalock. 2009. Hospitality in college composition courses. *College Composition and Communication* 60 (4): 707-27.

Haswell, Janis Tedesco, and Richard H. Haswell. 1995. Gendership and also the miswriting students. *College Composition and Communication* 46 (2): 223-54.

Haswell, Richard H. 1970. Narrative point of view in Wordsworth's *Lyrical Ballads*. *Papers on Language and Literature* 6: 197-202.

———. 1998. Searching for Kiyoko: Bettering mandatory ESL writing placement. *Journal of Second Language Writing* 7 (2): 133-74.

———. 2007. Acrostic: Subtext and Countertext. Online. http://comppile.tamucc.edu/comppanel_40.htm.

Haswell, Richard H., and Janis Tedesco Haswell. 1996. Gender bias and the critique of student writing. *Assessing Writing* 3 (1): 31-83.

Haswell, Richard H., and Min-Zhan Lu, eds. 2000. *Comp tales: An introduction to college composition through its stories*. New York: Longman.

Heller, Agnes. 1992. Death of the subject? In *Constructions of the self*, ed. George Levine, 269-84. New Brunswick, NJ: Rutgers University Press.

Herman, Judith Lewis. 1997. *Trauma and recovery*. New York: Basic Books.

Herrington, Anne J. 1992. Comparing one's self in a discipline: Students' and teachers' negotiations. In *Constructing rhetorical education*, ed. Marie Secor and Davida Charney, 91-115. Carbondale, IL: Southern Illinois University Press.

Herrington, Anne J. and Marcia Curtis. 2000. *Persons in process: Four stories of writing and personal development in college*. Urbana, IL: National Council of Teachers of English.

Hillman, James. 1975. *Re-visioning psychology*. New York: Harper & Row.

Hitchcock, Alfred. 1927. *Bread loaf talks on teaching composition*. New York: Henry Holt.

Hockey, Susan. 1980. *A guide to computer applications in the humanities*. Baltimore, MD: Johns Hopkins University Press.

Hölderlin, Friedrich. 1998. *Selected poems and fragments*. Translated by Michael Hamburger. New York: Penguin Classics.

Horner, Bruce. 1997. Students, authorship, and the work of composition. *College English* 59: 505-529.

Illich, Ivan. 1982. *Gender*. New York: Pantheon Books.

Iser, Wolfgang. 1993. *The fictive and the imaginary: Charting literary anthropology*. Baltimore, MD: Johns Hopkins University Press.

JanMohamed, Abdul, and David Lloyd. 1997. Toward a theory of minority discourse: What is to be done? In *Postcolonial criticism*, ed. Bart Moore-Gilbert, Gareth Stanton, and Willy Maley, 234-47. New York: Longman.

Johnstone, Barbara. 1996. *The linguistic individual: Self-expression in language and linguistics*. New York: Oxford University Press.

Jordan, Terry G., John L. Bean Jr., and William M. Holmes. 1984. *Texas: A geography*. Boulder, CO: Westview Press.

Josephs, Ingrid E. 1997. Talking with the dead: Self-construction as dialogue. *Journal of Narrative and Life History* 7 (1-4): 359-67.

Jung, Carl Gustav. 1953/1983. *Collected works*, ed. Herbert Read, Michael Fordham, and Gerhart Adler. New York: Pantheon.

Kameen, Paul. 1999. Re-covering self in composition. *College English* 62 (1): 100-11.

Karp, David A., Lynda Lytle Holmstrong, and Paul S. Gray. 1998. Leaving home for college: Expectations for selective reconstruction of self. *Symbolic Interaction* 21 (3): 253-76.

Kawash, Samira. 1997. *Dislocating the color line: Identity, hybridity, and singularity in African-American narrative.* Stanford, CA: Stanford University Press.

Kirsch, Gesa. 1999. *Ethical dilemmas in feminist research: The politics of location, interpretation, and publication.* Albany, NY: State University of New York Press.

Knoblauch, C. H., and Lil Brannon. 1984. *Rhetorical traditions and the teaching of writing.* Upper Montclair, NJ: Boynton/Cook.

Krog, Antjie. 1998. *Country of my skull: Guilt, sorrow, and the limits of forgiveness in the new South Africa.* New York: Three Rivers Press.

Kukla, Rebecca. 1996. Decentering women. *Metaphilosophy* 27 (1-2): 28-52.

Labouvie-Vief, Gisela. 1980. Beyond formal operations: Pure logic in lifespan development. *Human Development* 23: 141-61.

———. 1994. *Psyche and Eros: Mind and gender in the life course.* Cambridge, England: Cambridge University Press.

Labov, William. 1972. *Language in the inner city: Studies in the Black English vernacular.* Philadelphia, PA: University of Pennsylvania Press.

Lanzmann, Claude. 1995. *Shoah: The complete text of the acclaimed Holocaust film.* New York: Da Capo Press.

Latour, Bruno. 1987. *Science in action: How to follow scientists and engineers through society.* Cambridge, MA: Harvard University Press.

Leonard, George B. 1968. *Education and ecstasy.* New York: Dell.

Levinas, Emmanuel. 1969. *Totality and infinity: An essay on exteriority.* Translated by Alphonso Lingis. Pittsburgh, PA: Duquesne University Press.

Lifton, Robert Jay. 1993. *The protean self: Human resilience in an age of fragmentation.* Chicago, IL: University of Chicago Press.

Linde, Charlotte. 1993. *Life stories: The Creation of Coherence.* Oxford, England: Oxford University Press.

Locher, Frances Carol, ed. 1980. *Contemporary authors.* Vols. 85-88. Detroit, MI: Gale Research.

———. 1983. *Contemporary authors.* Vol. 108. Detroit, MI: Gale Research.

Lunsford, Andrea A. 1980. The content of basic writers' essays. *College Composition and Communication* 31 (3): 278-90.

Lunsford, Andrea A., and Lisa Ede. 1994. Collaborative authorship and the teaching of writing. In *The construction of authorship: Textual appropriation in law and literature*, ed. Martha Woodmansee and Peter Jaszi, 417-438. Durham, NC: Duke University Press.

Marinara, Martha. 1995. Theory, self, and rhetoric or, what to do with Ariadne's thread. ERIC Document Reproduction Service, ED 397428.

Martin, Jane Roland. 1985. *Reclaiming a conversation: The ideal of the educated woman.* New Haven, CT: Yale University Press.

Maslow, Abraham. 1962/1968. *Toward a psychology of being.* New York: Van Nostrand Reinhold.

Mason, Bobbie Ann. 1993. *Feather crowns.* New York: HarperCollins.

Mason, Gordon. 1988. Behind the writing. *Use of English* 40 (2): 19-26.

Matsakis, Aphrodite. 1996. *Vietnam wives: Facing the challenges of life with veterans suffering post-traumatic stress.* New York: Sidran Press.

McAdams, Dan P. 1988. *Power, intimacy, and the life story: Personological inquiries into identity.* New York: Guilford Press.

———. 1993. *The stories we live by: Personal myths and the making of the self.* New York: Morrow.

———. 1996. Narrating the self in adulthood. In *Aging and biography: Exploration in adult development*, ed. James E. Birren, et al., 131-48. New York: Springer.

Mellon, John C. 1979. Issues in the theory and practice of sentence combining: A twenty-year perspective. In *Sentence combining and the teaching of writing*, ed. Donald Daiker, Andrew Kerek, and Max Morenberg, 1-38. Conway, AK: L and S Books.

Mencken, H. L. 1917. *Book of prefaces*. New York: Alfred P. Knopf.

Michaelson, Sidney, and Andrew Q. Morton. 1973. Positional stylometry. In *The computer and literary studies*, ed. Adam Jack Aitken, Richard W. Bailey, and Neil Hamilton-Smith, 69-83. Edinburgh: Edinburgh University Press.

Miller, Nancy K. 1997. Time pieces. *Narrative* 5: 60-66.

Miller, Susan. 1989. *Rescuing the subject: A critical introduction to rhetoric and the writer*. Carbondale, IL: Southern Illinois University Press.

———. 1993. *Textual carnivals: The politics of composition*. Carbondale, IL: Southern Illinois University Press.

Mitchell, Sally, Victoria Marks-Fisher, Lynne Hale, and Judith Harding. 2000. Making dances, making essays: Academic writing in the study of dance. In *Student writing in higher education: New contexts*, ed. Mary R. Lea and Barry Stierer, 86-96. London: Open University Press.

Moi, Toril. 1985. *Sexual/textual politics: Feminist literary theory*. New York: Methuen.

Monastersky, Richard. 2002. Revising the book of life. *Chronicle of Higher Education*(March 15): A14-A18.

Moore, Virginia. 1954. *The unicorn: William Butler Yeats's search for reality*. New York: Macmillan.

Morgan, Thaïs E., ed. 1994. *Men writing the feminine: Literature, theory and the question of genders*. Albany, NY: State University of New York Press.

Mumford, Michael D., S. Scott Wesley, and Garnett S. Shaffer. 1987. Individuality in a developmental context, II: The crystallization of developmental trajectories. *Human Development* 30 (5): 291-321.

Murray, Donald M. 1990. *Shoptalk: Learning to write with writers*. Portsmouth, NH: Boynton/Cook Heinemann.

Neisser, Ulric. 1988. Five kinds of self-knowledge. *Philosophical Psychology* 1 (1): 35-59.

Nelms, Gerald. 1992. *An oral history of Janet Emig's case study subject "Lynn."* ERIC Document Retrieval Service, ED 345 277.

Newkirk, Thomas. 1997. *The performance of self in student writing*. Portsmouth, NH: Boynton/Cook.

Nielsen, Joyce McCarl. 1990. *Sex and gender in society: Perspectives on stratification*. Prospect Heights, IL: Waveland Press.

Norris, Dwayne, Scott Oppler, Daniel Kuang, Rachel Day, and Kimberly Adams. 2006. *The College Board SAT writing validation study: An assessment of predictive and incremental validity*. Research Report No. 2006-2, College Entrance Examination Board, New York.

Ondaatje, Michael. 1992. *The English patient*. New York: Random House.

O'Reilley, Mary Rose. 1993. *The peaceable classroom*. Portsmouth, NH: Boynton/Cook.

Osterhout, Lee, and Phillip J. Holcomb. 1993. Event-related potentials and syntactic anomaly: Evidence of anomaly detection during the perception of continuous speech. *Language and Cognitive Processes* 8 (4): 413-37.

Owens, Derek. 1993. Composition as the voicing of multiple fictions. In *Into the field: Sites of composition studies*, ed. Anne Ruggles Gere, 159-75. New York: Modern Language Association.

Ozouf, Mona. 1997. *Women's words: An essay on French singularity*. Translated by Jane Marie Todd. Chicago IL: University of Chicago Press.

Parker, Alan Michael, and Mark Willhardt, eds. 1996. *The Routledge anthology of cross-gendered verse*. New York: Routledge.

Phillips, Jane. 2006. *James Tiptree Jr.: The double life of Alice B. Sheldon.* New York: St. Martin's Press.

Piercy, Marge. 1982. *Parti-colored blocks for a quilt.* Ann Arbor, IL: University of Michigan Press.

Plato. 1926. *Timaeus.* Translated by Robert Gregg Bury. New York: Heinemann.

———. 1951. *Symposium.* Translated by Walter Hamilton. London: Penguin.

Plutarch. 1871. *Morals.* Vol. 2. Translated by William Watson Goodwin. Boston, MA: Little, Brown.

Polkinghorne, Donald E. 1988. *Narrative knowing and the human sciences.* Albany, NY: State University of New York Press.

Poovey, Mary. 1988. *Uneven developments: The ideological work of gender in mid-Victorian England.* Chicago, IL: University of Chicago Press.

Powell, Fredric A. 1974. The perception of self-uniqueness as a determinant of message choice and valuation. *Speech Monographs* 41: 163-68.

Pratt, Annis V. 1981. Spinning among fields: Jung, Frye, Levi-Strauss and feminist archetypal theory. In *Feminist archetypal theory: Interdisciplinary revisions of Jungian thought,* ed. Estella Lauter and Carol Schreier Rupprecht, 97-126. Knoxville, TN: University of Tennessee Press.

Randall, William L. 1996. Restorying a life: Adult education and transformative learning. In *Aging and biography: Exploration in adult development,* ed. James E. Birren, et al., 224-47. New York: Springer.

Reiger, Terry. 1996. *The human semantic potential: Spatial language and constrained connectionism.* Cambridge, MA: MIT Press.

Riegel, Klaus F. 1973. Dialectical operations: The final stage of cognitive development. *Human Development* 16: 345-76.

Ritvo, Rosemary Puglia. 1975. *A vision B:* The Plotinian metaphysical basis. *Review of English Studies: A Quarterly Journal of English Literatures and the English Language* 26: 34-46.

Roberts, Holland D., Walter V. Kaulfers, and Grayson N. Kefauver, eds. 1943. *English for social living.* New York: McGraw-Hill.

Rubin, Louis D. 1967. *The teller in the tale.* Seattle, WA: University of Washington Press.

Russ, Joanna. 1990. Letter to editor. *Extrapolation* 31: 83.

Ruth, Jan-Erik, and Gary Kenyon. 1996. Biography in adult development and aging. In *Aging and biography: Explorations in adult development,* ed. James E. Birren, et al., 1-20. New York: Springer.

Saddlemyer, Ann. 2002. *Becoming George: The life of Mrs. W. B. Yeats.* Oxford, England: Oxford University Press.

Sass, Louis A. 1992. The self and its vicissitudes in the psychoanalytic avant-garde. In *Constructions of the self,* ed. George Levine, 17-58. New Brunswick, NJ: Rutgers University Press.

Scholes, Robert. 1998. *The rise and fall of English.* New Haven, CT: Yale University Press.

Scott, Fred Newton. 1909. What the west wants in preparatory English. *School Review* 17: 10-20.

Scott, Paul. 1962/1985. *The birds of paradise.* London: Granada.

———. 1963/1985. *The bender.* London: Granada.

———. 1968/1998. *The day of the scorpion.* Chicago, IL: University of Chicago Press.

———. 1972/1998. *The towers of silence.* Chicago, IL: University of Chicago Press.

———. 1975/1998. *A division of the spoils.* Chicago, IL: University of Chicago Press.

———. 1986. *My appointment with the muse.* London: Heinemann.

Sennett, Richard. 1990. The rhetoric of ethnic identity. In *The ends of rhetoric: History, theory, practice,* ed. John Bender and David E. Wellbery, 191-231. Stanford: Stanford University Press.

Shay, Jonathan. 1995. *Achilles in Vietnam: Combat trauma and the undoing of character*. New York: Touchstone.

Shields, Carol. 2002. *Unless*. London: Fourth Estate.

Smith, Craig R. 1970. Actuality and potentiality: The essence of criticism. *Journal of Philosophy and Rhetoric* 3 (3): 133-40.

Smith, Paul. 1988. *Discerning the subject*. Minneapolis, MN: University of Minnesota Press.

Snyder, C. R. and Howard L. Fromkin. 1980. *Uniqueness: The human pursuit of difference*. New York: Plenum Press.

Spivak, Gayatri Chakravorty. 1995. *Imaginary maps: Three stories by Mahasweta Devi*. London: Routledge.

Steiner, George. 1989. *Real presences*. Chicago, IL: University of Chicago Press.

Stern, Carol Simpson, and Bruce Henderson. 1993. *Performance: Texts and contexts*. New York: Longman.

Sternberg, Janet, ed. 1980. *The writer on her work*. New York: Norton.

Sternberg, Janet, ed. 1991. *New essay in new territory. Vol. 2 of The writer on her work*. New York: Norton.

Sternglass, Marilyn. 1997. *Time to know them: A longitudinal study of writing and learning at the college level*. Mahwah, NJ: Lawrence Erlbaum.

Stierstorfer, Klaus. 2003. Introduction. In *Beyond postmodernism: Reassessments in literature, theory, and culture*, ed. Klaus Stierstorfer, 1-10. Berlin: Walter de Gruyter.

Stillinger, Jack. 1991. *Multiple authorship and the myth of the solitary genius*. Chicago, IL: University of Chicago Press.

Swim, Janet K., Eugene Borgida, Geoffrey Maruyama, and David G. Myers. 1989. Joan McKay versus John McKay: Do gender stereotypes bias evaluations? *Psychological Bulletin* 105: 409-29.

Tanner, Jennifer Lynn. 2006. Recentering during emerging adulthood: A critical turning point in life span human development. In *Emerging adults in America: Coming of age in the 21st century*, ed. Jeffrey Jensen Arnett and Jennifer Lynn Tanner, 21-58. New York: American Psychological Association.

Thernstrom, Melanie. 1990. *The dead girl*. New York: Simon and Schuster.

Thomas, Francis-Nöel. 1993. *The writer writing: Philosophic acts in literature*. Princeton, NJ: Princeton University Press.

Tiptree, James, Jr. 2000. *Meet me at infinity*. New York: Tor.

Tomlinson, Barbara. 2005. *Authors on writing: Metaphors and intellectual labor*. New York: Palgrave Macmillan.

Torrance, Mark, Glyn V. Thomas, Elizabeth J. Robinson. 2000. Individual differences in undergraduate essay-writing strategies: A longitudinal study. *Higher Education* 39: 181-200.

Trilling, Lionel. 1976. *Beyond culture: Essays on literature and learning*. Garden City, NY: Anchor Books.

Trimbur, John. 1994. Taking the social turn: Teaching writing post-process. *College Composition and Communication* 45 (1): 108-18.

Tversky, Amos, and Daniel Kahneman. 1974. Judgment under uncertainty: Heuristics and biases. *Science* 185: 1124-31.

University of South Florida. 2008. ENC 1101 first year composition. http://collegewriting.us/FrontPageDocuments/NewProjectWebs/Collaboration.htm.

Van Dyck, Barrie. 1980. *On-the-job writing of high-level business executives: Implication for college teaching*. ERIC Document Reproduction Service, ED18558.

Wachtel, Eleanor, ed. 1993. *Writers & company: In conversation with CBC radio's Eleanor Wachtel*. New York: Knopf.

Waddell, Martin. 2002. Interview. http://www.jubileebooks.co.uk/jubilee/magazine/authors/martin_waddell/interview.asp.

Waldrep, Tom, ed. 1985. *Writers on writing*. Vol 1. New York: Random House.

———. 1988. *Writers on writing*. Vol. 2. New York: Random House.

Wall, Susan, and Nicholas Coles. 1991. Reading basic writing: Alternatives to a pedagogy of accommodation. In *The politics of writing instruction: Postsecondary*, ed. Richard Bullock and John Trimbur, 227-46. Portsmouth, NH: Boynton/Cook.

Watson, Ken. 1981. *English teaching in perspective: In the context of the 1990's*. Sydney: St. Clair.

Weatherall, Ann. 1998. Re-visioning gender and language research. *Women and Language* 21 (1): 1-9.

Welch, Nancy. 1996. Worlds in the making: The literacy project as potential space. *Journal of Advanced Composition* 16 (1): 16-80.

Welty, Eudora. 1941. *A curtain of green, and other stories*. Garden City, NY: Doubleday.

White, Robert W. 1952. *Lives in progress: A study of the natural growth of personality*. New York: Holt, Rinehart, and Winston.

Wilkinson, Andrew. 1980. *Assessing language development*. Oxford: Oxford University Press.

Williams, Raymond. 1976. *Keywords: A vocabulary of culture and society*. New York: Oxford University Press.

Witte, Stephen P. 1987. Pre-text and composing. *College Composition and Communication* 38 (4): 397-425.

Woolf, Virginia. 1950. Mr. Bennett and Mrs. Brown, *The captain's death bed and other essays*. New York: Harcourt Brace. 94-119.

———. 1957. *A room of one's own*. New York: Harcourt, Brace and World.

———. 2003. *A writer's diary*. New York: Harcourt Brace.

Wordsworth, William. 1974. Essay on morals. In Vol. 1 of *The prose works*, ed. W. J. B. Owen and Jane Worthington Smyser, 103. Oxford: Clarendon Press.

Yagelski, Robert P. 1999. *Literacy matters: Writing and reading the social self*. New York: Teachers College Press.

Yeats, Michael B. 1998. *Cast a cold eye*. Dublin: Blackwater Press.

Yeats, William Butler. 1925. *A vision*. London: T. Werner Laurie.

———. 1959. *Mythologies*. New York: Macmillan.

———. 1961. *Essays and introductions*. New York: Collier Books.

———. 1964. *Letters on poetry to Dorothy Wellesley*. London: Oxford University Press.

———. 1978. *A critical edition of Yeats's A VISION*, ed. George Mills Harper and W. K. Hood. London: Macmillan.

———. 1986. *The collected letters of W. B. Yeats*. Vol. *1,1865-1895*, ed. John Kelly. Oxford: Clarendon.

———. 1992. *The automatic script: November 5, 1917-June 18, 1918*. Vol. 1 of *Yeats's VISION papers*, ed. Steve L. Adams, Barbara J. Frieling, and Sandra L. Sprayberry. Iowa City, IA. University of Iowa Press.

———. 1992. *The automatic script: June 25, 1918-March 29, 1920*. Vol. 2 of *Yeats's VISION papers*, ed. Steve L. Adams, Barbara J. Frieling, and Sandra L. Sprayberry. Iowa City, IA: University of Iowa Press.

Young-Eisendrath, Polly. 1988. The female person and how we talk about her. In *Feminist thought and the structure of knowledge*, ed. Mary McCanney Gergen, 152-72. New York: New York University Press.

INDEX

ABOUT THE AUTHORS

JANIS HASWELL is a professor of English at Texas A&M University–Corpus Christi. She teaches undergraduate and graduate courses in British literature for the English Department and composition in the university's First-Year Program. She is the author of *Introduction to the Raj Quartet* (1985), *Pressed Against Divinity: W. B. Yeats and the Feminine Mask* (1997), *Paul Scott's Philosophy of Place(s): the Fiction of Relationality* (2002), as well as some thirty articles in both literature and composition. She is currently the review editor for *The Journal of Teaching Writing*.

Her administrative titles have included assistant chair of the department of humanities, coordinator of the English graduate program, and director of the university honors program. She received the Excellence in Teaching Award from the College of Arts and Humanities in 2002, and the University's Excellence in Scholarly and Creative Activity Award in 2003. She was also a faculty fellow at the United States Holocaust Memorial Museum in 2004.

RICHARD HASWELL, now emeritus, was for twenty-nine years at Washington State University, where he directed the composition program and the cross-campus writing-assessment program, and taught courses in rhetoric, romanticism, and postmodern literature. He then spent nine years at Texas A&M University–Corpus Christi, where he held the Haas Professorship of English and added courses in young-adult literature, contemporary poetry, and language in society.

He is author of *Gaining Ground in College Writing: Tales of Development and Interpretation* (1991) and co-editor of *The HBJ Reader* (1987), *Comp Tales: An Introduction to College Composition through its Stories* (2000), *Beyond Outcomes: Assessment and Instruction within a University Writing Program* (2001), and *Machine Scoring of Student Essays: Truth and Consequence* (2006). His journal publications range from studies of Baudelaire's plagiarisms, to quantitative experiments in the evaluation of second-language student writing, to translations from the French and the Spanish. In 2000, with colleague Glenn Blalock, he launched *CompPile*, an online, open-access bibliography of scholarship in composition and rhetoric, now the largest and most utilized in the field.